END
TO END

The Land's End to John o'Groats
Cycling Record: A Story of Obsession,
Hallucination and Happiness

PAUL JONES

Little, Brown

LITTLE, BROWN

First published in Great Britain in 2021 by Little, Brown

1 3 5 7 9 10 8 6 4 2

A CIP catalogue record for this book
is available from the British Library.

Hardback ISBN 978-1-4087-1273-3

Typeset in Adobe Garamond by M Rules
Printed and bound in Great Britain by
Clays Ltd, Elcograf S.p.A.

Papers used by Little, Brown are from well-managed forests
and other responsible sources.

Little, Brown
An imprint of
Little, Brown Book Group
Carmelite House
50 Victoria Embankment
London EC4Y 0DZ

An Hachette UK Company
www.hachette.co.uk

www.littlebrown.co.uk

For Mum, for the lift

Contents

List of Illustrations

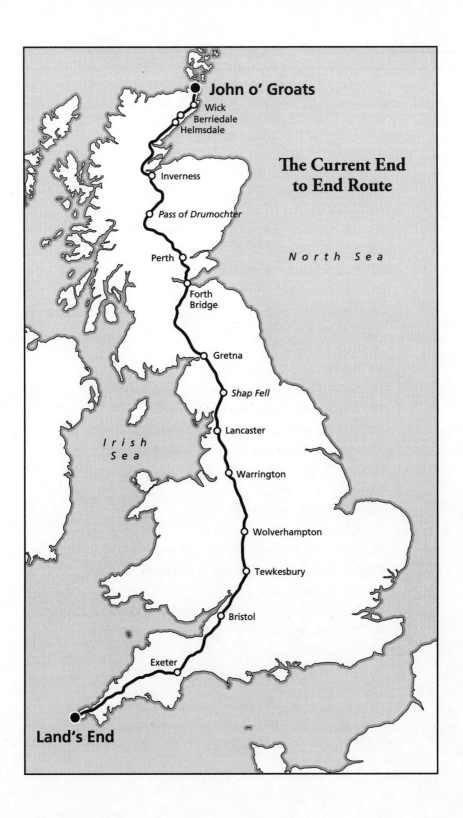

The Current End to End Route

John o' Groats

Wick
Berriedale
Helmsdale

Inverness

Pass of Drumochter

Perth

Forth Bridge

Gretna

Shap Fell

Lancaster

Warrington

Wolverhampton

Tewkesbury

Bristol

Exeter

Land's End

North Sea

Irish Sea

1

Everyone makes it to the start

Sunday, 19 August 2018

This is not *Poldark*. There are no remnants of tin mines, no rugged Celtic cliffs standing firm against the inchoate fury of the sea, no Cornish beefcake, half naked, emerging from the foam. It is grim, grey and cold, even in the winter weather in the heart of summer. It is the end of the line, a road that stops, a footpath that tails off with nowhere to go except into the ocean or back the way you came. It has less in common with Atlantis, more with Severn Beach or Withernsea: desolate places leading from somewhere to nowhere, with no prospect of further travel. I don't know if I was expecting some sort of Celtic myth hovering in a fine mist rolling in off the Atlantic, Cornishmen chanting and Britt Ekland dancing in the interstices of a sinister stone circle, but whatever it was, this is not it. Land's End is underwhelming. It was underwhelming for Harman and Blackwell, who were likely the first to undertake the End to End journey by bike in 1880. The pair found the view disappointing even from the vantage point of their penny-farthings, or 'ordinaries' as they were known. Writer John Hillaby, too, was far from overwhelmed; 'it was misty', and he 'couldn't see much', except for the hotel and 'shacks of trinket vendors'.* But I'm here, standing silently and contemplating the journey ahead – the schlep through Cornwall, onwards into the unknown.

I have been here before. As children my sister and I insisted Dad take us to Land's End after a day out at Flambards Cornish theme park. It was nowhere near as close as any of us suspected, Dad included, and seemed even further in an ageing bright yellow Ford Cortina, purchased for £185. My sister had been watching *Willow* and *Labyrinth* over and over, she had vague fantasy imaginings of unicorns being tamed by a young Tom Cruise, or David Bowie waving a crystal ball. I thought of *Robin Hood*, with Jason Connery, because that was my mythical touchstone.

'Is this it?' my sister said when we got there.

'Yes,' said Dad. Always taciturn, always literal.

My dad said the Cornish were a funny old lot. He was right, but we were from Devon, so couldn't really comment too force-fully on our neighbours. People in glass houses shouldn't have sex with members of their immediate family, or so the saying nearly goes.

I knew then but would have struggled to express it as neatly as my sister managed. It's a frontier, a no-place, a full-stop. You can't go through it to go anywhere. We weren't looking for anything in particular, perhaps a Tintagel-type experience. We were

---

* John Hillaby, *Journey Through Britain* (London: Constable and Company, 1968), a seminal account of a walk off the beaten path from Land's End to John o'Groats.

A ROUGH SEA OFF THE LANDS END. *Dear Florence* ———————. *We forgot the the fowl — Mary* —————

unusual in that regard. People travel to Land's End in search of something; maybe they are looking for the thing they can't see, or thinking of the presence of America, the knowledge that if they carry on going it's the next thing that will loom out of the ocean. There is a sense of people far away, massed on the other side of the grey sea, a leviathan, a diaspora, people gone and not returning. Apart from such fancies, people go to Land's End so they can turn around, embark on a wobbly diagonal and end up at a similarly bleak, unprepossessing bit of headland 840 miles in the other direction.

Today, a layer of salt is stratified in the air, a solid crunch edging on the wind which rustles in from the Atlantic, a serrated beading that abrades the skin. It whistles around a strange tiny bothy, a squat construction designed to shelter people gazing out at the depth and breadth of the ocean. The Atlantic lies still and depthless. Grey, windswept faces try to separate the grey horizon from the grey ocean. Grey people nurse cups of grey tea in an austere conservatory wrapped around the white walls of the last building in the west. The apathetic angular shape of the hotel squats awkwardly, like a long-drop toilet cascading into the sea against the low cliff edge. White was the colour, resisting the tidal salt marks the main imperative, but now it too is grey, a rainbow of grey among grey elemental forces, signifying time and nothingness. They look out through UPVC double glazing, staring at the people in the bothy who in turn stare out at the ocean. Seagulls swirl above, symmetrical ticks flung and bent back, each one a letter V, shaped and then folded on the eddying jetstream.

People come here to start a journey. They tick it off their list. They do it to beat a record, or to try to beat a record. They do it for charity. They do it because someone died, or someone is dying. They do it for none of these reasons – just because it is here and it leads to there, along a narrow strip of road, and it makes for a nice few weeks. Sometimes they do it simply because they want to do it, because life is short and journeys shape meaning. They do it because it is quantifiable. It is a way of making sense of the world around them; it's something with a definitive outcome. I am drawn to this one, the outcome, the idea of the journey and the simplicity of the challenge: start here, ride for a long time – days, nights and weeks – and go as far as you can go. I love to tour, to travel huge distances over several days, see the landscape change and inhabit a space removed from everything else, the routines of time that govern the working day or the brainpower given over to work. The journey helps make sense of the non-journey time. Sometimes there is so much noise – from work, from decisions taken or not taken, relationships, family, friendships, and everything else, the wall of data and served adverts – that getting on your bike and heading out the door is the only way to make sense of it. It helps with the endless search for answers.

I am doing it because I am obsessed with the End to End, the challenges and hallucinatory madness of the record. It is

a finite, measurable challenge. When you get there you have to turn round and come back again. The distance is also at the very edge of what bike racers and endurance athletes can achieve. Those who manage to break the record sometimes go for the 1000-mile record as well; it's the furthest fixed distance on the Road Records Association book. As though 840 miles isn't enough, they 'add on' another 160 just because it seems silly not to. Cycling in the UK is obsessed with fixed distances, the time trial, 10, 25, 50 and 100 miles, then the 12- or 24-hour where the winner is the one with the biggest mileage. The End to End and the 1000 record represent the absolute limit. They are ridiculously long time trials, the rider against the clock. There is nothing else, just the brutal nature of the challenge. It is all or nothing, no second place. Sleep deprivation, mental and physical exhaustion, rain and wind mean there are stories to tell.

I am doing the End to End because I have time on my hands. I am staring out at the turbulent sea and trying really hard not to see it as a clumsy metaphor for my life right now. I left my job as a secondary school headteacher despite having no other job to go to, and with plenty of rage against the world. My ceaseless ambivalence and tendency to overthink were not helpful. This is a shame, because they are my two biggest strengths. I feel like the protagonist in an Arthur Miller play; the little man, a tiny walking tragedy. I reacted against accepted notions of leadership, the endless carousel of empty ideas and management theory, training exercises, self-aggrandising blogs and tweets, role plays and empty words. I failed to reconcile the challenges of inner-city teaching with the requirements of austerity measures, or more accurately I failed to acknowledge the fact that it was impossible to reconcile these two things. Having a visceral dislike of accountability measures, Ofsted readiness and current curriculum reform in hindsight wasn't helpful. I said none of these things in my letter of resignation; instead I typed 'I want to spend more time with my family and less time at work'. People keep asking me about things with confused concern. I reply in truisms: *it wasn't the right thing for me*; *I wasn't cut out for it*; *other people are better at it than me, more robust*. I don't talk about the other reasons that lurk below the surface of a sea of anxiety and self-doubt. I have lost my confidence and sense of self; it is undermining the important relationships in my life in frightening ways. I am no longer stressed about work, I am stressed about the absence of work and what to do next. So it goes.

The sea and the scenery at Land's End offer some palliative warmth because the End to End brings certainty and definition. The 'free' time I have now is far from empty, it is the opposite of free time; it is angst-laden time, filled with a formless terror of what might happen next. I allow the End to End to squeeze everything else to the periphery, at least for a time.

John Hillaby's *Journey Through Britain* sits in a growing pile of End to End-related literature back on my desk at home. He writes about the 'skull cinema', the reel of images and thoughts that unspools as you move through the landscape, a trance-like state acquired when passing through 'persistent ordinariness'. The book is surrounded by a mass of End to End confetti in the form of random Post-its. The wall is covered with imperatives – *speak to this person*, *do this ride*, *go here*, *ring so-and-so* – stuck next to peeling luminous squares of thoughts scrawled upon waking in the dead of night. The floor is carpeted with back copies of *Coureur*,* a magazine edited by Jock Wadley, because I am captivated by Wadley's writing and photography; it is a celebration of British cycling in texture and colour. I have spent hours poring over the pages, disappearing into the narratives between and behind the pictures, the hand-drawn illustrations and the distinct editorial voice. I got side-tracked, entirely, by a sequence of events in 1958, when two cyclists from the margins of the sport, Dave Keeler and Reg Randall, two amateurs with a particular passion and strength for 24-hour time trials, battled it out to lower the End to End record. A picture in the middle of one page showed three people walking up and over Aultnamain in northern Scotland through a murk of mist and dank air. In the middle, Dave Keeler, on the right and left supporters. The fog is a net curtain. It is 4 a.m., or thereabouts, and there's a way to go. At 6 feet 2 inches he looks enormous, 'the giant of the End to End'.† Jock Wadley illuminates the images he took with compelling, incisive prose, seeming to understand everything and know everything, a voice from within cycling.

It feels like all this is crammed into my Carradice saddlebag, the bike propped against the famous signpost as I try to get a

---

* *Coureur* ran from 1957 to 1968, redefining the relationship between writing and cycling in the UK. It became the touchstone for *Rouleur*, probably the closest modern equivalent.
† 'Dave Keeler: The Giant of the End to End', *Coureur*, August 1958, p.16.

photo amid a huge gaggle of Russian tourists. I am exploring
the extraordinary narrative of the End to End, the journey and
the people who aspired to beat the record, and the only way I
know how is to meet the people and ride the route. I can sense
and see Michael Broadwith riding away from the same spot two
months earlier, on his way to tackle the men's record. I think
back to the trip I took with his support team, driving through
the day and night at 20mph, watching and writing. Memories
of his extraordinary ride are superimposed on the things I'm
looking at now, principally the narrow road away from the hotel,
a gentle cadence through aimless groups of people, optimism in
plentiful supply with 842 miles to go.

I gaze out to sea in the way that you are supposed to, wistful,
optimistic, melancholy – studied – but the wind stings my eyes,
forcing them closed, then stings my eyelids. Tomorrow I am going
to ride to Bristol in one go, an attempt to knock off the first 212
miles in the fretful time I have available. I plan to leave at 5 a.m.
and get there before nightfall, then I will pause and plan the rest
of the ride. It is the beginning of the book and the journey. I think
of previous long bike rides I've undertaken: four days in Devon
and Cornwall with friends, rolling into a youth hostel in Hartland
at twilight; a tour through west Wales and the Beacons, riding
along the Usk Valley and over the Gospel Pass; a joyful two weeks
meandering from Barcelona to St Malo. After each one I felt fortified and renewed, inoculated even, better able to cope with the
world I was heading back to. I hope that tomorrow and the days
to come, spread over the next few months, will be restorative. It is
a physical journey, through the undulating terrain of the island,
but also an imaginative one. I want to see the topography of the
island from the width of a bicycle tyre, to sketch a line the length
and breadth of the island and to join the dots on an unfeasibly
large scale, to dissect a brain slice of the country.

But in this present moment the riding bit seems foolhardy.

I can do lots of things on a bike, but endurance riding is not one of them. I have ridden long distances, as much as 127 miles, but that was one of only two century rides I have ever done. I don't really see the point in doing absurd distances. I like to watch the audax* champions and Transcontinental lunatics as a very slow-moving dot on a virtual map rather than join their quest for utter degradation and fatigue, sleeping for seven micro-seconds in a farmer's gateway with a discarded copy of *Razzle* and a used prophylactic for a pillow. It is a vicarious thrill.

My preparation involved riding to work and back, 17 miles each way, through a Mendip winter. Most days it was fine, just over an hour on the bike. However, on one occasion I bonked so indescribably hard that I was reduced to eating blackberries and a half-rotten windfall apple found at the side of the A37. I had to scrub off the viscous, cloying diesel residue from the unrotten side before eating it. The 'bonk' stalks all cyclists – a catastrophic collapse in blood sugar which leads to disaster. Cycling clubs abound with myths and legends of *défaillance* – the time a chum was reduced to picking up discarded energy gel wrappers on the side of a French mountain to suck out a homeopathic amount of sugar. It tends to happen after 70 or 80 miles of hard riding in the hot sun, not during a ride home from work. All things considered, I am not the best person to tackle a 'stage' at least twice as long as anything I've ever done.

But these are specifics; I hope that I will find space and time to breathe, make sense of what a chaotic year it has been, resolve tensions and ambivalences and begin to feel better. I think of everyone else who has stood here with a bicycle and thought

---

* Audax (Latin for 'bold, daring') is a form of cycling in which participants attempt to cover long distances within a set time limit.

about the journey ahead, their names and stories. I start with Mike Broadwith in 2018, then hurtle backwards to G. P. Mills, and further again to Harman and Blackwell nearly 140 years ago. Everyone makes it to the start.

2

Harman and Blackwell run the gauntlet of the natives

Tuesday, 20 July 1880

I 'm glad it's not just me who struggled to cope with the reality of Land's End. C. A. Harman and H. Blackwell saw it for what it was: 'a fine mass of broken rock, but not as impressive as one could wish or expect.' I'm not sure what they were expecting; the name gives it away: the Land does End. Maybe their crucial mistake was bypassing Flambards.

Like most muscular Christians of the Victorian era it is all surnames and initials. At some point H. B. decided it was a challenge worth doing and pitched the deal to C. A. H. If the ride had been attempted before in this form it hadn't been documented, and so it came to pass that these two gentlemen started the ball rolling.

Over twelve days in July 1880, Blackwell kept a detailed diary which was later published in the cycling magazine *The Wheel World*, beginning with the ongoing disappointment of the Cornish start line; although when 'compared with the "other corner", it is simply grand'. It's what's in the middle that matters, like an Arctic Roll. Get through the stale, cold sponge and joy awaits. The account is full of idiosyncrasies, telling observations, dark humour and a traveller's sense of excitement in the mundane and the unusual. As Alan Ray* observed, both men exhibited 'the explorer's attitude to their surroundings . . . pioneering urges . . . and a preoccupation with bathing facilities'.

I am struck by a sense of admiration for how they undertook the challenge on a penny-farthing or 'ordinary', the saddle 8 feet from the ground, with some 900 miles to travel on rough, shape-shifting roads, running the gauntlet of 'the natives', as they put it. The journey seems incomprehensible to me now, but through the joyous and colloquial tone of Blackwell's prose, its observational eye, it comes to life in waves of contemporary colour.

The journey begins on the night train from Paddington to Penzance. Profound disappointment ensues when they realise not only are their tickets not checked on the train, but the station is also lacking in staff. Like two students heading home for reading week, they are gutted that they shelled out on a ticket when they could have chanced it. On arrival at Penzance they ride the short distance to Land's End and their point of departure. The plan is to stay at the hotel and then leave in the morning. Time expands and elides as they wrestle with 'slippery macadam', the road arguing and hurtling its way towards the sea, unsettling our intrepid travellers:

> It was a continuance of what is picturesquely termed undu-
> lating country, but which can more haply be termed 'deuced
> hilly'. How to describe the surface of this road without using

---

* Alan J. Ray, *Cycling: Land's End to John o'Groats* (London: Pelham, 1971).

the swears is a puzzler. Where there was not a big hole like a small grave, there was a rock like an adult gravestone, only it generally had the decency to lie down; with here and there a small cliff sticking up playfully in the middle of the road.

I am drawn into the baroque and seemingly anachronistic world of the Victorian swears, wondering what words they employed, whether the full Anglo-Saxon fuckery of our times existed back then. Perhaps they went for *rantallion* ('one whose shot pouch is longer than the barrel of his piece'), or *bescumberer* (shit-thrower), or *cacafuego* (braggart, literally 'shitfire'), or maybe they're just enacting the role of the *smellfungus* (archetypal fault-finder in all things). I imagine all, possibly at the same time, in an explosion of righteous metropolitan effrontery. I like them even more.

The two of them provoke feelings of familiarity despite the archaisms and their resolute Victorian sensibility. They are the aliens, navigating through a strange land – Marlow travelling upriver in *Heart of Darkness*, Jerome Newton across the Midwest in *The Man Who Fell to Earth* – and it isn't long before they start discussing 'the natives' residing in a landscape of dark satanic mills and bucolic, bleak countryside. They are as close in time to William Blake as we are to Philip Larkin, which gives a clearer indication of their social and physical landscape.

The pair struggled with the rolling hills right from the start, walking through Helston, up and down, on and off, to Penryn, with no respite on the downhills. A 50-inch gear, rider hovering 8 feet above the ground, with a stirrup brake rubbing on the solid tyre, made for much soiling of breeches on any descent bigger than a molehill. Rain and more rain led to a constant search for shelter, with 'all sentiment washed out'. The end of the first day saw them reach a 'dreadfully muddy' Bodmin at 58 miles.

Devon offered much of the same: unnavigable roads beneath a shimmering sheen of drove-driven slurry and rain, rutted surfaces, and inquisitive and aloof locals. To cap it all, they were struck by a series of savage mechanicals. The rubber came loose from Blackwell's rear wheel, requiring re-gluing and a pause for the cement to set. The dangers of the ordinary bicycle were a constant threat: 'I slipped my pedal with the usual accompaniment of such indulgence, bending crank, handle-bar, and head, and throwing hind wheel out of the track. The crank got put right at first blacksmith's, but the handle-bar and head had to wait until we reached Exeter.' They continued 'swearing at the bumping road', rather than absorbing the picturesque sights, and it is painfully obvious that the Devon county line offered nothing but joy, and a plea for divine intervention: 'the suffering that charming county annually inflicts on our brother wheelmen will take a lot of wiping out in the big settling day'. The Horsemen are coming for you, Devon.

Towns and cities sit on a binary spectrum, bucolic versus 'smoky', with Bristol falling into the latter camp, Tintern unsurprisingly the former. Hills were too steep to ride up and too steep to ride down, and ferries were the order of the day, earlier at Plymouth, Torpoint, and then at Aust to cross the Severn. Accommodation was sought out one way or another, often using the Bicycle Touring Club network of guest houses but at other times a coaching house or inn, regardless of availability:

The New Inn, at St. Owen's Cross near Ross. I kicked lustily at the door, and a light soon appeared. We roughly forced our way in, in spite of the landlady's remonstrance and repeated avowal that she had no bed to spare, and were soon seated in the comfortable bar-parlour discussing hot whisky with 'mine host' who, being a mechanic by trade, was much interested in my double ball bearings, while the missus, seeing the impossibility of getting rid of us, was knocking up a bed, into which we turned a little after midnight in fine trim for appreciating a good night's rest.

The presence of people on bikes was a relatively unusual sight: the iron horse drew admiration and confusion in equal measure, causing widespread 'astonishment of the natives' in Shrewsbury. Ablutions were sought; 'being a big town, we flattered ourselves we could get a nice hot bath there, a thing rarely met with in even good country hotels; but no, the proprietor of the baths groaned ... the inhabitants of Shrewsbury were, he supposed, better provided for in their houses than most places, or else never washed at all, as he never had an enquiry for hot water excepting from visitors'.

No doubt refreshed after their cold ablutions, the duo continued in their eternal battle with the road surfaces – cobbled streets, black cinder tracks, more 'villainous roads' – and added 'smoky Wigan' to 'smoky Bristol' in their black book of polluted places. The natives were restless, and more tales of the recalcitrant troglodytes emerge, this time 'the operatives of Preston, men and women, and their doings' scrambling the metropolitan minds of Harman and Blackwell. 'The amount of ale put away by some of the men was simple derangement to a well-constituted mind; glass after glass, or rather the contents, following one on the other as though no such a thing as intoxication existed.'

More mechanicals, before the reckoning on this pre-Tour, pre-myth, pre-heroic bike adventure, creating the myth and defining the narrative. A journey of firsts: the first riders to do the End to End, the first to write about Shap Fell in Cumbria. They roll through Kendal, only for Harman to hear 'language, not fully expressed by the term strong, from H.B.', who was again struggling with his rear tyre, resorting to tying it on with wire and string, ready for the climb ahead, out of Kendal and upwards over Shap Fell, and at around 9 miles a very long climb indeed. In fact, 'the biggest and roughest hill I ever crossed. First four miles we were able to ride, thanks to favourable wind, then came a tedious three miles walk and push up country, barren and desolate beyond description; and first mile down we had to walk, or rather hop, being much too rough to allow us to mount. This road, I should think, can never be used excepting for cattle, such was its rough condition near the top.' Like a parochial Petrarch, swapping Ventoux for Shap, Blackwell had now defined the hill in literary terms.

After several days of riding, the effort began to extract a price. Falls were a given; a gust of wind, a rough surface, a pothole, a lack of concentration, any momentary lapse could be cata- strophic. Harman was struggling to cope with a knee injury and was unable to straighten the leg on the pedal stroke. They swapped machines, as H. B.'s was smaller. The run to Edinburgh took longer than anticipated, 'having to walk up every bit of every hill', with 'just the hundred miles' in the bag for the day. Some positives were found, mostly in the gaps between the rain: 'Dunkeld ... looked lovely in the dusk ... the very spot one would select wherein to end one's days.' They carried on to Loch Ericht Hotel in the Highlands – cue another scathing and surreal TripAdvisor report: 'It might easily be mistaken for a large stable, no sign of any sort being up. We were kept waiting for tea while they hunted down a sheep for our chops.' They feasted on fresh mutton that evening. The next night the welcome was slightly more ambivalent: 'An old-fashioned inn and old-fashioned landlord who greeted us from the bedroom window ... trying to sleep off his animal and alcoholic spirits.'

More ferries, Kessock, then Meikle, hoicking the ordinaries up and on to the small boats, 'two each, boatmen, passengers and bicycles, being more than the cockleshell was ever designed to hold, and the sea running up in a most amusing way to any but the ferried. There we sat, almost inside the machines.'

By the second Saturday the end was in sight, with the 'simply vile' Helmsdale standing in the way. Blackwell provides a glimpse of a now changed environment, where fishing dominated the land and seascape: 'looking back to Helmsdale and seeing the immense fleet of fishing boats lying off, an idea can be formed of the enormous proportions to which this business has grown, the whole sea being covered with the sails of these hardy little craft' – a staggering sight which assailed their London senses, filling it with 'the very essence of Billingsgate'.

The further north they travelled the more remote, removed and isolated they felt. There seems to be an underlying suspicion of the area, a reading of the landscape as bleak, unyielding and beyond the pale: 'a few wretched cottages scattered about, all seeming to have a common interest in the moor or waste surrounding; not a tree to be seen, or sign of vegetation, excepting where some cottager had by Herculean efforts cleared a few feet whereon to raise a sickly and disappointed looking crop of oats, and only wanting a few stone walls and pigs to remind one irresistibly of the West of Ireland'. The Celtic regions are conflated into a picture of pre-modern misery, of subsistence, populated by serfs and terrifying lunatics:

We saw, clinging to a post, a maniac, screaming and bellowing with all the power of an unrivalled pair of lungs, who, upon our approach, interested himself at a heap of stones and, picking out one to his fancy, pitched it at my wheels with such precision as to hit the back fork. Thinking no good could come of our dismounting to argue the question with this poor idiot, we hurried on, acquainting the first constable we met of the fact. He treated it as quite a common occurrence, and not worth his consideration, as he (the madman, not the

bobby) was only one of a whole family who were all in the
same boat, mentally, and generally confined themselves to the
amusement of mutilating one another. We had to rest con-
tent with this testimony to the offender's harmlessness, and
trusted that the next bicyclist in the neighbourhood might
get through without having his skull battered in.

The narrative peters out the closer they get to the finish, the
'20 miles to John O'Groats' requiring 'no description'. 'There
was nothing to be seen but bleak moor and ditch. I cannot help
expressing my disappointment at the celebrated terminus, and
surprise that so many tourists should ever go so far, when there
are so many better roads and so much more interesting country
down South. A cold, wet coast this, at the best of times, but a
paradise to the fisherman and collector of shells.'

In completing the ride, Harman and Blackwell established
the bookends for the journey; two grim endpoints linked by a
trip through time and space. The publication of Harman and
Blackwell's account by *The Wheel World* helped establish the
journey in the popular imagination and created a mark for
other, more ambitious cyclists to follow. It was no accident.
Blackwell was a contributor and doubtless had the journey in
mind as an ideal narrative construction; he knew it would write
and read well. In this respect he is no different to those following
in his tyre tracks nearly 140 years later.

Despite its hardships and disappointments, the journey had a
lasting impact on their lives. Their subsequent return to London
was not entirely welcome, having to leave the freedom of the
road behind to 'begin again our everyday drudgery'.

3

George Pilkington Mills
dispatches the dogs

Monday, 5 July 1886

Pictures of a rider, from a lifetime long ago. No voice, no recording, just sepia-tinted images. G. P. Mills is unblemished; looks serious. His kit is immaculate: light tweed and cotton plus fours with matching jacket and cap, beautiful leather shoes. A strange array of bicycles, from the ordinary right through to the safety, steadily changing angles with a slow progression towards the horizontal axis, the point at which bike design achieved an equilibrium unbroken until the advent of plastic. He comes alive on the page – the sound of tyres on grit, the pulse. He breathes again as I type. I can hear him, his voice, the urgency of the race.

George Pilkington Mills was a key heroic figure in the late nineteenth century, a proto-modern cyclist who undertook crazy feats of endurance riding, made the headlines and attracted professional sponsorship. Two things stand out: his youth when attempting distance records, and the number and compressed nature of his record attempts. He thought nothing of doing several obscenely long rides or competitions in a short space of time, including three 24-hour races in one week, defying our contemporary sensibility and neatly framed expectations of how you train, taper and pedal.

He was born in Paddington in January 1867 to relatively wealthy parents, his father a manager of a cotton firm. They moved to Streatham, and then from 1881 he was a boarder at Redland Hill House School in Bristol (the school is still there, now a Steiner institution), which he left to become an apprentice civil engineer. Having just turned eighteen, he joined the Anfield Bicycle Club – now the oldest cycling club in the land, then a nascent collection of passionate roadmen and women. He then founded the North Road Cycling Club and embarked on a succession of attempts to redefine the framework of long-distance cycling, all within nine years, from 1886 to 1895. It acted as a call to arms for heroic pioneers. Six successful End to End attempts were made on a variety of machines, plus various place-to-place records, an excursion to the continent to take on the French and a series of 24-hour races. It also marked the start of formal checking and detail, with the formation of the Road Records Association (RRA) in 1888, which took on the responsibilities for all place-to-place records.

G. P. Mills lived through the first great golden age of cycling following John Kemp Starley's invention of the safety bicycle in 1885. Roads were colonised by pioneer cyclists, cars having yet to make a dent in the popular imagination. For context, Peugeot wasn't founded until 1891, and by 1903 only 30,204 cars were produced in France: compare that with the 14 million vehicles sold in Europe in 2015. Popular culture responded in favour of the bicycle as a galvanising force of modernity – until the sudden arrival of the motor car. Witness the car-drunk figure of Toad in *Wind in the Willows*, in thrall to the physical and sensuous rush of pleasure ... 'the magnificent motor-car, immense, breath-snatching, passionate, with its pilot tense and hugging his wheel, possessed all earth and air for the fraction of a second, flung an enveloping cloud of dust that blinded and enwrapped them utterly, and then dwindled to a speck in the far distance'. Toad's reaction – 'The poetry of motion! The real way to travel! The only way to travel! Here today – in next week tomorrow! Villages skipped, towns and cities jumped – always somebody else's horizon! O bliss!' – horrifies his friends. In contrast, the Welsh poet W. H. Davies laments a lost sense of time and space, recoiling in silent horror at the relentless acceleration and mechanisation of modern life: 'No time to stand beneath the boughs / And stare as long as sheep or cows.'*

It is a tipping point, the late Victorian era seeing the benefits of technology on bicycles until suddenly rendered obsolete in the aftermath of mechanisation and the Great War by a second, darker phase of modernity. Cycling linked well with late Victorian ideas of muscular Christianity, exploration and the masculine pioneer. The advent of the railway had removed coaches from the road, leaving them empty. Pioneer cyclists adopted them, but the roads were grim: unmetalled, no surface dressing, at times two cart tracks through fields, each track existing on widely differing geometric planes. It was a gravelly combination of dust, pebbles and cow shit, slurry in the rain, dusty desert in the scorching sun. And we complain about chip and seal.

For Mills, and others in the 1880s and 1890s, the empty roads conferred a limitless freedom on the individual, sparking the birth of cycling clubs and prompting a full embrace of the

---

* 'Leisure', by W. H. Davies.

leisure movement. In the absence of cars, the bike became a revolutionary means of personal mobility, allowing people to go much further and faster in the same amount of time. Factories like W. D. & H. O. Wills in Bristol became an integral part of the bike boom, riding the wave of clubs that emerged in the 1890s, donating trophies and supporting excursions. Outdoor cycling tracks appeared in most towns – at Carmarthen, Bootle, Brighton; there were twenty-seven tracks in London alone. For all the satirising force of Pooter, it was a pursuit with popular appeal, both in terms of the masses and the more peculiar and extreme speed merchants, those with the thirst for rapidity exhibited by Mills and others.

G. P. Mills wasn't the first to attempt the End to End at speed. He was employed as a pacer on Lawrence Fletcher of the Anfield's tricycle End to End attempt (all records at this point were paced). He rode from Gloucester to Edinburgh on a 53-inch ordinary, then carried on when he realised the next pacer lacked the same power and speed, completing the 650 miles to the finish. A year later, on 5 July 1886, he took up the challenge on a Beeston Humber Ordinary, again on a 53-inch with solid tyres (it wasn't until 1887 that J. B. Dunlop began experimenting with pneumatic tyres, leading to their commercial debut in 1890). The weather was hot and the roads were a scree of dust and gravel. Mills later recalled that they 'very much resembled a shingle beach'.* Fellow Anfielders helped with the record attempt, sorting out where to stay, organising food and marshalling – a prototype of the organisational network deployed on nearly all records since: a combination of a cadre of direct support and informal support along the route.

Mills rode day and night, with the exception of forty-five

---

* Alan J. Ray, *Cycling: Land's End to John o'Groats*, p.24.

minutes of sleep taken at Gloucester. His encounter with the
Garry Pass near Killiecrankie was nearly a disaster. One of the
risks of being on a high-wheeler were wind gusts through gaps;
rider and entourage were blown from their machines while
heading up through the pass, but uninjured. Mills pressed on
to Edinburgh before taking any further rest, stopping for four
hours once across the ferry. The Scottish arterial roads were no
better, some were much worse, a recurring problem being the
gradual conversion of road to railway, with track laid across the
top of the camber. Mills invariably took to the heather, followed
the cart tracks or pushed around the obstacle. He teetered into
John o'Groats after 5 days, 1 hour and 45 minutes, beating the
previous record, held by Lawrence Fletcher, by fifteen hours.

Mills' ride drew admiration from the press, who were awestruck by both Mills and the Anfield Bicycle Club. *The Wheel
World* wrote: 'The Anfield encourages its members to emulate
their doughtiest deeds; and whilst London is seething in a

G. P. Mills in Bordeaux–
Paris, 1891

Nadar © BNF/France

continual turmoil of racing-path squabbles, Liverpool asserts its priority to recognition as the home of the best bath of road-riders on earth.' Along with unceasing admiration for the Liverpool club came wonderment at the achievements of Mills, who had 'knocked the previous record into a cocked hat ... a feat of stupendous endurance. We are further astonished by the news that he is so little distressed as to be determined to start again, this time on a tricycle.'

The penny-farthing record stood for 133 years, until Richard Thoday proved he was made of the right degree of madness and determination. The RRA refused to ratify this new record, possibly because, as Thoday freely admitted, 'a penny-farthing is lethal if the slightest thing goes wrong'. He gave a unique insight into the challenge that they both faced:

> The road conditions would have been far worse; I can't imagine how he felt at the end. After four and a half days of riding I was seeing double. For me, it was a journey of personal discovery and finding out what I'm capable of. I found my limit; the ride was physically brutal. I tried to ride again a few days later but was incapable – it took me several months before I was able to cycle properly again, unlike G. P. Mills who was straight back out again. I feel much closer to G. P. now than I did at the start of the ride and I'd swear I felt his ghost riding near me at dawn on the second day out on the road.

Mills was indeed back racing straight away, attacking the 24-hour ordinary record and winning the North Road with 288 miles. Just five weeks later he took on the tricycle End to End record. He hadn't seen the trike he was due to ride until arriving in Penzance, at which point he adjusted the saddle and rode off through the most abysmal weather to obliterate the trike record by twenty-nine hours, finishing in 5 days and 10 hours. It created a further ripple of admiration. Fans included F. T. Bidlake, a man who was instrumental in the RRA and seen as the founding father of time trialling: 'he knocked more than a day off each of the previous bests, in a sort of double event, riding virtually without sleep, certainly no more than a wayside nod'.* The machine used was a Cripper – missing only the letter L in terms of a better description of its side effects, and weighing a mind- and limb-altering 75lb.

By 1891 the technological revolution in cycling meant that Mills could ditch the ordinary for a safety bicycle. It weighed in at a substantial 50lb and was furnished with a new set of Dunlop pneumatic tyres. Mills left Land's End at midnight on Sunday 29 September. Within the first 10 miles he'd lost his first pacer after a collision with a cart. Club members from 'First and Last C.C.', a Penzance-based cycling club (now sadly defunct), came out at 1 a.m. to assist with pace-making and escorted Mills up and through Bodmin in a rolling cavalcade of riders. A big crash somehow took out everyone except Mills, who sailed serenely on to Taunton, getting through the hilly stuff and towards the edge of the Somerset levels in 13 hours and 43 minutes. It's an ordinary stretch of road, the Mendips on one side, Brent Knoll on the other, a steadily rising ramp which continues up and over Redhill to Bristol.

On reaching the outskirts of Bristol, Mills cracked and switched his 23kg safety for a pacer's lighter weapon, saving some 6kg. (Moving from 23kg down to 17kg is hardly the stuff of lightweight dreams – anything over 8kg for a racing machine these days would be seen as morbidly obese – and shows the additional burden carried by those early endurance riders.) He

---

* Les Woodland, *This Island Race* (Norwich: Mousehold Press, 2005), p.33.

pressed on through Bristol, past coaching inns and toll bars to the city limits marked at Redland with Horfield the northern-most point, a linear village, and Filton some distance adrift. The travelling circus recorded 256 miles in the first twenty-four hours, stopping north of Worcester at midnight for a hot meal. The perils of pneumatic tyres meant punctures and more switching of machines for the run to Warrington, where biblical rain heralded his arrival into the borough.

He reached Penrith after forty-three hours in the saddle and took thirty minutes' sleep. The rain continued to sluice down and the adventure nearly came unstuck, once again in the Garry Pass. Mills momentarily fell asleep in the saddle but somehow avoided a fatal fall into the river below. After a fourth night of minimal rest, and with only 54 miles to go, the silent, sinister fingers of sleep deprivation grabbed hold. He stopped at Helmsdale and a pacer was instructed to visit a nearby chemist to find 'something to keep him awake'. He returned with a white powder which he swiftly tipped into a cup of tea for the somnolent rider.

Within seconds Mills felt alert and in tune with the rapid cadence and speed required. He jumped up on to the saddle, moved off and darted along the road until he was 'flying dementedly'. He shed each of his pacers and roared along until his eyes began to glaze once more. Mills entered a fugue state, somewhere between sleeping and waking, eyes empty of reason, legs a blur, somehow pedalling onwards for a further 35 miles. Just 3 miles from the finish, at 4.50 a.m., he dropped from the bicycle. No one could rouse him from the deepest of sleep. He was far into the recesses, lifeless; 'a somnambulist on wheels, he fell in a heap and went on sleeping in the mud'.* Concerned

---

* *Bicycling World*, 30 October 1891.

helpers carried him to bed in a nearby cottage and waited. Some seven hours later, Mills awoke with a start, shocked by the time. 'I leaped from my bed, I could not waste a moment. In hot haste I dashed along the road with all the vigour I could summon.' Mills ripped through the last ten minutes and beat the record by fourteen hours and twenty-eight minutes, with 4 days, 11 hours and 17 minutes.

In the aftermath of the achievement, Mills tried to piece together the last hours of the ride, having no memory of events between Helmsdale and Wick. He asked his pacer what he had given him. 'Cocaine,' came the reply – according to a doctor, 'enough to kill two men'. In those days cocaine was a key ingredient of patent medicines, seen as a minor tonic, with undocumented side effects. Mills was saved simply by dint of the excessive energy he expended immediately following the overdose. He had unwittingly counteracted its effects – constricted blood vessels, and increased temperature, heart rate and blood pressure – and ridden along with other substantial side effects shaking themselves loose around him: tremors, muscle twitches, auditory hallucinations, changes in depth perception, the gnashing of teeth. Mills 'confessed' to the episode in a letter to *Cycling* magazine some twenty years later – insofar as anyone can confess something that they didn't administer, although these days he might still fall foul of 'strict liability' laws.

Following the record his reputation as an endurance pioneer began to reach the continent. Mills and others were travelling vast distances unaided, something beyond comprehension in recent memory; they were rewriting our knowledge of what could be achieved, how far and how quickly, through human effort. Technology has recalibrated our sense of journey time, but in an age of railways and nothing more, the distances attempted on safeties and ordinaries were heroic, mythical. The stayers of the era became celebrities, and G. P. Mills was the

most celebrated of all. He was invited by *Véloce Sport* magazine
to take part in the inaugural Bordeaux–Paris, planned to be
the longest road race ever seen. He headed across the Channel
as part of a five-strong British contingent, the rest a roll call of
Victorian nomenclature: Monty Holbein, Selwyn Francis-Edge,
P. C. Twentyman and J. E. L. Bates. They may have looked
like archetypal country gents in plus fours and caps, but they
knew exactly what they were doing. Footrests were installed on
the forks for the descents and road-tested woollen jerseys and
'knickers' were preferred, in contrast to the outmoded French
with their long trousers and bicycle clips.

Despite an early fall, Mills extended the peloton like an
accordion player stretching for the loudest notes, and he
reached Angoulême at 10.30 a.m. The Mayor and an excited
civic committee had prepared hot baths, a full three-course
dinner, a range of refreshments and freshly made beds. Much
to their chagrin, Mills and his team paused only to wolf down
some soup before charging straight on. They had no time to
stop and stare. The group continued to peel off seconds and
minutes, hurtling along between the plane trees at 14mph,
picking up carefully stationed pacers along the way. At Tours,
he ate a raw steak and a 'specially prepared stimulant'.* It was
pre-Choppy Warburton,† but drug use was commonplace. Just
five years later Arthur Linton was to win Bordeaux–Paris under
Warburton's supervision, as observed by a colleague:

> I saw him at Tours, halfway through the race, at midnight,
> where he came in with glassy eyes and tottering limbs, and in
> a high state of nervous excitement. I then heard him swear – a

---

* *The Bicycle*, 21 November 1945, p.10.
† Famous trainer of bicyclists, beset by allegations of 'doping'.

very rare occurrence with him – but after a rest he was off again, though none of us expected he would go very far. At Orléans at five o'clock in the morning, Choppy and I looked after a wreck – a corpse as Choppy called him – yet he had sufficient energy, heart, pluck, call it what you will, to enable him to gain 18 minutes on the last 45 miles of hilly road.*

Warburton's involvement in cycling ended abruptly once his riders started dying, but the use of stimulants within sport and recreational life remained common.

Fortified by soup and stimulants, Mills won the race by an hour in 26 hours and 36 minutes. The great French hope, Laval, was five and a half hours adrift. The last of the thirty or so to finish came in two days later. At 358 miles in total, it was a third the length of his usual racing distance, not much more than a sprint.

An oft-recycled part of the Mills myth: he liked to shoot. He rarely left home without his trusty Colt revolver and always took it when training or riding. 'When the dogs come, as surely they will throughout the countryside, there is one solution only. Dispatch them with a careful aim. In this way the racing cyclist can escape serious injury and unwanted attention.' During that Bordeaux–Paris he shot and killed five. Allegedly.

Mills was 'a king among those of the road',† pushing the boundaries of what was thought possible. He took part in the North Road Club annual 24-hour race and travelled across to Holland to race, declaring in strident tones, 'I astonished the natives, winning the 100-kilometre road championship by half an hour.' On 5 June 1893, Mills attempted his fourth End to

---

* *Sporting Life*, 25 July 1896.
† *Strand Magazine*, vol. 1, January to June 1891, p.527.

End record, again on a Cripper tricycle. The Cripper had a much closer resemblance to modern machines than other bicycles of the era, chiefly because the steering had shifted to the front, getting rid of the track-rod steering and making it quicker to corner and more stable. It is not without a certain aesthetic beauty, but not built for racing.

Mills had been hit by a severe bout of blood poisoning earlier in the year, requiring an operation to save his foot, but it didn't seem to hinder his build-up to the event. The main issue during the attempt seemed to be a bout of 'cholera' at Gloucester, cured with 'forty drops of chlorodyne',* a patent medicine consisting of Samuel Taylor Coleridge's favourite,† laudanum, mixed with cannabis tincture and chloroform. Mills was able to continue, and he rode into the middle of the modern age of railway expansion. The road between Carrbridge and Inverness was being subsumed by track-laying. He used rutted cart tracks through the moorland heather, covering 20 miles in four long hours. It failed to deter his progress as he reduced the tricycle record to 3 days, 16 hours and 47 minutes for the 900-mile trek. All this on a tricycle weighing over 50lb, on rutted roads, in awful weather, while recovering from cholera and blood poisoning.

Mills made a fifth attempt in 1894, this time on a 'safety'. The Garry Pass loomed again as the capricious adventure-wrecker of choice. While he was rolling along a shying horse bolted, pulling a trap over and causing a huge crash, affecting all the riders. Mills was injured, his thigh bone visible, a gleaming white surface at the bottom of a deep, wide slash in his leg. They cannibalised the pacers' machines to create one working bicycle,

---

* Alan J. Ray, *Cycling: Land's End to John o'Groats*, p.27.
† 'I have in this one dirty business of Laudanum an hundred times deceived, tricked, nay, actually & consciously LIED' – Coleridge in an 1814 letter to a friend describing his addiction.

stapled the wound together, and he managed to continue. More wet weather left the party in a filthy condition; hostelries and hotels refused them admission on account of the layers of grime, so they pushed on, lowering the record to 3 days, 5 hours and 49 minutes. He had reduced his first record by over two whole days.

Mills' last effort was the tandem record in 1895, with kindred spirit T. A. Edge, also of the North Road. They opted for an Olympia tandem tricycle, where the pilot sits perilously on the front, as though perched on the edge of a ducking stool. Emergency braking was managed by sticking the leg in front of the tyre, which allowed them on least one occasion to escape a stray flock of sheep. For this sixth End to End record, Mills and Edge managed 3 days, 4 hours and 46 minutes.

At the age of twenty-eight, Mills was done. He continued to work in the cycle trade – a common career path for ex-professionals, even now – and put his experience of bicycle design to practical use. He started as a designer with Humber, in Beeston, preparing the frame for the provision of a new gearing mechanism by Henry Sturmey and James Archer ahead of their first patent application and development of planet-geared three-speed hubs. He moved to Raleigh in 1896 as works manager, constructing and equipping the new Lenton factory, which went on to employ over four thousand workers. He was awarded the DSO in the First World War, then returned to engineering. He died on 8 November 1945, aged seventy-eight, in Croydon. So much for the contemporary views of doctors in the 1890s who predicted a foreshortening of life expectancy – as much as ten years per long ride.

Mills' cycling career was defined by acceleration on many levels. His remorseless riding led to the overhaul of records by incomprehensible margins. It also marked an acceleration in bicycle design, as manufacturers moved away from the ordinary towards the important diamond frame construction. Perhaps more importantly, Mills reflected the essence of the times, a proto-modern world where time and space were expanding and accelerating, pushing the horizon away but bringing it closer at the same time, allowing for far greater distances and speeds. Along with the paced track teams of the day, he was part of the vanguard of heroic pioneer cyclists, riding at incredible pace, linking together the extremities of the map. This was a world of new, unforeseen speeds, of the photography pioneer Eadweard Muybridge and split-second times, a world where the railway disgorged passengers from the pastoral into the metropolitan in the blink of a dislocated and disconcerted eyelid. Mills was a key part of this expansion of time and shrinking of distance, a source of wonder and anxiety in a world typified by the H. G. Wells short story 'The New Accelerator', in which the protagonist imbibes a tincture that changes his perception of himself and the world for ever: 'Remember you will be going several thousand times faster than you ever did before, heart, lungs, muscles, brain – everything – and you will hit hard without knowing it. You won't know it, you know. You'll feel just as you do now. Only everything in the world will seem to be going ever so many thousand times slower than it ever went before.'*

_____

* H. G. Wells, 'The New Accelerator' (http://www.online-literature.com/wellshg/16/ – accessed 20 November 2018).

4

The westward train was empty and had no corridors

Monday, 20 August 2018

I wake at 5 a.m. and begin by banging doors, again and again, the double bangs of huge industrial fire doors. My sleep was interrupted by noisy Spaniards banging doors again and again and their rabid noisy squiggles of drunken Spanish. I am keen to ensure they are aware of the importance of my endeavour. I hear movement, rumbling from the room next door, grumbling, and I feel as though the first part of my mission is complete. Breakfast is a hardboiled egg and bread I brought with me from Bristol.

Nothing is moving between the soft dark and light. The youth hostel slips away over my shoulder, subsiding into the hidden valley before falling away slowly to the sea. The notch of the valley is framed by the capital As of tents in the garden against the velour blue of the approaching dawn; the deep blue sky seems to soften the sound of the gravel crunch beneath my cleats.

I am attempting to see, in a small, fathomable way, what it

is like to ride for a very long time. I know I will need to rest afterwards, before repeating the exercise with another long stage early next year, away and up through the Midlands corridor. The north of England and Scotland will be later again, in the summer, when I have more time – days, a week – rather than the hours available today. My decisions have been shaped by the 'free' time available, the commitments of my temporary part-time job and the permanence of family.

I barely touch the pedals. To touch the pedals is to exert energy, and to exert energy is to burn matches, and burning matches is bad. I use the word 'crepuscular' all the time, ever since someone told me it was their favourite word and then I made it my favourite word, but finally I *am* crepuscular, for a few fleeting moments, as the grey light oozes in like molasses, a commingled blue and grey. The wind is behind me, and I am grateful – genuinely, quasi-religiously, worthy of prayer to something or someone – as I begin to trace a line up through the middle of the county.

I ride through Cornish villages and towns where silence holds and no one is awake, much less going to work. No one stops to ask me where I might be going, and I am disappointed because I want to say 'I'm going to Bristol' and bask in the confusion and madness of their response. I want people to know I'm doing this crazy thing. At 6 a.m. in deepest Cornwall no one cares.

The lanes give way to the main road and the ride begins in earnest. Finally, I see two people on road bikes. They ask me where I'm going and I say, 'Oh, just Bristol,' and they look at me like I am an idiot or lying or both.

It is mining country, or it was mining country. The remnants of minerals and china clay are still here. They found alquifou in the dense minerality of this landscape, used by my mum many years later to create the greenish tint for her pottery glaze. The land above is scarred, the land below crossed by veined tunnels. It has been a long time since industry ruled the county. Even for Harman and Blackwell the landscape was one of change: 'on all sides were traces of the departed glory of the tin district; old mines with chimney shafts by the dozen pointing gloomily to the sky, as if calling it to witness the state of decay'. There must be fewer of them now, but there are more than I imagined. Riding on out of Bodmin towards the moor they stand on either side, reminders of grim industrial times, of smoky and pitted landscapes, at odds with our prelapsarian ideals of this county where the chimneys now occupy a bucolic postcard-sized space in our imagination. Men would travel for three hours to reach the seam 3000 feet below, work for four hours, then return. The Cornish experience remains one of marginalisation and struggle, where the forces of youth and innocence battle with the grasping age of experience, high capitalism, second homes, neglect from the centre. It is a county that grasped Brexit as an opportunity for severance and recompense but which can only end up further away from the centre of things.

The main road is vile, my first taste of the route for record rides. It is not through choice, but out of necessity; on a long, long day there is no alternative. I want to get to Bristol before nightfall. I could use the lanes but the zig-zags and grippy surfaces add hours and miles to the total. I stick to the A30. It is a steady trek uphill. I think of the riders who take this route on their record attempts; any ideas that this might be a scenic or enlightening journey are dispelled. It is speed and time. Mike Broadwith, who I followed on his epic journey a couple of months ago, messages me later. I have appointed him as my mentor, even though I haven't told him he has been appointed and I am unlikely to tell him.

MB: Someone asked me about riding the A30 as a recce. I said it was a shit idea.

PJ: Through Cornwall, that one?

MB: Yes that one, what do you think? You rode it.

PJ: It is a shit idea you are correct.

Mike has said he will come and meet me and ride alongside
for a bit. I have mixed feelings. I wanted company but I was terrified of what company meant. I was torn between telling people
what I was doing and not telling anyone anything, because if I
told them then I would *have* to do it. In the end I told everyone
and I decided to raise money for young people's mental health
in Bristol. It felt like a good thing to do. I had spent years trying
to support young people in schools while community initiatives
were pollarded under the consumptive dogma of austerity –
because, you know, it's mentally ill young people who should
pay for the global financial crisis. By doing it at least in part for
somebody else, the taint of narcissism, the *whyness* of the endeavour, could be deflected. And I would *have* to do it.

The A30 is horrid. A tide of tarmac besmirching the middle
of Bodmin Moor, a prehistoric landscape of russet-coloured
heath, cairns and tors, standing stones and circles. The dual carriageway rolls upwards and it feels unsafe. I struggle with traffic
'suck', the swooshing vacuum of huge lorries passing close and
pulling me outwards into the void of moving air. I used to love
traffic suck when racing alone in time trials; it was 'free speed'.
Today, I am less enamoured. No one wants or expects to see a
cyclist on a road like this. During record attempts the support
vehicles create a buffer, slowing up the inside lane. Here there
is nothing and I resort to riding on the hard shoulder, a strip of
gritty, spiky tarmac. I hate it. I go on hating it for two hours. I
even ask a police officer if it's legal to ride on the A30. He looks
at me like I'm a complete idiot – which I am, clearly – and says,
'Yes, but it's not recommended.' Eventually, at Launceston or
thereabouts, I achieve escape velocity and find a quieter road.

I tick off the milestones: 50 miles, then 100. I make a mental note to tick off mile 127, the furthest I've been. My mind adjusts to the madness of the distance. Eighty miles seems like nothing, 100 means only 100 to go. Boredom isn't quite the correct word. I lapse into a state of flow, of self-preservation, coping with my rubbish legs and terrible fitness. I think maybe I've cracked it, the art of riding slowly enough. Just don't stop. It has taken a long time to learn how to take this long to do things.

I take a known short cut. The roads are worse, but it goes through Tiverton, where I went to school. I want to look and see what has changed. The answer is everything. The school is gone, replaced by 'executive' houses. I recognise the path we used to follow by the River Exe. I look over the embankment wall and can see the younger me walking in a crocodile with other school friends, none of us knowing what the future held but hoping it held something, knowing that what I hoped the future held was not this. It was twenty-six years ago, before life unfolded like one of those maps which can never be folded back in the same way. It was before I lost my mind for a time, fought to get it back again, found my pride and self-belief, then lost them again, only to look for them once more on a long section of straight road through Devon and Cornwall. We were obsessed with the fighter jets we would one day surely be piloting. We would hear the roar and see them swoop low over the Exe Valley. There was no room for baggage in the SEPECAT Jaguar, our fast jet of choice in 1985.

I miss the simple certainty of childhood. I'm still trying to work out why I'm doing this, or what the journey will lead to. I am impulsive and make bad decisions. I am the sum of bad decisions, of which this journey may or may not be one. I hope I am going to achieve something at some point in this ride, some-thing transcendent. Everything will become clear, somewhere on a luminous ribbon of tarmac. It might be today when I'm in the depths of riding further than I have ever ridden before.

I stop for garage food and feel lifted by the spiritual persua-
sion of sugar and endorphins, the surge in feeling and energy, a
crackling in my mind. Endorphins are my favourite. I wonder
if people mistake endorphins for a sign from God. All it takes is
a heady combination of the dancing light from clouds, a bit of
sepulchral mist, some fatigue, all mixed in with the elation from
endorphins and a fragile ego, and BOOM, God is speaking,
imparting wisdom, a lightning bolt of *do this now*. I am welling
up, in that way I almost well up when confronted with some
sort of hinted truth, like when I see a small dog shivering with
cold, or a squirrel's back legs twitching because it was hit by a
car but not enough to kill it, just to make it shudder to death. It
is a welling of regretful tears at things happening that shouldn't
have happened, seeing the shadow of my younger self walking
alongside, unburdened by what is to come and dreaming of fast
jets. I think of Louis MacNeice and how his poetry defines the
way I feel with a precision I cannot reach:

> I do not want to be reflective any more
> Envying and despising unreflective things
> Finding pathos in dogs and undeveloped
>   handwriting . . .*

The ceaseless patter of the A38 keeps me company, a gossipy
noise which soothes my mind – the hypnotic rumble of tyres on
a lumpen surface, the steady rattle of the bike – and I'm back
thinking of ordinary things. I keep eating. It is hard to eat on long-
distance rides. I never knew this. I assumed a ravenous hunger
would conquer everything, but my stomach feels wrong. I remember author and endurance cyclist Emily Chappell describing long

---

* 'Wolves', by Louis MacNeice.

rides as 'an eating competition'. I guess it is, but I didn't realise the competitive aspect was trying to eat in the first place.

I know Mike is going to appear somewhere near Wellington and I am afraid of not being able to keep up. I was afraid of not making it this far, of getting off my bike and crying a long way before Wellington. It feels ludicrous: man who rides from Land's End to John o'Groats in under forty-four hours offers to keep a hapless chopper company on a slow-motion crawl through the West Country. There is considerable scope for embarrassment. Before I can overthink, he appears at a roundabout with a jaunty wave. We join up and tap along the main road and into the flat familiarity of Somerset, moving up country. It is meat and drink for him, a bun run, a skip out for a quick 100 miles. I am grateful for the wheel and grateful that I feel OK, and we talk aimlessly as we roll along at about 15mph. I'm anxious about my ability to last the distance. I feel like it's a normal level of concern. I think about how Mike did nearly 20mph for 842 miles, or that if he left on his record ride at the same time as me this morning he would currently be near Worcester.

At which point Mike reads my mind and says, 'I'll show you the power I rode at for the entire End to End. It was 210 watts, 280 on the climbs. I'll show you on this bit of road.'

I'm sceptical because I have no idea what 210 watts means. The acceleration is steady but final. I try to force through the pedal stroke but he is gone and I am happy to let the elastic snap. I realise that riding at nearly 20mph for 842 *metres* is beyond me after 120 miles.

The ride settles again, and I am grateful for the company. The roads are quiet as we bowl along the edge of the levels and then up through a notch in the Mendips and past the airport to begin the fast run-in to Bristol. Friends come out to say hello. Best man and cycling chum Steve Green stands at the finish line of the time trial course where we did our first ever race together and offers up treats. Some long-distance ultra-nutters join us at Shipham for the ride in, and suddenly we are a group and we are chatting about everything and nothing as the sun subsides languidly into the landscape, draining the colour away until everything is a blue-green wash and the city lies stretched out before us like a crowded picnic rug. The bridges are visible in the far distance – I point them out to Mike, because I know he likes bridges. He is impressed. Three suspension bridges in the same widescreen sweep, each one a fluorescent tube of moving light against the darkening blue.

The ride seems shortened, time-compressed, the journey reduced to an arpeggio, not the symphony it seemed at the beginning. Stage one is complete. Fifteen hours of riding has been reduced to a series of memories and flow, some of it buried, doubtless to return in another twenty-six years' time.

On the A38 with
Michael Broadwith

5

Women will not die by the wayside

Tuesday, 19 July 1938

If bike racing in the UK has a founding father, it is Frederick Thomas Bidlake. There are three longstanding cycling institutions in the UK: Cycling Time Trials (CTT), the Road Records Association and the Cyclists' Touring Club (CTC); British Cycling is the latecomer. Between them they encapsulate the cultural background of cycling and its parochial British identity, somehow removed from those rogue continentals with their fancy ideas. F. T. Bidlake was a founding member of all three. He has a revered trophy and a very nice garden in Bedfordshire named after him.

However, Bidlake was very much in keeping with late Victorian morality: he didn't like ladies riding bikes. He was not alone; there was open anxiety at the potential for social and physical change, with 'lady cyclists' causing consternation. Towns and cities across the land were scandalised. Take the streets of Nottingham in 1893: 'women, in addition to the degradation of riding a bicycle, have further unsexed themselves by doing so in man's attire' – and so it continues, with words like 'demoralising', 'weak-minded', 'illegality' and 'reprobated'.* The horror is visceral in Derby a year later: 'when the rider of the iron horse belongs to the "emancipated" section and wears her hair with the brevity of a man's ... and smokes a cigarette as she dashes through the villages, it poses a sex problem to the gazers'.† Roll forward to the fin de siècle and Lord Salisbury wades in on the topic of 'rational dress',‡ an 'offensive, absurd and comical costume'.

Bidlake seemed driven by a latent fear of ladies and the erosion of Victorian certainty. He retained his sense of moral panic for many years, relying on the hefty power of verbosity to make his point. At one point he came out against knickerbockers; they were an object of 'contumelious ridicule'. I suspect 'contumelious' was an archaism even then. It's a Jacob Rees-Mogg of a word, riding on to the page dressed in plus fours and blowing a bugle. I do a bit of A Level language analysis, whack it in the Google Ngram Viewer which checks word frequency in every book and text over time. It delivers the goods: 'contumelious' peaked in usage in the 1810s, a full hundred years prior to Bidlake's anachronistic charge into the politics of gender and his terror at the prospect of ladies riding quickly. The most febrile point of his outrage was reached in 1912 in an editorial for *Cycling* magazine:

> Cycle racing for women is generally acknowledged to be undesirable. My ideal of a clever lady rider is one who can

---

* *Nottinghamshire Guardian*, 18 November 1893.
† *Derby Mercury*, 22 August 1894.
‡ *Illustrated London News*, 1 July 1899, p.7.

ride far, who can ride at a really useful speed, who mounts hills with comfort, and makes no fuss or show of effort. The stylish, clever lady stops short of being a scorcher, but if women's races were to be organised, the participants would have to run to their limit, or else make a mockery of racing. And that limit is not pleasant to contemplate ... the speed woman is dishevelled, grimy and graceless. I believe in a high standard of cycling ability as really worthwhile attaining by women, but not as racers ... Imagine women dressed for speed, on bicycles built for speed, in attitudes necessary for speed, grabbing speed food and finishing dead to the world.*

It speaks of a desperation to retain some sense of a permanently fragrant woman. Bidlake may have been instrumental in the development of bike racing in the British Isles, but he left a legacy of gender inequality, a deeply chauvinistic Victorian mindset which took some dispelling. His involvement in the RRA and then the Road and Time Trials Council from 1922 saw many of these values enshrined in the written and unwritten rules of competitive cycling. This was a man who viewed continental massed-start racing as 'a superfluous excrescence'. Cycling was a threat to patriarchal authority.

Under his watchful eye the men carried on riding. George A. Olley set the record twice, in 1907 and 1908, bringing it down to 3 days, 5 hours and 20 minutes. Tom Peck lowered it later that year to 2 days, 22 hours and 42 minutes, a record that stood for twenty-one years. In that time the geography of the island changed; cars colonised the landscape, bridges put ferries out of business, and times and distances came down. It seems like a typical lull in record breaking, and in many ways it was. When

---

* 'Should Lady-Cyclists Ride in Races?', *Cycling* (UK), 25 July 1912, p.75.

the record is rewritten a psychological shift seems to occur and it dampens the enthusiasm to take it on. Bringing it within three days seemed significant; when Dick Poole brought it inside two days in 1965 his record stood for fourteen years. Jack Rossiter, in 1929, and then the legendary Australian Hubert Opperman, in 1934, reduced the record a bit more, before Sid Ferris took the last pre-war End to End record in 1937. Ferris was an accomplished rider, sponsored by Raleigh and Sturmey Archer. He was obsessed by detail, with careful and exact preparation. The press made hay over two things: he was a vegetarian and he had one eye. A tasteful graphic in *Coureur* in 1958 depicts him as a pirate waving a carrot impaled on a cutlass. Ferris was chasing the record set by Opperman (depicted riding a kangaroo riding a bicycle in the same illustration), and it wasn't until the last third of the ride that he edged ahead. The Hounslow ace took 2 days, 6 hours and 33 minutes to complete the distance.

Hubert Opperman

For women, the challenge was recognition and acceptance – the RRA was an exclusively male organisation. Instrumental in breaking down both the practical barriers to participation and the ideological fog spread by Bidlake in his writing was journalist Lyn Stancer, known as Petronella. Her columns in *Cycling* were widely read and unequivocal in their support for women's cycling, forming a compelling counterpoint to Bidlake who wrote for the same publication. Petronella's stance was radical, both explicitly and implicitly. She was an advocate for freedom of movement, freedom to race, freedom of dress and of everything else. It was a post-suffrage battleground for equality which reached outside the parameters of the sport. In 1927, American sociologist Crystal Eastman was living in London. She was quick to recognise the physical and intellectual power of bicycles as being 'the beginning of women's emancipation'. As historian Peter Cox neatly summarised, 'they offered the opportunity for unchaperoned, autonomous and independent mobility: precisely those codes of action constrained by rigid social roles. Eastman and other militant feminists campaigned through the 1920s for the abolition of laws and provisions for the special protection of women, arguing that equality for women must mean equality at all levels.'*

The National Cycle Archive at Warwick has a set of lanterns taken by Petronella when touring across Europe and the UK. It is a breathtaking representation of a different England: pre-war, quiet roads, a joyful, Edenic emptiness. The images highlight the liberating power of the bicycle, the emancipatory nature of touring as a physical act. 'The gently revolutionary'† Petronella

---

* 'Women, Gendered Roles, Domesticity and Cycling in Britain', in Peter Cox (ed.), *Cycling Cultures* (Chester: University of Chester Press, 2015), p.179.
† Ibid, p.182.

Petronella sheltering from the rain

Lantern from the Warwick National Cycling Archive
MSS.328/N104/K/10/90, Modern Records Centre,
University of Warwick

also challenged notions of acceptable clothing, confronting
Bidlake's revulsion at 'rational dress'. 'It is about time that girl
cyclists were allowed to dress as they like (within reason) and as
they consider most suitable for the type of riding they prefer . . .
I say it is time that all these things should come to pass. I have
not the slightest hope that they really will, and even if I did have
any hope at all I expect that it would be entirely dashed to pieces
when I read the replies that I shall surely get to these remarks.'*
Her ambition, wit and pragmatism served as a response to
patriarchal power and the marginalisation of women. On many
levels Petronella was an inspirational and important force for
change in the world of cycling and beyond.

It is a significant point of cultural transformation. The
combined efforts of a small group of women, their energy,

---

* *Gazette*, October 1937, p.342.

commitment and strength, created lasting change in the post-war era. This group included Evelyn Parkes, Billie Dovey, Lilian Dredge and Marguerite Wilson. They were pioneers, opening the door to everyone else who came afterwards, from Ethel Brambleby to Beryl Burton, from Eileen Gray to Lizzie Deignan and Emily Chappell. They formed the Women's Road Record Association (WRRA) in 1934 to ratify place-to-place records, but not the End to End. They were hesitant about the biggest place-to-place of them all, fearful that the sight of women suffering might be seen as degrading and thus set back their quest. There was also a reductive desire to avoid any 'male precedent'. This involved trying to ensure record attempts were undertaken with female observers, timekeepers and so on, to prevent men from seeing things they shouldn't perhaps see. This proved unworkable and was abandoned before too long.

The End to End was added to the books as a standard distance for women in 1937. The first attempt was by Lilian Dredge, a year later. It is a landmark moment. Dredge was an incredible rider; she had ridden the World Championship in Belgium in 1934 and taken several place-to-place records in the first few years of the WRRA. Male voices proclaimed 'she'll die by the wayside' and 'the slimming will be carried to extremes and she'll be worn to a shadow'. There was also a conspicuous lack of support from the industry – normally so quick to get the men on their bikes. However, the frame-builder Claud Butler stepped in to help with logistics and equipment, and he signed her up as a professional. The initial schedule was set for five days and seventeen hours, well outside G. P. Mills' effort on an ordinary, but it allowed for 'sleep stops', which were seen as essential because she was a woman.

The entourage set out from Land's End at 4 a.m. on Tuesday, 19 July 1938. Dredge opted for a cutting-edge Osgear 3-speed – the specified gearing for the Tour de France in 1937, the first year gears were allowed. It features an ungainly hanging front arm used to change gear on the back, pushing the chain down. She took hurried meals at roadside cafés, while grape juice and Emprote (a 1950s energy drink consisting of dried milk and cereal powder and very high in protein) were handed up by roadside helpers. After 231 miles in the saddle she slept at Gloucester. By the end of the second day she had reached Kendal, at 424 miles. Thursday saw the Shap and then the Grampians, with a break at Guay on the old road to Pitlochry. She arrived at John o'Groats at one in the morning, stopping the clock at 3 days, 20 hours and 54 minutes, eighteen hours of which were spent sleeping.

Given the circumstances and the weight of expectation – both to fail and to succeed – it was an important ride, opening up the distance for women and setting a competitive marker. After nine hours' sleep at John o'Groats, Dredge went on to complete the 1000 miles, finishing in 4 days, 19 hours and 33 minutes. The WRRA, far from being open to the 1000 record, threatened to disallow it because no notice of the attempt had been given; it came down to a battle of wills between Petronella (in favour) and Jessie Springhall, the secretary, who wanted the mark expunged. Petronella won the day.

In 1939, Marguerite Wilson became the second lady to attempt the record. In a short space of time Wilson had acquired a reputation that transcended gendered expectations. She redefined what was thought possible and achieved a level of fame that shifted outside the narrow confines of domestic cycling. In this respect Wilson can be seen as a forerunner of Eileen Sheridan and Beryl Burton. Post-war record holder Sheridan recalled meeting Wilson at the Royal Albert Hall in 1945. 'I admired and had read about her. I was the 25-mile national champion and received my medal and I saw her talking to some friends. I went and asked her for her autograph, and she scribbled it and I thanked her, but she didn't talk to me because she didn't know who I was, but I knew who she was – gosh, she was *Marguerite Wilson!*'

Wilson started out with the Bournemouth Arrow in 1934, for the simple reason that it was supportive of women riding and racing; in her own words, 'the male members of various local clubs resented the intrusion, the women were half hearted when they knew they had not the support'.* She was a tourist and racer, combining the two by riding to races, camping out, racing, then riding home. She covered huge distances in search of women's events, challenging the view that 'her ilk should stay at home, get themselves tidied up and wait for the phone to ring'.† She became enthralled by the thrill of competition, seeing a 'good tear up' as 'the real joy of cycling', but even so, she didn't tell her parents where she was going or what she was doing. 'I tucked my home-made tights into my bag and crept out.'‡

Having cleaned up in the locality, Wilson began to look further afield and put a team together for the North Western Ladies 25 promotion. It required a lot of logistical planning. Rather than ride and camp, they opted to drive, having access to a clubmate's tiny Morris two-seater. They crammed it with three riders, one supporting chap, three bikes and all their equipment. They stuck the helper in the 'dickey' with the bicycles – essentially a fold-up seat in the boot. They still needed to strap one bicycle to the bonnet, with Wilson noting that 'it impeded my vision no little extent'. It is also worth mentioning that she had never driven a car before. At about half distance

---

* William Wilson & Marguerite Wilson, *The First Star of Women's Cycling* (Poole: CMP (UK) Ltd, 2015), p.14.
† Ibid, p.13.
‡ Ibid, p.21.

they ran out of petrol because they didn't realise cars required fuel. Eventually they arrived at race HQ at 2.30 a.m. Digs were out of the question so the four of them 'slept' in the car. The next morning Wilson won the race, the Arrow took the team prize, and they drove home to Bournemouth.

Wilson rapidly became a standard bearer for women's cycling, winning regularly at multiple distances, including 12-hours. In 1938 she moved to Sevenoaks and joined the West Croydon Wheelers, one of a handful of clubs in the south-east that sought to expand opportunities for women. Rosslyn Ladies, with Lilian Dredge, Florence Uren and others, were the core of the WRRA. Wilson gained additional miles by riding home on Friday and back from Bournemouth on the Sunday. With a new level of support and a wider sense of the possibilities, she turned her attention to place-to-place records.

The ambivalence of the trade and leading figures within the press was slowly eroded by Petronella, Marguerite Wilson and others through a combination of a burning desire for equality, force of personality, ambition and a series of startling achievements by WRRA members. Billie Dovey rode nearly 30,000 miles in a calendar year – 80 miles a day – often touring and giving talks in the evening. She gained sponsorship from Rudge-Whitworth and Cadbury's, who sent her 5lb of chocolate each month. It did much to dispel the unhelpful myth of female fragility and the dangers of cycling for the 'womanly' temperament. Both Lilian Dredge and Marguerite Wilson arrived at the right time: road records were dominating the cycling magazines and making headway in the national media, featuring in the papers and on Pathé newsreels, with riders becoming celebrities, feted for their derring-do. Things were changing, even if it was framed through a gendered filter: for men, the adventure and suffering; for women, the adventure, but tempered with a clear reinforcement of domestic values – how lovely they looked when riding, how quickly they got home to cook dinner.

Marguerite Wilson began targeting records in 1938, including London to York, which brought her to the attention of Frank Southall, the 'records manager' for the Hercules Cycle and Motor Company, who insisted they get her on the books. Southall was a revered rider at the time, a former Olympian and 'crack cyclist'. He had been involved in an Ashes-style battle for place-to-place records with the Australian Hubert Opperman. It filled the pages of the press who termed the rivalry 'The Wheel War'. Opperman took various place-to-place records and went home, Southall then retook them. Opperman returned from Australia with a crack team of Antipodeans to take them back – cue publicity shots of Opperman training on rollers during the long journey by sea. Bankrolling the attempts were the two big bike brands, BSA and Hercules, each hoping that their bikes would prove fastest and gain publicity. In 1934, Opperman lowered the End to End to 2 days and 9 hours. He returned home, satisfied with his achievements, and subsequently set out to redefine Australian place-to-place records. They are continental in scale and emotion, the most terrifying among them Fremantle to Sydney, a 2900-mile crossing – well over three consecutive End to Ends. He fell asleep while riding, crashed and had perilous encounters with snakes ('I landed the bike on top of it, hard') in a thirteen-day adventure into the dark heart of the continent, a latter-day Voss on pilgrimage: 'I do not need a map. The map is in my head ... I have to imagine it ... I will make my own map. The country is mine.'*

Having retired, Southall had assembled an all-male team, including pre-war tyros Cyril Hepplestone and Shake Earnshaw.

---

* Patrick White, *Voss* (London: Penguin Modern Classics, 1966).

Hepplestone had an impish smile. Earnshaw looked scary and angular. Three Belgian professionals rounded out the group. Southall took a high-tech approach, block-booking the Winter Garden Hotel in Kingston upon Thames, creating an indoor training centre with rollers and a treatment room. Into the middle of this came Marguerite Wilson.

What followed is hard to comprehend, then and now, as Wilson overshadowed the men on the team and embarked on an unmatched sequence of record rides. She started on 4 April 1939 by setting a straight-out 50-mile record. Six days later she broke both the London to York and 12-hour records, managing 230 miles for the latter. Eight days after that she took the London to Brighton and back. It was her fourth record in a fortnight. On 13 May she took Edinburgh to Liverpool, 22 May London to Portsmouth and back, 2 July London to Bath and back, and Land's End to London *and* the 24-hour on 21 July. Both her

The Hercules Road Records Team

peers and the press ran out of superlatives: 'I have never seen a fitter or less tired-looking girl', 'truly a wonderful ride', 'the most phenomenal ride I have ever seen'; she is a 'record-smasher', 'the most amazing proposition on two wheels'; but the comments also included the more familiar trope of the 'blonde bombshell'. However, this amazing sequence was only a warm-up for the biggest one of all. The End to End was scheduled for September.

Marguerite Wilson's aim was to reduce Lilian Dredge's record by seventeen hours, the bulk of this coming from a tighter sleep schedule. There was some anxiety about the weather: women were expected to go, regardless of the conditions. On her place-to-place rides earlier in the year she'd regularly contended with a block headwind when 'conditions weren't right for a men's attempt'. It seems it was OK to send Wilson or Dredge out in the eye of a storm whereas Olley or Ferris would have the luxury of waiting. With the Hercules team in support, Wilson waited for three days at Land's End for better conditions, but to no avail. She rode away from the grey hotel into the teeth of a horrid easterly, so fierce that the Hercules PR cameraman was sent flying from his ladder by one sudden gust of wind. It was a race against time, as always, but a greater shadow loomed: the imminent threat of war. It coloured the mood, nationally, but also had a practical implication – the threat of blackout and the impact on night-time riding should hostilities be announced.

The wind dented her progress through Cornwall. A stop for tea at Sticklepath, near Okehampton, forms the most famous image from the ride and the cover of Isabel Best's *Queens of Pain*. An unruffled Wilson sips from a china cup, a picture of club-run calm. In the first twelve hours she rode 193 miles before stopping at Kidderminster for her first sleep, using the support caravan. The schedule proved ambitious and she was behind all the way to Kendal; Shap was the turning point. She climbed with ease on a lowest gear of 66 inches. In contrast,

Marguerite Wilson on Shap Fell

Michael Broadwith's biggest gear in 2018 was a 54-inch. Gear inches are technical things – when the wife is struggling to sleep I talk to her about the benefits of a 65.8-inch around Bristol and the Mendips – but in simple terms Broadwith's bike in 2018 was much easier to ride uphill than Wilson's in 1939.

A three-hour sleep at Lanark marked two days on the road and 632 miles. By now the wind was kinder, with sunshine beginning to peep through. The Garry Pass sparkled in the late summer sun and her confidence was up, the last big climbs negotiated without alarm. She finished the ride in 2 days, 22 hours and 52 minutes. After a brief rest, she then prepared for an 11 a.m. assault on the 1000.

Daylight slipped away and a blanket of cloud hung heavily over the landscape. The blackout left Wick in complete darkness, but Wilson finished safely in 3 days, 11 hours and 44 minutes. The sun sank in the early evening sky, easing into the broiling water off the coast. A destroyer lurked in the Pentland Firth, heading to Scapa Flow.

Two days later, war was declared and things changed quickly. Wilson stopped riding in 1941; she held all sixteen WRRA records. She served as an ambulance driver, then worked on BOAC Catalina flying boats out of Poole Harbour. The big bike companies switched to munitions and the war effort. After the war she moved to Canada and took part in a massed-start bike race, where the anecdote states she came fifth in a men's bunched race on a brakeless 78-inch track bike. Eventually she returned to the UK, but fell foul of the professional–amateur divide and was unable to race again. The authorities refused to readmit her to the amateur ranks and even threatened the Arrow with sanctions if she acted as a starter for a race.

In 1949 she had spinal surgery for a back injury and was unable to ride again. She disappeared out of the limelight and into family life, playing golf ridiculously well and bringing up her daughter. However, she suffered from depression, and in 1972, at the age of fifty-four, took her own life. In recent years her story has been placed firmly back where it belongs, at the forefront of cycle sport, by family member William Wilson who has an amazing archive of Marguerite's papers and photos, but also by Isabel Best in her brilliant book, and Ian Cleverley of *Rouleur*, who passionately advocated her inclusion in their hall of fame. She was the first woman to be employed as a professional cyclist, and the first to win the Bidlake Memorial Prize, itself a beautiful riposte to that man's views.

After the war it fell to Edith Atkins to get things moving again. Like Eileen Sheridan, her near contemporary, she was from Coventry and less than 5 feet tall, but unlike Eileen and Marguerite Wilson she remained an amateur. After taking several place-to-place records she received offers from both Dunlop and Raleigh, but rejected both. She didn't want the additional pressure, preferring to work with husband Ron, who coached and supported. As a result, money was tight, limiting the amount and type of support for her rides. They made do with one supporting vehicle and Atkins remortgaged her house in order to finance her attempts.

In the run-up to her End to End one place-to-place ride stands out. It started as the London–York. She completed it in record time, but opted to carry on riding, taking the 12-hour 'straight out' record. She didn't stop there, rolling onwards to set a new record for London to Edinburgh, before finishing the ride at the 24-hour mark, setting another new record of 422 miles and becoming the first woman to break the 400-mile barrier. It is a spectacular achievement: one day, four records. According to Ron, 'I knew I had a champion, and I was right.' After six days' rest she turned around and did Edinburgh to London. Two weeks later she tackled the End to End. Throughout this period she was riding an incomprehensible 300 miles a week in training, fuelled on a diet of raw eggs every 20 miles.

The End to End was an exercise in solidarity, with extensive support from the WRRA and the pre-war pioneers. Lilian Dredge helped on the road while her husband Freddie manned the phones in London. Petronella was there, handing up and supporting Atkins throughout an incredible ride. She set the first women's amateur record for Land's End to John o'Groats, eight days after her Edinburgh–Glasgow–Edinburgh record, beating Marguerite Wilson's professional record by nearly five hours. She finished in 2 days, 18 hours and 4 minutes.

For a tangible and touching reminder of an important time, head along to the Coventry Transport Museum. Her bicycle is on display alongside Eileen Sheridan's. It speaks of the power of the bicycle, clearly, but also of a time when a cadre of brilliant and committed cyclists transformed a sport. The WRRA absorbed vituperative anger and anxiety and broke down barriers through compelling journalism and action. They demonstrated beyond any doubt that women's endurance riding and racing was here to stay, narrowing the gap between the women and the men to the extent that both records stood at less than three days. They were pioneers in the truest sense of the word, in a way we should all aspire to be – by being better, not taking no for an answer, and confronting adversity and challenge head on. And they opened the door for one of the greatest bike riders the UK has ever seen, Eileen Sheridan.

6

Eileen Sheridan and the row of mermaids

Friday, 9 July 1954

I've lived in at least thirty places in forty-three years. It's been a peripatetic existence forged by my mum and dad's compulsive escapism, an expatriate lifestyle and their belief in the security of rootlessness. There are no accumulated memories for me, no ghosts lurking in a house laden with familial iconography. No childhood voices echoing through hallways, boxes of possessions in the loft and old crinkled photos. The contrast provided by Eileen Sheridan's living room is sharp, vivid. Two nights ago, I watched a Pathé newsreel from the early 1950s of Eileen Sheridan. She was sitting in an armchair with her son, Clive. She was wearing the Hercules head badge on her burgundy top, an indication of her professional status. The voiceover told us how Eileen is 'no ordinary woman', she does 'training with a capital T'. Sixty-five years later and I'm sitting opposite Eileen who is in the same chair wearing the same coloured top.

I was nervous about meeting Eileen Sheridan because lots of people had met her before, had tea, talked about her amazing life and asked her lots of questions. I recalled an interview Jack Thurston did some years ago, her playful tones and inspirational stories told in asides, each belying the magnitude of the achievement. I thought about writing her story by reading all the other stories, but knew I wanted to ask the questions myself. I discussed it with Isabel Best and she told me to get on with it. I wrote a letter. Three days later the phone rang and Eileen Sheridan was on the line. It was in the diary.

I always feel nervous when meeting people for interviews. I'm calling on strangers, wanting to talk to them about their lives, and there is no guarantee they'll be the person I think or hope they will be. I'm even more nervous when I'm meeting someone who was born in 1923. I stumble through Brentford accompanied by the screech of ring-necked parakeets nesting in colonies in Kew, just across the Thames. Eileen has lived in the same house in Isleworth since 1953. It backs on to the Thames, the ait (river island) there a lump of trees falling down into the revolving water of the river, forcing the sluggish waters around it. The parakeets and geese compete in decibels with the lumbering jets overhead, floating in leaden spirals downstream to Heathrow. The parakeets then flock outwards beyond the urban limit, towards Reading, westwards, vying with red kites in the race to Bristol. The place feels like a historic and unchanging portrait of village life juxtaposed with a city of noise and colour.

I bring biscuits, but I shouldn't have. Eileen has the biscuits ready, dense chocolatey ones, more chocolate than biscuit. I offer a hand by way of greeting, and she responds with a chuckle. 'Oh my, we are formal today aren't we!' I am disarmed in an instant, enraptured. 'If you want to know about a slow one, you're on to the right person. I would hate anybody to think that I thought

I was greater than all the girls that are riding now, because I'm not. The times the ladies are doing these days, they are fantastic.'

I feel overwhelmed by the combination of humility and inspiration. I want to be like Eileen Sheridan, to recognise the good in everyone. She grabs hold of time and shakes it around me; months, years and decades cascade as the sun streams through sash windows. We talk backwards through time, spanning the generations between us with joy. We skip through decades in a flush of excitement like teenagers, unaware of the world around us, consumed by the romanticism of cycling and of stories, the immediacy transcending the years between us. She leans forward and I am transfixed.

> It's such a long time ago, it feels different. I didn't mention a thing about the war in my book.* I didn't think I should in 1955. I was seventeen and living in Coventry – the blitz was all around us. I remember the shock of the flattened city. I carried my bike because I couldn't ride through the still-burning rubble. The men at the cathedral, the firemen were black, filthy, they'd been working all night. It was a dreadful thing to see. We got through that. Bikes and cycling were our blessing.

She is moved by the memories and the trauma, their power to shock still visible. Hackneyed notions of hardship and extreme cycling are realigned. I recall Vic Clark† in 2012 writing about

---

* *Wonder Wheels: The Autobiography of Eileen Sheridan* (London: Nicholas Kaye Limited, 1956).

† Vic Clark was National Hill Climb champion three times in a row, from 1946 to 1948. It's a niche and unforgiving discipline, and I met him in 2012, when he was ninety-four years young.

hill climbers; how he was moved to Kendal as a toolmaker, his factory bombed in the destroyed city. I think of the racer Alf Engers being buried beneath the rubble of his father's bakery in 1944 while the three night-bakers downstairs were killed. I think of how life is much easier now, in so many ways. I think of how sitting on your hands and watching Netflix for twelve weeks during a coronavirus lockdown is a sacrifice but not the same sacrifice our grandparents made.

Vic Clark lived near me and rode a tandem with his wife, Connie. He was a brilliant rider, a very small, light man. When Connie came out on the club run funny things happened. On one occasion at the cake-stop we went in for our tea. The room and walls looked dirty and dark. I used to pour out for the boys, so I was always last to get to the cake. I heard somebody saying, 'That cake, what's that green stuff?', and someone else piped up, '*Oooh*, that's pistachio.' Everyone tucked in. After a minute or so someone else said, 'That's not pistachio, that's *mould*!' and everyone rushed to the window to get rid of it. I had a narrow escape!

Eileen and Ken married in 1942 in Coventry. He was an engineer working away from his home in London. The feeling of those last few years of war is of a profound sense of community, a gradual reparation from the collective trauma of a city destroyed, ameliorated by an escape into the countryside.

I feel lucky, looking back. I was just riding around the countryside, to Warwickshire, Derbyshire, the Peaks, the Dales. We cycled everywhere and had great times. Coming back from the tea place was always a good tear-up, we used to love that. I was on an ordinary ladies' BSA step-through, with a very large bell which my father had carefully screwed on for me. I didn't have another bike until I was twenty-one. Ken bought me a beautiful little Claud Butler Continental, second hand. He had a French frame. It was black with fine gold lines, and it looked very superior to mine.

In the mid-1940s Eileen began racing. Suzy Rimmington was the fastest rider of the era, winning the inaugural women's 25-mile championship in 1944. Eileen looked up to her, saw Rimmington as somehow made of different raw materials, so far ahead, unattainable. It is the nature of competition. When we do match or overtake them, it's accompanied by disbelief and dissonance.

She was wonderful, she really tanked along. She always looked flat-out whenever you saw her. The first time I beat her I didn't believe it. I went up to the timekeeper. He wasn't best pleased because I was querying the timer. We had one National Championship and that was the 25, and I won it in 1945, beating Suzy. She hadn't even had the trophy from the first year by that point, so we shared it for six months each, which seemed fair. In one 50, Suzy was starting two minutes behind me. I was always a slow starter. We got to the far turn and when I could see Suzy coming, I just said, '*Sue!*' She'd made up two minutes to get to that point and it shocked me. I wasn't concentrating on the speed. I couldn't believe I was so stupid. I went like mad and I got a minute and a half back and the word had gone around – *Rimmington's caught Sheridan* – and I came steaming in and she came in foaming at the mouth . . . It was hilarious fun!

Sheridan raced throughout 1945, before giving birth to Clive in 1946 and taking a break.

I had a C section because I couldn't start labour, the baby's head wouldn't go down. It's not much fun now but in those days it wasn't very good. It was a massive operation. Clive was starving and my milk went because of the shock of the birth. They kept me in for three weeks, that was normal. I had to sit up. But they kept taking the baby, kept him in a separate room because he was too ill, but they didn't tell me. They'd bring in the others and I'd say, 'You've forgotten my baby,' and she'd say, 'No, Mrs Sheridan, we haven't.' Why didn't they tell me? You'd go through so much and you needn't have done because it was a terribly worrying thing, wondering what has happened to the baby.

After recuperation, she started thinking about riding again. Ken would put her bike outside, make sure it was ready for her to head out if she wanted to. She regained fitness and form and began racing again, with startling results. In 1948 she set 30- and 50-mile competition records in time trials before deciding to move into endurance events and the 12-hour time trial.

They set us off at two-minute intervals. I had a feeling that I had gone off course because I hadn't caught up with anybody. It might have been because I was pacing it, I knew it was a 12, but I panicked, turned round and began to ride back. I saw a man getting on a motorbike, and I called out, 'Which way to Wetherby?' and he said, 'You're going the wrong way, love.' I had been right all the time. I turned and rode like mad because it was such a shock.

Eileen set a new record for the 12-hour time trial with 237 miles, a near 20mph average speed, adding a staggering 17 miles on to the previous record. Only 6 miles less than the men's winner, it was a result which gave notice of her ability to ride fast for a long time. She took things easier over the winter and laughs at the thought of her extravagance. 'My racing weight was 7 stone 12. During winter I'd go up to 8 stone 6 – I would have been enjoying wines and things.'

In 1950, Sheridan improved her 50 record and won the National 100-mile Championship with an average speed of nearly 22mph. It was part of a sequence of achievements which saw her awarded the prestigious Bidlake Prize. 'It was a great honour, especially as he didn't like ladies.' She laughs at the thought of his reaction. There remained an underlying scepticism that a woman could manage such feats, but it seemed to make Sheridan more determined the following year. 'My aim was to equal or better last year's performance, if only to convince people – and there were not a few of them – who just would not believe that a girl could cover 237 miles in twelve hours. Some even had said that I cut out a part of the course, and one particularly assertive racing type was sure a mistake had been made in the calculations.'

Eileen also dabbled in the track. Most cities had at least one velodrome. She won the Midland sprint championship in 1947 and then lined up for the National Championship at the Butts in Coventry. 'I was no track rider. I'd go down, take the mudguards off and the saddlebag, sometimes with a bit of help. Suzy cut across me, but I should have been ready for it. I was pleased with second. I used to do a lot of pursuits with Mary Capel; I'd work hard into the wind and work it so we could pull together. We had lovely times; it was a great thrill. They were really lovely girls.'

The shift from time trials towards place-to-place records came about after a conversation with the secretary of the WRRA, Mary Rawlinson, in 1950. She felt Sheridan was the one to tackle Marguerite Wilson's records. At 5 a.m. on an acerbic October morning Sheridan set out with her supporters from

Birmingham New Street Post Office, aiming to reach the central sorting office next to St Paul's Cathedral in five hours. The Metropolitan Police had been alerted. 'A mobile police officer went ahead on a motorbike to give warning . . . light after light went green . . . traffic was halted . . . how their eyes must have popped when they saw a little girl in black sweater and shorts go tearing by!' With a thirteen-minute margin of success, plans were immediately drawn up for a second ride, this time London–Oxford–London, with another early start ('it was cold and dark at 4 a.m.'). She beat the record, and then the 'social season' beckoned: club dinners, dances, presentations, all culminating in the annual RTTC gala event at the Royal Albert Hall, featuring Fausto Coppi pedalling on rollers on a rotating platform in the centre of the stage under moving coloured spotlights.

Sheridan's focus on road records had opened the prospect of sponsorship, just as it had for Marguerite Wilson. 'Raleigh offered £500 for *all* the records. If you think of the miles – nothing else, just that it was not a huge amount. They knew that I was quite green. We were just married; we wanted a house and needed the money. Ethel Crowther of Mercian advised me to meet them. I thought the world of Ethel and Tom Crowther.* I cycled from Coventry to the office at Raleigh to meet at Mercian in Derby. I turned it down.'

After the 12-hour, Hercules got in touch. They had been regular sponsors before the war, including of Marguerite Wilson, and they offered 'a wonderful contract'. However, they lacked their pre-war resources, leaving Sheridan unsettled. The solution was simple: they appointed Frank Southall.

---

* Ethel and Tom owned Mercian Cycles which had opened in 1946; this is Ethel's first appearance of many in this book.

'I was so lucky to get him; he knew what it was about. He got used to my style in the end!' Southall's involvement was a godsend. He had managed Wilson and knew the game inside out. However, any illusion that professional status would lead to better conditions, a studied wait for the right weather, were some way wide of the mark. Sheridan was sent out regardless. Many of the records started in the very small hours, in freezing early spring.

One of the early ones was so cold, Monty [Southall, Frank's brother] said I rode like a crab. I couldn't get any breath in my body. I was struggling. I wanted to make some money; it was my job. My father always came out to see me. On London–Holyhead he opened the bedroom window to pouring rain and a headwind. He thought I'd never start and went back to bed. The chain kept falling off. By the third time I was *furious* and slung my bike to the side of the road. I'd been going into this awful headwind for hours. Monty said, 'Ride on to the Master,' meaning Frank, and I said, 'To hell with the Master, I'm *getting in*.' Frank and Monty had a terrific row. Frank opened the door and said, 'To hell with the Master, eh?' and I said, '*Yes*.' On London to York it was lashing with rain. On Portsmouth and back I broke a blood vessel in my throat trying to breathe because it was so cold; I was bleeding in the throat and it was hardening. I got the record by two minutes, one of Marguerite's. I had a resting pulse rate of 42bpm but always felt I could do with bigger lungs.

Early in 1952, misfortune struck during training for the season ahead. Eileen was out in freezing conditions and wearing five sweaters to fend off the cold. The main road was clear, with 'brilliant sunshine alternating with deep shadows cast by

PA/PA Archive/PA Images

Eileen Sheridan, 1954

the trees'.* She failed to spot a wooden chock from a lorry and went straight over the bars, spending the next three weeks in hospital and having seventeen stiches in her forehead. 'Mother said I looked as though I had a square head.'

Once back to fitness, Eileen continued to target records, racking up publicity for her sponsors. She appeared regularly in Pathé newsreels, promotional films for Dunlop's and Hercules' own PR material. Next was Liverpool to London, a mere 201 miles. August saw Liverpool to Edinburgh, up over the Shap and the Devil's Beeftub – key climbs on the End to End route – beating Frank Southall's pre-war men's record in the process. London to Bath and back featured an 'enormous white owl swooping out of the darkness to attack me'. The rides became longer and more unforgiving, the last attempt for the 1952

---

* Eileen Sheridan, *Wonder Wheels*, p.82.

season 287 miles of purgatory from Land's End to London. Slowly she was stitching together the separate sections of the End to End route.

As she made her way through the Cornish countryside, people were cheering her on; peeking from doorways, waving from cars. It was odd. Record rides were enacted under a cloak of secrecy, in line with strict RRA rules. Someone had tipped off the press with timings and route information. By the time she arrived in London a substantial crowd was waiting at Hyde Park Corner. Sheridan blames Hercules: they wanted her to carry on for the 24 even though she wouldn't be able to claim it, seeing it as good publicity for the company. It is easy to see the relationship as benign, but Sheridan was a paid employee and at times it caused problems. She had a second attempt at Land's End to London. They were stuck at Land's End, waiting for the wind to change. However, Hercules wanted her at the Earls Court Cycle Show the next day and insisted she get moving, only for the ride to be abandoned at Bodmin.

In 1953, Ken and Eileen moved to Isleworth. The money from Hercules had been significant, allowing them to buy a house and live closer to Ken's relatives. Eileen encapsulated the values of the time, a post-war rationality and assertiveness, but combined with a desire to support the family within the prevailing patterns of domesticity. It is reflected in press coverage of the time which seemed to revolve around her abilities to ride *and* be the model housewife at the same time. A 1956 newsreel is subtitled 'Housewife Cyclist' with a stentorian voiceover proclaiming how 'she runs her Isleworth home as an expert housewife should. Cooking is Eileen's principal hobby, and she loves trying out new recipes.'* A similar narrative featured in

---

* 'Housewife Cyclist', Pathé News (1956).

print: 'In addition to her housewife duties she finds the time to be a champion cyclist ... no wonder she wins races, she has to, to get back in time to catch up with the housework.'* Sixty-five years later, Eileen is nonplussed. 'It's just what they used to say; they were very annoying at times. I didn't take a lot of notice to be honest. It's how it was then.'

Flushed from their successful relationship with Sheridan, Hercules moved to sign Ken Joy to challenge the men's place-to-place records. In an echo of Eileen's battles with Muriel Maitland on the Butts track, Joy came up against Bob Maitland and the two fought tooth and nail in the mid-1950s.

Ken Joy rode for the Medway Wheelers, a club immortalised in song by Wild Billy Childish – in my house at any rate, although perhaps not in those houses unaware of the outsider artist. It tells the story of his mother who was a member of the club at the same time as Joy:

> She joined the Medway Wheelers in June 1944.
> She grew up in Wigmore, wanting to see the
>   big outdoors,
> Cycling on a Hobbs Supreme, lightweight, made
>   to measure.
> Medway Wheelers, Medway Wheelers!

As well as being the only song ever to feature a Hobbs Supreme, it lists club-run and hostelling destinations Torquay, Clovelly, Dungeness and North Wales, and speaks of meeting 'Rita at the Tuck-in, getting lost in the fog ... Ron and Reg Abell'. It's a paean to a lost era, before cars crushed the optimism of the cycling leisure movement.

---

* *World Sport*, May 1953.

Ken Joy left the Wheelers to sign for Hercules in 1953, by which point he had won the British Best All-Rounder (BBAR) four years running at record speeds, and held the 100-mile and 12-hour time trial records, as well as a number of place-to-place records. Throughout 1953 he rewarded the faith shown in him by Hercules, breaking eight RRA records, including Land's End to London in 12 hours and 54 minutes. Two of Joy's RRA records still stand. Many of the records were broken and then rebroken by Maitland within weeks, maximising publicity in the press who loved a good rivalry and remembered the BSA v. Hercules battle between Southall and Opperman before the war. Maitland rode for BSA, but joined Hercules in 1954. Joy rode the Tour of Britain in 1954, Maitland the Tour de France in 1955, as British cycling took its first wobbly steps on the continent.

By 1954, Eileen Sheridan had one aim – the End to End. A few early-season place-to-place records were targeted. Edinburgh to Glasgow and back was knocked off by fifteen minutes. Both Ken Joy and Sheridan tackled Edinburgh–York on 5 June. Eileen then took a 'break' to have a tilt at some of the Irish records. The attempts weren't embargoed, and huge crowds turned out to watch. Eileen took fifteen minutes off the *men's* record for Galway to Dublin, then did Cork to Dublin two days later, where she was shouldered high by the crowd in a scene of jubilation. All that remained was the unfinished business of Land's End to London, which she took apart, completing the 287 miles in under fourteen and a half hours, before carrying on to Cromer to bag the 24-hour, completing it in 442.5 miles and beating both Marguerite Wilson's professional record by 46 miles and Edith Atkins' brilliant 422-mile mark. For Eileen, it was the culmination of her efforts, and perfect preparation. 'I always hoped I would do the End to End. I didn't even really think about it, which is just as well, because it's amazing the state you can get into on that record.'

Her bike had four gears, the lightest at 72 inches very heavy; for comparison, day-to-day riding or commuting on fixed tends to be a 68-inch. Lighting was also an issue with two full nights of darkness to come. 'I had a little front lamp, an old rear lamp, that was it. Monty would put the headlamps on as much as he could, that would light up a bit of the road at times.'

They waited at Penzance for the weather to break, before heading out with a westerly wind on Friday, 9 July 1954, at 10 a.m. The support wagon was rather different to Eileen's request for 'a little caravan with a bed in and a loo'. An enormous flatbed lorry with a caravan precariously mounted on the back turned up at Penrith. Separate, at the end, was a small toilet.

It was a stupid thing. I had to hold on to the wires and stagger on the parapet of the flatbed lorry to go to the loo. I'd be seen going towards the hedge instead and they'd try and stop me. There was a ladder going up into the caravan, the loo was between the two, you wouldn't believe it. They had to help me up the steps to make sure I didn't fall off; it was higher than I was. I couldn't have done it on my own. Frank was furious about it and I felt sorry for him. Marguerite had a simple caravan, not this stupid thing!

The first 10 miles felt like 'a training spin', but the southerly winds impeded progress on the long drag up to Jamaica Inn and she was down on schedule at Launceston. At Exeter, the support team began to join the entourage; first former Olympian Stan Butler, then Lilian Dredge. 'You can't look at Lilian's time without realising that things were much more difficult for her than we ever knew. The men didn't like women racing at all. They didn't want them to go riding through the night, it was expected that they sleep – but the clock wouldn't stop.'

With the shift north towards Bristol the wind was more

obliging. They successfully navigated the city centre with support from Bristol club members and Boy Scouts. The shift up through the industrial heartland was marked by the onset of rain at Whitchurch. Shap presented no obstacle; 'my speed never dropped below 10mph, even over the final stiff incline for which I used my 72-inch gear'. She covered 432 miles in the first twenty-four hours before taking a break at Carlisle for 'hot broth ... a change of clothing ... a blanket bath and a short nap of fifteen minutes'.

At Beattock it rained and the wind shifted round, blowing down the climb. The challenge of the long slog wore away at her reserves of mental strength. 'The editor of *Cycling*, H. H. England, was stood at the side of the road. He said, "I'm so sorry, Eileen" – he didn't expect me to go on. I didn't want to give up, but I was questioning myself: would I be strong enough?' It was in the balance, but she pressed on through the dark, before picking up pace as she rode towards Stirling.

By late Saturday afternoon the prospect of a second night weighed on the mind, with Drumochter summit 'appearing like a monstrous forbidding shadow, streaked here and there with snowdrifts'. The headlamps from the following car threw shadows against the rock 'like a huge cyclist going past'. Dawn at 1500 feet saw the temperature drop further, an intense frost causing painful feet. Frank gave her his socks, then waited barefoot for another pair to arrive with the caravan. Such are the privations – two nights without sleep and intense cold, a struggle for the helpers as well as the rider. The descent towards Inverness was welcome, but not without additional problems – this time her hands. Sheridan was reduced to gripping the bars with her thumb and the webbing between thumb and first finger because she had 'a blister as big as an orange on both hands; my thumb joints felt as if they were being pulled off. I hadn't realised how bad they were. I put on two pairs of gloves and Frank re-taped the bar with sponges.' It was too much for Nurse Crew, who wept once Eileen headed out again. Nurse Crew had a bit of an ordeal, all told. She stayed in the caravan as it moved up over the big climbs of the Ord of Caithness, peeking out at the 300ft drop to the sea below before cowering inside to avoid seeing or thinking about the dangers.

Both Helmsdale and Berriedale were taken on foot, as planned. Confidence was high, with just the coastal run down to John o'Groats to come. But the wind had other ideas, coming in off the North Sea with spite. It became a struggle against time and movement, monitored wordlessly by the endless wooden telegraph poles lining the road.

They went on for ever, rose and fell away into the distance each time I breasted one of the many hills, more and more telegraph poles along the rough road. Frank had got a few people out to cheer, saying 'a little suffragette has just come from London'. I was cold and had all the layers on, including Frank's lovely Hercules sweater. I swear my eyes were closed. I sprinted to the timekeeper at the door of the hotel. Everyone rushed up to congratulate me, I was tired but elated and needed sleep. Ken said, 'You won't bother to go on for the thousand,' and I said, 'What's another 130!' But I don't believe that anybody *doesn't* have a tough time in the thousand.

When I started it felt as though my thighs were being torn until we got on to smooth road. I was exhausted, just trying to keep my eyes open. Frank called out to me, 'Can you do a third of a mile faster, because you'll get the men's record?' and I said, '*No.*' It was worth him asking, but I wasn't strong enough. If I'd tried I might have killed myself. You then go through a third night without sleep. It's so lovely when you lie down. They cooked bacon and eggs, a big plateful. I

couldn't eat it because of the big thick gloves and foam for my
blisters, so they fed me. I began seeing things. I was always a
bit artistic, and at home I was planning on doing a mermaid
on the wall with shells – I was going to hang the shells, put
them round on the wall – and I was thinking about this
mermaid and I thought, Ooh yes, that'll be nice. The next
moment I saw a row of mermaids in the road. I saw a group of
people stood on the bend; they said, 'You turn here, Eileen.'
I'll swear they were there, and I turned, and Frank called
out from the following car: 'Eileen, where are you going?' I
saw what I thought was a major road ahead sign and people,
I waved ahead, and when I got there, there was no one. An
enormous glass tumbler appeared, and I had to swerve to miss
it. I was dreaming, I was just far, far away.

Eileen with Frank Southall, Lilian Dredge to her right, then Mary Rawlinson;
Stan Butler to Frank's right; Monty far right, looking away

By the early hours of the morning Eileen was struggling to stay upright and awake, being 'drawn to the verge as if by a huge magnet' and crying with exhaustion – the unrelenting effects of sleep deprivation and physical exertion. A final sleep was called with 30 miles to go. She took an hour, and on waking implored Nurse Crew not to wake the helper in the bunk opposite: it was another trick played by an exhausted brain, for there was no one there. Having lowered the End to End record to 2 days, 11 hours and 7 minutes, she completed the 1000 miles in 3 days and 1 hour, by that point beyond tired and unable to sleep. Incredibly, her time was just two hours and twenty minutes slower than the men's record.

By the time Eileen Sheridan finished her cycling career she had transformed perceptions of women's cycling and transcended the sport. She held all twenty-one WRRA records by the end of 1959. The End to End record was out of reach for the next thirty-six years and her 1000 record lasted until 2002. We talk a bit more, about the *Daily Mail* Air Race, which Eileen was asked to do in 1959, and about her canoeing, when she was pestered into paddling on the Thames and within a short space of time became the national K2 champion. Nothing is ordinary in this life lived to its fullest. I resolve to do more with my minutes, to ride more, write more, have more fun, cope with adversity better.

I get up to go, anxious not to outstay my welcome.

'We'll have a cuddle, won't we?' she says.

Formality dissolves, and I am smitten by the lovely Eileen Sheridan.

7

Dave Keeler finds a new way to save on bus fares

Friday, 30 May 1958

This chapter is about Dave Keeler walking out of the fog on Aultnamain. It is a picture which started the process of writing this book. I was lost in the sepia tint of past times. This chapter is about being 6 feet 2 inches and 13 stone and how big your bike needs to be. But it is also about being 5 feet 2 inches and going by the name of Reg Randall. Lastly, it is about Jock Wadley, who wrote amazing stories with beautiful photographs, sometimes taken by him and sometimes by the mythical Bernard Thompson, and the beautiful magazine called *Coureur*.

There was a comparative lull in men's attempts after Sid Ferris had rearranged the record in 1937, though the deranged tricyclists were busy, with two tandem tricycle records and three trike records in five years. The tricyclists seem to suffer; it's further, harder and more terrifying. Some of them also like

Dave Keeler in the fog

to do it on a tandem tricycle which is like an articulated lorry
and probably harder to manoeuvre.

The RRA was in rude health. Eileen Sheridan's press coverage
and profile ensured that the End to End was seen by the public
as a worthy endeavour and a key feature of domestic bike racing.
A day after the start of her attempt, John Arnold and Albert
Crimes set out on a tandem tricycle. John Taylor, End to End
archivist and a current member of the RRA, is a big fan of the
tandem crews and the tandem tricyclists, as was contemporary
Jock Wadley, who followed both attempts. After starting 'like
the clappers' they slowed to a halt while Crimes, struggling
with stomach-ache, collapsed in the long grass with waves of
nausea. Wadley was already on the road following Sheridan, so
he carried on to join Crimes and Arnold.

Wadley belongs to the golden era of 1950s and 1960s cycling
writers, toiling away in offices and on the road, their words read
by a select band of enthusiasts but not widely known. There is
a line, from journalist Dick Snowdon and Petronella, coursing

through to Wadley and onwards to Geoffrey Nicholson and his captivating account of the Tour, on again to Max Leonard looking at what it takes to come last, Herbie Sykes bringing lost voices out of the past, and Emily Chappell defining a race across a continent in open, lucid prose. They are writers committed to defining the thing they love in the way they want to write it, characterised by texture and colour.

Jock Wadley describes the tandem trike in lyrical terms and is nothing if not subjective. *Coureur* is full of glossy pictures from the Tour, an obsession with Fausto Coppi, and the burgeoning massed-start races in the UK. The tandem trike, in contrast, looked like something from a pre-industrial past, which was a part of the draw – it was reminiscent of the madness of the heroic era. However, Wadley knew that Crimes and Arnold were far from the pipe-smoking eccentrics normally found on a tricycle. In Albert Crimes he saw a thread running back through time, as though he'd just stepped out of the forge after fixing an axle by hand in the midst of a 250-mile stage of the Tour. He describes the machine itself as an 'obsolete contraption' and 'long barrow', but something took hold in his imagination. Wadley recalled a previous sighting of the pair attempting a place-to-place record: 'we came across a dozen chaps standing round an island at Ollerton. We expected to see a pair of old codgers ambling along at 15mph, instead we saw two athletes taking the wide island on two wheels at 25mph and leaning out like sidecar passengers, flattening out before tearing off down the road ... cornering with one wheel a full foot in the air.' A bath at Abington 'looked like a tank of oil after they got out'.

The End to End proved a tough challenge, and it nearly came unstitched at Carlisle. Crimes continued to fight his battle against illness from the stoker's seat. Wadley gave up hope, predicting a struggle to the Grampians whereupon the crew would 'die in the mountains'. They got through, picked up speed and hurtled to the finish. There are two things of note here: first, it shows Jock Wadley's commitment to the cause by watching two End to End attempts in four days; second, their time of 2 days, 4 hours and 26 minutes was an *all-out record*. Two people on a bastard-heavy 'obsolete contraption' had gone faster than any individual cyclist before. It was a catalyst for individuals to reclaim bragging rights from the demented pair.

Dave Keeler was first out of the blocks. He was born in Letchworth, and initially raced for the Letchworth Cycling Club on a shiny Hetchins fixed wheel. In the late 1940s he studied engineering at Nottingham and became involved in the nascent student cycling scene. He established the university cycling club and went to the World Festival of Youth and Students in Budapest in 1949, coming back with a gold medal and trophy. His enthusiasm led to the formation of the British Universities Cycling Union, and he donated his Budapest trophy to be awarded to the winner of the annual 25-mile championship. On leaving university he became a development engineer and joined the Vegetarian Athletic and Cycling Club. Both his parents were vegetarian and it chimed with Keeler's internationalist and progressive outlook. The 'Vegetarian' stands along with the Clarion as a club with a clear ideological purpose – socialism in the case of the latter – and although both have diminished slightly over the years, they remain an important part of social and cycling history. Keeler was following in the footsteps of George Olley and Sid Ferris, both staunch vegetarians who had previously held the End to End record.

Keeler was a formidable opponent on the track and over shorter distances; he towered over the opposition and rode a huge 25-inch frame. He wasn't afraid to do things differently, and this extended to equipment choices. Keeler used a Mercian with a Paris–Roubaix gear set-up which was already anachronistic in 1958. Changing gear involved unbolting the rear wheel to adjust the tension – while riding. It appealed to Keeler's scientific brain: no derailleur and no pulley wheels equals less friction. He also said he 'didn't intend to change gear all that often'. Tom and Ethel Crowther's Mercian frames were increasingly the default choice for endurance riders in the UK. Keeler had used his at the World Track Championship at the Velodromo Vigorelli in Milan in 1951, coming second in the pursuit. It was a good year: he also won the Herne Hill invitational, set a 25-mile competition record (twice) and won the National Pursuit title at the Butts in Coventry. One memorable report in *Cycling* describes him as 'the tall vegetarian automaton'.

Keeler planned to go early, explaining afterwards in an interview in *Cycling*: 'I was looking for the balance between condition and rest and I preferred an early attempt. It got it out of the way.' There were minor issues, living in Paris being the main one. He had moved there for work, but it meant he was out of the UK domestic racing scene and at risk of losing form and fitness. He managed two weekend rides of 200 miles, a club 500 and the London–Southampton–Dover–London record. The End to End was scheduled during a two-week holiday to the UK. The idea that a record attempt could be slotted in around work commitments raised a few eyebrows in the RRA community. This approach had been successful before – a tandem crew, Innes and Thompson, broke the End to End in 1939, had seven hours' sleep and then went back to work on the Monday – but it wasn't typical.

Once again Jock Wadley went along for the ride, by now a seasoned commentator on all things to do with the End to End, including the effect on the support crews. 'The truest test of friendship is to put three men in a car at Land's End, and if they get out at John O'Groats still calling each other by Christian names then they really are friends.' He had doubts over Keeler's ambitions: 'I consider him to be entirely the wrong size for this kind of job, at 6 feet 2 inches and 13 stone 2 pounds, that weight cannot be anything but a disadvantage.'

Conditions were good, and Keeler was inside Ferris's record at Okehampton. It was seen as in need of an update, and Keeler hoped to beat the record by six hours, using a tapering schedule: four 12-hour blocks, 250, 230, 210 and 180. 'What I actually did was 242, 217, 188 and 175.' Again, gears were huge by today's standards, with only five compared to a choice of eleven or twelve these days.

Prior to his attempt, most riders factored in at least some sleep; Keeler went without. He reached Bodmin in just over two hours, Tewkesbury in twelve hours. He was down on the ambitious schedule, but it didn't matter: 'schedules are of relative value, and of more benefit to the helper; we went for two days in the wild hope that there would be a strong helping wind all the way up'. Ethel Crowther, now a veteran of attempts, joined at Derby. John Arnold was out at Warrington and again at Gretna. At Carlisle, Keeler came across the start of the Tour of Britain time trial stage, encouragement from the peloton cheering him through. It was the first one to be sponsored by the Milk Marketing Board – apt for Keeler who drank the stuff by the tankerful. However, road closures and diversions left him lost on the way out of the city, losing time and adding on mileage. Things were back together by Penrith, but not before a catastrophic hour of barely 10 miles' progress.

By the time he reached the Shap he was suffering from nagging back pain. Despite being four hours ahead by the 'second sultry afternoon' Wadley still harboured doubts. 'The first gruelling 24 hours knocks every bit of class out of the rider. The second 24 is ridden on courage. The fire had gone out. Although preserving his beautiful style, the speed went down to club run level.' He lost contact with his helpers after the border and the sudden sense of isolation rocked his confidence. Wadley mused on the idea that short sleeps lead to rapid increases; he'd seen it with Arnold and Crimes on their bonkers run north at high speed. Keeler preferred to 'ride slowly and surely for five hours, rather than stop for one and hurry for four'. Keeler reflected after the event on the challenge of dealing with expectation, where everyone is an expert and advice is freely given. 'It's easy to sit in a car and say he shouldn't freewheel so much and should attack the hills. But maybe the rider has a couple of legs that don't feel like legs, but lumps of lead, and what he wants to do is give them as much relief as he can.'

The back pain continued, but stoicism ruled the day. Further questions rattled around the following car. How could he possibly cope when subsisting on his restrictive and faddish diet of vegetarianism? And were those strange gears to blame? The hardened team recalled how when things got tough at the top of the Shap, Albert Crimes demanded a plate of fried liver. For Keeler it was poached egg sandwiches and crustless squares of bread, gallons and gallons of milk, more eggs and more milk. Crimes had savage stomach pain, Keeler nothing beyond hiccups.

Time appears never to have been an issue. The buffer was huge and as long as he kept going, Keeler was always likely to take the record. The struggle was mental more than physical – 'it seemed endless; the flatter roads were harder than the hills, I thought Perth would never come' – just a constant battle into the distance, trying to narrow the mileage to a manageable concept.

In 1958, the route from Perth to Inverness clung to the fast-flowing River Garry, holding tightly to General Wade's military track. It makes for a longer but more beautiful journey than the uncompromising A9. It is the same route I followed in the summer of 2019, through tree cover and steep-sided banks as the landscape becomes stereotypically Scottish, far removed from the tedious steppes of Lanark. Wadley felt spring had stayed late somehow, writing of 'primroses, cowslips, bluebells, lilacs, rhododendrons' at the side of the road in a wide sweep of different colours; the season had vanished in the south but was holding on in the north. Keeler had toured the Grampians as a schoolboy, pre-war, stopping for drum-ups, navigating the edges of the mountains.

Caithness was misty, a still from every Macbeth film ever made, even Akira Kurosawa's *Throne of Blood*. Out of the fog of Dunkeld, the swirling, primordial soup of time and nature, appeared club mate Jim Purves, standing at the side of the road with a bottle, waiting for Keeler to emerge from the ink. Purves worked for London Transport. Keeler appeared, expressed surprise and took the bottle, Jim's comment stretching his grin from ear to ear: 'Here, Dave, think of all the bus fares you're saving.'

The final stretch, through the 'millions of telegraph poles' recalled by Eileen Sheridan, was distressing, and a sense of loneliness and isolation settled on his thoughts. There is a solitude on the road on the End to End that isn't the same as any other form of racing, not even time trialling; there are no rivals to catch, just the ghostly figure of the record holder – in Keeler's case Sid Ferris, from some twenty-one years before, riding the same route, somewhere back down near Gretna, pedalling incessantly, waiting to catch you if you fall. The ghosts of the route become figures in the mind, their time and progress a permanent note in the book, while the lone figure attempting the ride exists in a form of purgatory.

However, it was as good as done, and Keeler took the record by three hours. He rested for forty minutes, then took on the 1000, looking fresh and ready to go. The sun was up and the weather kind. Despite the conditions, the attempt fell apart quickly. Keeler was overwhelmed by fatigue and fell asleep on the road. Faced with a choice of an hour's sleep or carrying on, they called it off. Wadley reflected after the event: 'Keeler comes out intact, with a loss of 5lb in weight and no unpleasant memories. A horrible pasting on the final 6 hours of the thousand might have written *finis* to his career. One must be prepared for some gruesome sights in the 1000.' He viewed Keeler as 'a middle-distance man with enormous potentialities who wants to go on being an amateur cyclist'. His warmth towards Keeler and the End to End record is clear: 'having followed all or part of seven rides, it's one of the most absorbing of all aspects of the sport'. Wadley gave Keeler a lift back – he had never learned to drive. On the long, long journey Keeler pointed out all the places he had been when touring. He grilled the journalist on the history of the event. Even in the aftermath of his success he wanted to know about those who had gone before.

Dave Keeler carried on riding and working. He stayed in Paris for nine years, long enough for three of his four children to be born in Versailles; the fourth had to make do with Watford General. He never lost his sense of scientific exactitude. He knew that there were 1279 cats' eyes on the North Orbital between the Hatfield Tech turning and the Rainbow Garage. He had ridden the road so often, usually into a west wind, that he had counted them all.

Reg Randall couldn't be more different to Dave Keeler. Randall had the nickname 'Tubby', which seems odd for a racing cyclist: as a breed they are obsessed with weight. I can only think of one other – Paul Bennett, who became known as 'Porky', but seemingly with good reason. Bennett broke the competition record for 25 miles in 1965 with a 54-minute ride. He then descended into alcoholism after being overlooked for the 1964 Olympics. By the late 1970s he was in hospital and given six months to live. His answer was to get back on his bike, at 18 stone. He managed to get down to 12 stone, but his weight fluctuated. He stayed healthy and raced into his seventies, before dying at seventy-five. Pictures of Bennett show why he was called Porky. Pictures of Randall don't provide similar proof of tubbiness. I asked Janet Tebbutt, whom Randall helped on her End to End in the 1970s, to shed some light on it. 'Reg was only about 5 feet tall but what I would call "thick set", so very strong,' she replied, delicately. The nickname stuck, and Wadley used it in print throughout his report.

Like Keeler, Randall was a committed clubman. He was heavily involved with the Harlequins Cycling Club in west London, at one point its general secretary, then club captain, before stepping down to 'social secretary' when focusing on the End to End. He was modest, self-effacing, as though somehow unaware of the high esteem in which he was held, both as a rider and a person. He was unmarried at the time, allowing him to focus on the thing he loved most: riding bikes and the fellowship of cycling clubs. Whereas Keeler had out-and-out speed, Randall seems to have been an archetypal stayer who turned in huge mileages. A standard training week, especially in the run-up to a long-distance effort, would be 500 miles. I struggle to hit that in two months. It is an enormous number, on the edge of acceptable. It takes a certain kind of physique and strength to process it without ending up washed out and ill. Touring miles were a central part of Randall's cycling; he spent time riding across Europe and Scandinavia, chalking up over 10,000 miles per year. His succinct reason: 'I have always liked lone riding and long-distance rides.' In the year preceding the End to End he'd go out all day from his home in Hayes, head west, then turn back at the coast and get back to the Harlequins club hut before it closed with a wry comment like 'there's fog in the Bristol Channel'. With this background and the fact that the record was due an update, an attempt on the End to End grew as an idea through 1958. 'It just snowballed. All along I was encouraged in a way I never thought possible. When people do that you can't let them down.' It was a significant shift for Randall, who preferred the comfort of obscurity to press coverage and expectation.

Outside the club, few shared his optimism. Wadley was pessimistic: 'he'll fight like a tiger in the second 24 hours. He must have a better wind than Keeler and I don't think he'll get it.' We all take on the mantle of expert in these situations, ready to be proved right and to bask in the collected aura of our wise pronouncements. Sometimes it needs a little more faith, as Wadley also acknowledged: 'I have seen highly organised professional outfits shivering in a northerly at Penzance for a month. However, luck does often favour the brave amateur who, months ahead, picks a day to coincide with his and his helper's holidays' – as though the sound of all the eggs going into the basket has a crazed providence to it. Randall is the 'plucky' little guy, David to Keeler's Goliath, at least physically, giving away a foot and a half in height.

His preparation was far from ideal. Randall crashed heavily on a descent three weeks before launch. He was found lying against a telegraph pole. He suffered severe concussion, with angry headaches, fatigue and depression in the run-up to the ride. Nevertheless, they stuck to the plan, despite continued rubbish weather. With two days to go the wind remained stubbornly unhelpful. With no time to mess around, they went on the appointed hour – 10 a.m., Tuesday 29 July – and hoped the conditions might change.

Randall started well, rolling through the undulations of Bodmin and Devon. The breeze picked up by mid-morning, giving Randall 'a punch in his short legs and a grin on his wide face', pushing him up through Bristol without any concern. The news from their man at the Met Office was mixed: the wind was rolling round to the south, but it was bringing rain. Wadley was reduced to ringing the 'checking stations' to get a sense of where Randall was. 'At 6.05 p.m. I asked the operator to get me West Harptree 205, which I assured her was somewhere in Somerset.'

At Lancaster, Randall hit the deck – by all accounts a bit of a habit. Fellow Harlequin Bob Anderson put it into perspective: 'I'm glad he crashed. He has to have at least one crash in every event.'

Wadley got the midnight train to Carlisle, which is a bit like the midnight train to Georgia in that they both leave at midnight, but not like the midnight train to Georgia in any other respect. He grabbed breakfast in the Moss café near the station then caught up with the team and Randall as 'he steadily munched into the huge plateful of miles he had ordered at Land's End'. Things were getting interesting. Wadley was initially obsessed by the difference in style: 'The tall, lithe Keeler sat as still as a rock for hours at a time, driving the cranks with the regularity of a machine; short, stocky, restless Randall was punching away at the job, beating time with his head to the rhythm of his pedalling. His bicycle behaved accordingly, rock'n'rolling from side to side. I was reassured by the team; "that means Tubby's feeling good. He only rides straight when he's suffering."'

The suffering was to follow, along with the bad weather. The sky turned the colour and consistency of black treacle, and Cumbria and Scotland were coated in a cloying layer of rain. The downpour accompanied the lone rider all the way up Beattock. Randall was in trouble, soaked through, frozen, unable to stop his teeth from chattering or his body from shaking. It was a horrendous experience, slow, dispiriting progress up the side of a mountain while 'chilled to the marrow'. They stopped at Crawford for more clothes, gloves, some soup and warm towels – a bid to stave off hypothermia and get things back on track. Wadley began to warm to Tubby's determination: 'Nobody would have blamed Randall had he accepted the chance to pack it up there and then and go off to the nearest hotel for a bath and a bed. 9 out of 10 would have done so. Reg the tenth got back on his bike and pedalled off into the gloom, his path now more than ever a zig-zag as he picked his way through the miniature lakes on the road.'

The hallucinations began to bite: three women seen at the side of the road, cheering, then melting into petrol pumps – tired eyes creating fictions. The consensus was that he looked 'a bit rough'; the situation called for more warm clothes, jerseys, layers of embrocation and hot drinks. Randall had a busy pedalling style, he rarely freewheeled; just a constant bundle of energy, trying to keep warm and steal every second on the road. He became convinced he was behind, fighting a losing battle, because of miscalculating his start time. In reality he was up, nearly all the way. Nearing 600 miles he was desperate for information, fighting with the cold and gear changes. He carried on, furious with himself and the elements; clothing was thrown into the verge as he fought to get back on terms, to narrow a deficit which didn't exist. Throughout the long night it was wet, the road under water for 50-yard stretches. It became 'a cautious grope through mist and rain' to Inverness.

Finally, the timing issue was resolved at Dunblane, the clock suddenly much friendlier. His mood lifted instantly. He looked happier and more relaxed, took on a bidon of soup and headed up and over Drumochter at midnight. The snow-capped peaks formed a moonlit strip of white bunting in the gaps between the dark cloud and the somnolent moorland below. It was an overtired Wadley's turn to be anxious: 'were 700 miles of heroic effort to be frozen, dead and buried in the blackness of a Grampian graveyard?' Randall didn't seem bothered, apart from wanting more of the custard tart he'd eaten at the previous break; he was 'really enjoying it', rolling along the River Garry, out through Inverness.

They negotiated a car crash at Beauly, the team helping while Reg was sent on. Disaster nearly struck at Aultnamain: Randall's brake cable snapped on the high-speed descent, leading to a monstrous rear wheel skid. 'We do have fun and games,' Reg said.

With 20 miles to go the record was in sight. Helmsdale was reduced to a hillock, Reg pushing the 64-inch gear with fluency and fun, provoking comparisons with Charly Gaul from the support team – had Charly Gaul come from the home counties and been nicknamed Tubby. Berriedale was one for walking, as for Keeler, as for everybody, except Tubby – 'my legs are too short to walk up here'. He danced over the top then down towards the line and pulled in at the hotel – the wrong hotel. A quick switch and hurtle to the right hotel and Randall beat Keeler's record by over an hour, lowering the time to 2 days, 1 hour and 58 minutes.

Like Keeler, he went on to tackle the 1000. Like Keeler, he started badly and got worse; he went off course, fell and hurt his wrist, couldn't stay awake. Like Keeler, he abandoned in the knowledge that the End to End was done.

Dave Keeler discovered the news while calling his local bike shop from a phone box at Staples Corner. 'I was shattered. I left the phone hanging and rode back home to Letchworth. I was ready to pack up cycling and take up golf.'

Two weeks later, Randall met up with fellow Harlequin Peter Bryan, his wrist now in plaster having broken it on the End to End. Randall's reaction showed his parochial priorities: 'this is the biggest disappointment of all. Planning and training for the record has meant that I have not been on one club run this year. I had promised myself that tomorrow would see me out with the lads, Sevenoaks for lunch and Lower Kingswood for tea.' This goes some way to defining Randall's appeal – his joyful simplicity and sharp humour, the amateur in every sense of the word, 'a champion of the cycling cause who has elevated the status of the clubman into the record books'.

8

Between the alphabetical storms from Bristol to Bradford

Monday, 18 February 2019

I feel pleased about my ride through Cornwall, primarily because I retained my dignity. It is a low bar, I accept that. I wanted to see what ridiculously long days felt like from a lay perspective, to get some sense of scale and the effort involved. Admittedly, I spent the entire time going as slowly as I could with the aim of getting to Bristol at some point, and in one piece. In the same time frame, Lynne Taylor, the current women's record holder, would have been at Wolverhampton and Mike Broadwith at Stoke-on-Trent.

I rest, return to work and begin planning the next bits. I have other commitments: part-time teaching, interviewing people for this book, being married, child-wrangling. I am part-time because writing for a living is not a viable proposition and I'm having 'a breather'. I went against the tide of accepted wisdom and resigned from my job with no job to go to. I feel better for it, but I am increasingly unnerved by the waterfall of anxiety and not-knowingness that cascaded out of a limitless blue sky. Instead of making one careful decision about what to do I try to make all the decisions at once, applying for every different job I can.

So I work part-time and try to find time to write this book and my thoughts are like a madman's shit. I go to job interviews and it goes well until I start crying, which is generally not seen as a good look. People don't see 'emotional honesty', they see 'damaged: avoid at all costs'. I over-explain my reasons, why I made certain choices. Every explanation seems to provoke further questions. Things used to be so certain; I had 'got' every job I ever applied for, now I get nothing. I am lucky if I get an interview. I struggle outside of work, at home. I don't know what else to do so I continue to plan the next bit of the journey. The lack of available time lends itself to another long, reckless ride, this time from Bristol to Bradford. I think it will solve everything. I think things through when out on the bike, so it stands to reason that another really big bike ride will solve all of my really big problems.

Bradford is a deviation from the classic End to End route. My mum lives there, and she has a camper van which she uses to go to Northumberland with her partner, Ian. They park up and watch birds returning from migration, a seemingly endless shimmering skein of geese, shearwaters and skuas. I have decided to requisition the van and driver for my adventures. It saves money, and in the cold grey light of part-time work this is a driving factor. The only minor caveat is an occasionally tempestuous mother–son relationship. We are too similar. We are anxious, impulsive. It can make for an abrasive pairing, both extreme highs and lows. I decide that everything will be brilliant. We will talk, hatchets will be buried, I will be calm, and it will be transformative for both of us. That is the plan. I'm going to ride away from things and find answers. I will become immersed in a sea of positive flow activity and the journey is going to redefine me and all of my relationships. I've read about people on journeys, salving their souls. Now this will happen to me, and I can write about it.

However, time has slipped away. Stage one took place in balmy temperatures with lots of daylight. It is now February and there is an alphabetical storm every weekend and it is dark. I will follow the A38 for as long as possible, then head through a narrow corridor between the peaks and Manchester, stopping somewhere near Oldham if necessary. I flirt with the idea of going straight through Buxton but I know the Peak District after 150 miles of riding is a bad idea. I stick with the post-industrial north, narrow green corridors and debris-strewn lanes. There are remnants of country lanes hidden within the urban sprawl, disconnected from the rural vernacular. They seem like erratics, strange boulders picked up by glaciers and dumped somewhere a thousand miles and a million years away; dislocated names next to a new-build estate, no longer calm, whispering havens of wildlife but shouty dogging spots and fly-tippers' paradises. Washing Pound Lane, once used as an overnight stay for drovers and cattle on the way to market, empties into the new-brick simulacra of Chiltern Avenue, Woodmarsh and Yewcroft Road, portmanteau places where the link between name and meaning is severed.

I get up at 5 a.m., trying not to wake the children. They are not shouty Spaniards and if they wake up early it is bad. Not so much for me, but for Helen, who will be left with two very tired and very young children for a fraught day and be sparing in her good luck messages from that point on. I am stealthy and get away without a sound, into the dark and quiet streets of Bristol where the temperature hovers just above freezing. I roll up an empty Whiteladies Road and on to Durdham Downs. This is where I joined Michael Broadwith on his End to End record attempt. Memories come up out of the tarmac, prompted by street-signs and sounds. I sat next to Steve Abraham for sixteen hours. Steve rode 72,388 miles in a year, or nearly 200 miles per day. He has a record for riding 7104 miles in a month, or 236 miles per day for thirty days. He told me stories about cheese and long-distance riding. Tommy Godwin had the record, at 75,065 miles. 'He never had a following car. He never had a tracker, no Garmin,' said Steve. I joked that maybe he used a stick in the spokes, counting it every time it clicked, then multiplied that by a really big number. Steve put me straight. 'He had a mechanical device, a Lucas odometer. He sent a postcard every hundred miles.'

Today I have no stick but I do have a Garmin GPS device, a small screen with a breadcrumb trail which I can follow through the darkness and along unknown lines of tarmac. It tells me I have a really long way to go, which makes me shift nervously in the saddle, which in turn makes me think of another Steve story, this time about an abscess.

He was supporting a rider in the Race Around Ireland, a horrific and long undertaking which can do terrible things to the undercarriage. It has a spiritual connection with the Race Across America and draws a similar profile of ultra-nutter. I remember seeing a documentary about the American race. A rider called Jim Rees went to his mental and physical limits. He had some sort of frame to brace his neck after his muscles could no longer hold his head up. He called himself a normal guy but he wasn't really. Steve told a story about another rider in vivid detail. 'This one chap was having all sorts of problems, the main one being an abscess on his bollock that was huge. We stopped at this garage and he disappeared into the toilet for an age. He came out and said, "That's killed two birds with one stone. Had a dump and burst me third bollock at the same time, made a horrific mess. I wouldn't want to be the next person in there."' I imagined a medieval charnel house, and placed Steve in the box marked 'outsider artist' – someone who operates on a different plane to the rest of us.

The early part of the ride is familiar, roads I have raced on many times. I climb up towards Almondsbury and startle early-morning dog walkers out of their silent possession of the pre-dawn. Possibility stretches out ahead and the only people awake are those foolish enough to be starting early or finishing very late. It suggests a quietness – what the world was once like, before it filled up with people. The view is uninterrupted across to Wales, with both bridges a strip of moving red and white light against the black abyss of the Severn. The M5 is a fluorescent tube lying in the flood plain. It is a Monday morning, and everyone is going to work. I have a funny feeling, like you get at funerals, when everyone else is doing normal things while I'm doing this thing that stops time and yet no one cares.

After 20 miles I have had enough. The cold seeps in and I want to stop. My hands and feet are cold, my forehead feels stretched and cold, my eyes are itchy and cold, and my lips are cold. I need to piss all the time because it is so cold and I keep stopping, maybe ten times before I get to Gloucester, each an opportunity to stop and turn back, to find an excuse not to do this thing that I said I would do but don't actually want to do. Although I know I need to do it because of this book and the promises I made, to myself and other people.

I think of the stayer's mentality. I think of people like Janet Tebbutt (more on her later), who get on their bikes and don't stop. I draw the obvious conclusion: I have neither the stayer's mentality nor the necessary depths of willpower.

The cold gives me a headache and I stop and eat ibuprofen and paracetamol. In a moment of clarity, I realise that stopping is the issue. Keeping moving is fine, but every time I stop I want to stop properly. There are hundreds of these small-scale dilemmas that are just the tiniest bit similar to an End to End, on a 1:72 scale model.

Dawn begins to break in diffused lines of paint, a watery wash of lighter blue. This ride will take a very long time and I must keep eating. Gloucester is awake and going to work and I pass through it quickly, and out the other side, trying to locate the A38 northwards. It is under water. Two consecutive week-ends of storms have wrought havoc on the Severn flood plain. The road is closed and no one knows what to do. People speak of floods as far as Tewkesbury. Some bright spark suggests I go via the Cotswolds. Delivery drivers panic and shout at the weather gods and everyone is angry. They are angry about the floods, that someone lets floods happen. It offers another ready-made excuse to stop and turn around and go home.

Suddenly, a cyclist comes the other way, through the deluge. He does a special thing with his pedals, keeping his feet out of the swamp. He offers sage advice in a Forest of Dean burr: 'Take the bypass at Tewkesbury, for you'll not get through the centre.' I set off through the middle, following the visible white lines until they disappear and the water inches upwards, then eventually recedes. The road hovers just above the water, sometimes dipping a shoulder into the inundation. I take a circuitous route through Tewkesbury, following further advice from an elderly couple, and then I'm through. Upton-upon-Severn is now under rather than upon. People stand by, gawping at flooded houses and pubs as pylons emerge from the primordial brown soup. I realise why people save the longer rides for summer. I realise I am making a terrible mistake. Then I realise it's too late to realise anything, so I carry on.

The towns get closer together – Worcester, Kidderminster, Stourport – until eventually it begins to blur into one long urban midland morass and turns into Wolverhampton. I come in on Penn Road. There is no cycling lane. Sometimes there is a vague apology of a cycle lane, a strip of degraded tarmac which comes and goes in right angles. The city is ringed by a bypass, huge roaring strips of road diametrically opposed to cycling. The Wolverhampton ring road is a sinuous river of evil. It forms a latter-day motte and bailey, with the interior a frightened cluster of 1960s concrete. I find it ironic that Wolverhampton was the thriving heart of the West Midlands bicycle industry for over a hundred years: Viking Cycles – sponsors of Paul Carbutt, who did the End to End in 1979; Sunbeam, Stallard, Hateley, Rudge-Whitworth.

I avoid the ring road, but then pile on to the main road to Stafford. It is another awful stretch of tarmac with piss-poor cycling provision. I feel like a participant in a case study on the creation of misery and antipathy within an urban landscape. I get close-passed more frequently than ever before, handlebars grazed by angry motorists. I get shouted at. In fact, that's not accurate. I get screamed at, repeatedly, by one man in a silvery car. He says GET OFF THE FUCKING ROAD YOU FUCKING CUNT. It is always a man in a silvery car. Just as it is always men who scream at other men. Just as it's always men who go into Subway to buy their lunch alone. I want to point out that a lone cyclist is not the problem, not the cause of traffic, of anger, of the repressed rage and bile, but he is gone in a millisecond of flaccid fury, driving ten minutes up the road to a date with destiny. I wonder if he has children and how he speaks to them. I wonder if he speaks to his mum with that mouth. Wolverhampton is a sewer. I crosscheck this later with a neighbour who lived in Wolverhampton for two years. She confirms that it is a sewer. I take a break and wheel my bike into a Subway to eat a sandwich, alone.

The main road to Stafford is a dual carriageway, replete with speeding vehicles and a higher risk of death. It is the End to End

ST. PETERS CHURCH.   WOLVERHAMPTON.

2314

Dear M,
I was so
pleased
to hear
from you
I am
sorry I
cannot
write
you a
letter. I
have got
to get tea
now, with
xxx love. Florrie

route, for better or worse, and I opted to do this bit because of one thing: the mythical Gailey roundabout. I am riding my bike on a dual carriageway in search of a roundabout. In all the interviews I did, people kept talking about it, this mystical amphitheatre. I know Mike Broadwith came out here to watch Christina Mackenzie attempt the record. Lynne Taylor talks about it because it isn't far from Cannock where she lives. It sits on the End to End course and for some reason has a resonance. I realise on arrival that the resonance, the noise, the thrum, the myth is all generated by me and based around the repetition of the word. It is a tedious, awful roundabout in the middle of a dual carriageway. Nonetheless, I take a picture of it.

I get drenched by an articulated lorry, a couple of feet away and moving fast. An entire bathtub of water has been tipped on to my right side. It goes in my mouth; a cupful of liquid, big gulps. I can taste the grit from the road and the salt. It's vile, and I can't get the taste out of my mouth. It's like a rotten roasted nut whose blackened husk you've absent-mindedly chewed while chowing through the packet. I place this ride, mentally, at the top of my 'worst rides of all time' top ten. This is not touring or some bucolic sojourn from coast to coast, it is something to be endured, an opportunity to catch diseases. Yet again I'm caught in the middle. In my spurious attempt to replicate or at least sample the full End to End experience, all I've managed to do is put myself in horrible places, on horrible roads, testing the limits of my willpower and determination and proving that I am not cut out for this.

The rain comes down thickly. My bike creaks, the brakes start to complain. I have disc brakes, a late concession to modern technology. They are great when they work, but they regularly stop working and I have no idea how to fix them. I tighten up the front and it seems OK; the back is a write-off. The rain comes down heavier than before, with more malice, scudding off the surface.

Eventually I move away from the trunk roads and take to the lanes, filling in a gap on the run to Stoke-on-Trent. These are the lanes that aren't really lanes; the leftover lanes that strayed too close to the city. The closer the countryside is to the city, the more the city pervades and undermines the rural. Cars rip along at dangerous speeds, using cut-throughs to skip from one urban space to another. The edges of the road are lined with rubbish – always fast food waste, greaseproof paper, plastic lids. Any gap or gateway is full of debris, builders' waste, fridges, plastic toy castles and bits of bed, a fly-tipped mess of consumer goods. The density of rubbish shocks me. In the road up ahead I spy something long and strange. It looks like a tree branch, a log of some sort. I draw closer and realise, with horror and hilarity, that it's a massive black dildo, the swollen member and bulbous end attached to a sturdy ball-bag, with life-like veins pulsing in the rain. I'm glad it's only a dildo and not the real thing, some stark sign of what happens to cyclists who stray into the Hilderstone-Moddershall triangle – they cut off your cock and balls and leave them in the road as a warning to other would-be tourists. I do the only thing I can do in the modern world: I take a picture and post it. The comments come flooding in. 'Fellowship of the choad' says one. I have to look it up. Apparently, a 'choad' is a penis that is wider than it is long. 'Saw plenty of those during our tour' say some American chums who rode around the UK. The lanes of the UK are paved with dildos. I conclude that there are certain factors that lead to a higher incidence of dildo sightings: proximity to a city; quiet country lanes; active dogging areas. Sandon is the hotspot.

I'm left feeling uneasy, a combination of road taste on the tongue and the associated image of the disembodied cock. I pedal on, trying to get away from the visceral imagery and sensual assault of the Midlands. I lurch, uneasily, into Stoke-on-Trent. I have expectations of a city with a strong industrial heritage, civic grandeur. These are not reified in rush-hour Stoke. The rain is teeming and I am soaked. The city seems to sit on a main road forging a straight line through the sprawl. I stagger into the first McDonald's I see and order chips, an indeterminate veggie product and a milkshake.

I want to stop. I am cold and wet. I text Mike, who doesn't know it but is assuming the role of spiritual mentor on this journey into the darkness – in person on the previous stage, only by message today.

PJ: I'm cold and wet, might stop.

MB: Classic Broadwith feelings. Can you manage 20 minutes from now?

PJ: Weather is abysmal.

MB: You're telling me. When I did my Feb half-term recce I thought I was going to die.

I realise I should think about carrying on because I'm not going to die and because that is what Mike would do and that is what he is telling me. Again, the trick is not to stop. At the same time, you have to stop at some points, to eat, to relieve the pressure on your bones, to look up from the road surface. Eventually I put all my wet kit back on, shoes, jacket and gloves so soaked that I had to wring them out in the sink and pools of brown water ran down the drain. Somehow, when I step outside the rain stops. The rush hour stays the same, but it seems like a miracle of sorts, of timing and agnostic prayer, and I press on, this time into the darkness which has closed out the day while I ate Veggie Dippers and chips, the food of champions.

One inescapable flaw in winter riding is that all of the semi-rideable, hard track paths are out of commission. Disused railway lines become sumps of waterlogged purgatory. I planned to avoid cycle routes that might be rivers of mud. Somehow, a section crept in, from Stoke-on-Trent to Congleton. Against my better judgement I opt to tackle the towpath. It saves me having to reorient and find the parallel road. The towpath doglegs around a lock-gate and on to a shiny piece of tarmac. It feels lovely after the relentless traffic and noise. The wind is behind me, it has stopped raining and I've eaten food; I feel superhuman, living fully in the moment. I trust in the trail and ride up through a valley, past the Chatterton Whitfield Colliery workings, a silent shadow on the hill-top against the near-black night. The valley has been landscaped, the industrial ravages of time smoothed over and replaced by greenery and trails and leisure. I opt to stay on the path when it turns to disused railway. I am relieved; no close passes, no soakings, no screaming, ranty men. Instead there are depthless potholes and filth. The back brake gives up entirely, the lever a phantom limb, rattling in the wind. Everything is covered in mud. I last for a little while before I seek the sanctuary of streetlights and tarmac, and as abruptly as they arrived, the euphoria and elation vanish.

After 160 miles I reach the edge of Greater Manchester, a sprawling conurbation with tendrils creeping out into the countryside along the main roads – Stockport, Hyde, Mossley, Stalybridge. It is dark, the rain returns, my brakes don't work, and it is snowing at Marsden. I don't want to die on the moors so I decide to stop at Saddleworth. I haven't done the full 198 miles I'd intended, it comes in at 175, with the rest to cover quietly in a shorter sprint tomorrow.

I wonder where this leaves my narrative. All along I'd known I had to do the route and had to do it in the time allotted. I have learned I can do these things; I can get on a bike and ride in shitty, horrible weather for twelve hours, dodging flood water and dildos. I've learned that achievement and enjoyment are not the same thing. However, in the days that follow I take delight in people's reactions to the ride. I feel a sense of vindication – that I *can* do things, that I *can* ride for long days and cover huge distances, that I am not the sum of bad choices in life. My self-esteem creeps up as I prepare for the next leg of the journey.

Somehow, by riding in a straight line northward in shit weather in February I have relocated the beginnings of a feeling of happiness, of reinforcement, of personal pride. My wife says she is proud of me for doing this stupid thing. And I realise that when I left my job, because I was stressed, because it was too hard, because I was unhappy, I lost things I could quantify, like the way people look at you when you run a school, the minor celebrity status which that confers in the local community, the gratification of being able to tell people what to do and to get things done. But I also lost things I couldn't quantify – certainty, linearity, progression, the supportive layers that come from working in a big institution, the understated strata of professional friendships, all vanishing overnight as I tinkered with the bolts to a trapdoor while standing on it.

And that left uncertainty, and lots of questions reared up at me like startled, angry snakes. What if I'd been more resilient? What if I'd held out a little bit longer; would the narrative have changed? Would I be someone different? And I conclude that I went as far as I could, because if I could have carried on I would have, but just like a ride over Saddleworth Moor and across the M62 at ten o'clock at night in low visibility and driving wind and snow is not sensible, neither is carrying on with a job in the face of the driving wind of stress and the tense misery of ambivalence.

The questions still hold though, like clouds of sleet in the sharp northern air, billowing and unresolved. I will take a break, wait for the weather to warm up and then do the rest, complete this journey in all of the ways that the journey is unfolding, both good and bad. And maybe I'll work this all out at the same time. It is becoming much more metaphorical than I'd imagined. I guess I'm living the dream, always banging on about how life is a metaphor for cycling, after the Dutch novelist and former competitive cyclist Tim Krabbé, and it seems I'm finally getting my wish, life mapping itself on to the bike ride to be turned into something literal. I live in hope.

Author photo

9

Dick Poole's list of towns

Monday, 14 June 1965

E arley is a strange place. It feels dormitory, looking at nearby Reading out of the corner of one eye. It forms an outskirt of large detached redbrick houses and mute cul-de-sacs. The street names disorientate, West Country by way of the Kennet and Avon: Clevedon Drive, Brean Walk, Radstock Lane, Kingsdown Close. Local names are forsaken in favour of local names from far away. I've driven from Bristol to find a simulacrum of north Somerset.

I'm here to meet Dick Poole, and I'm struck by how he lives *here*. How no one knows he lives here, or about the amazing things he did. Our estates are full of silent heroes sipping tea as they gaze out of the window, the runner, the artist, the lower-division footballer who years ago wrote his name on a far bigger canvas and meant something to people. Somewhere within each suburban housing area lives a man or woman who did something demented, unusual and amazing, unbeknown to their neighbours. Their deeds have long since slipped from the public memory. No one recalls the articles, the double-page spreads, the radio and television news reports. We look for contemporary heroes, ignorant of the ones next door, living in quiet, uninterrupted retirement. Such memories lie undisturbed until I come to Dick Poole's door, armed with a voice recorder and a box of biscuits.

Dick Poole is ageless. I don't mean he is not old, because he is. But he turns out to be much older than I had calculated. Poole set the End to End record in 1965. I think he must be in his early or mid-seventies. He looks about that age – healthy, funny, conspiratorial. I ask him. He is *eighty-eight*. I add him to my list of cyclists with ridiculous longevity, along with Eileen Sheridan, Vic Clark and others. I resolve to ride more. I recall that Clark rode 300,000 miles on one Brooks saddle. Poole kept a cumulative total of his *racing* mileage, not his training. He rode thirteen 24-hour races, ticking off 5807 miles in these races alone. I then look at his 12-hour figures – 6445 miles in twenty-seven events. Thus far we're up to a month of solid endurance racing, non-stop. I wonder if that's the bulk of his racing. Maybe he did a few 100s. I have a look in his ledger – it's immaculate. He did *over a hundred* 100-mile time trials. I can do the maths for this; it's 10,800 miles. He also did well over two hundred 50-mile time trials. I feel a bit dizzy and decide to have a sit down. As a key to a life free of illness I might have to seek something different. Olive oil. Herrings. Wine. Dark chocolate. Excessive miles on the bike spent racing.

His story is preserved in scrapbooks which lie across the table – faded newspaper clippings, artefacts, handwritten letters, black and white photos, certificates and logbooks, meticulously filled out with a clerical professional's hand, the spines long since detached, the binding a frayed mess of dry glue and string, but the ink bright and ageless, the mark made by the writer in the moment as true as any photograph, a prompt for a dozen reminiscences. The day of riding and the time recorded in blue ink dances before my eyes and swirls around the room as I see Dick Poole trace a line with his finger as surely as he wrote it sixty-five years ago. The memories well up from the depths of time and make themselves felt around the table. We talk over tea and biscuits about how Dick used to ride.

Four or five of us decided to go to Land's End and back over Easter. Thursday night we stopped at Basingstoke; it rained. Then from Basingstoke we went to Launceston, about 160 miles, got really wet again, then from Launceston we went through Bodmin, down to Land's End and back to Bodmin. Going over Bodmin Moor it hailed and snowed. [He laughs nervously, even now, to recall what it is like being stuck on a Cornish moor in Easter when the weather turns.] I'd got a racing cape on and it was beginning to fall apart. I was putting it on bit by bit while going up a hill and the hailstones were hitting the tops of my legs and it was so painful. I had the marks for days afterwards. We made it eventually. Oh God. I was in my early twenties. That was what we used to do, that and riding to races.

I think of the freezing rain when riding into Stoke in February 2019, and the primitiveness of being cold, how it makes you shake and cry. I see him shiver from the physicality of the memory.

People would ask, 'How was your weekend?' I wouldn't know where to start. A pal of mine said, 'Oh, I'm racing down at Blandford Camp, would you come and help?' I left at the crack of dawn to ride down there on time, 90 miles. He did his race, about 80 miles, said, 'Right, come back to the digs, and we'll have some breakfast and get the train back.' I got to the station and there were no more trains to London, so we had to ride home. As it happened, we got behind some lorry for miles and miles doing a steady 20mph; in those days the lorries would creep along and as long as you got on the back you'd be fine for ages. We got to Hook and stopped at a phone box to phone his mum to say what had happened, so that she could then phone my mum. We stopped at his overnight, just outside Staines. We piled up all the food we had in this phone box, scoffed it all, and carried on. I had to get up the next morning to go to work, from Staines to Liverpool Street. Another lovely lorry came along, I hopped in behind, all the way to Chiswick. I was a bit tired when I got to work. Someone asked how the weekend was. I mean, what do you say? 'Oh, great thanks, rode to Blandford Forum on Saturday morning, helped a guy race, rode to Staines later that day, stayed over, rode here this morning. And you?'

Poole was born between the wars in 1932 at Park Royal Hospital, a sprawling Victorian edifice, then the big infirmary for the west London suburbs. Now only bits of it are left; the refectory stands alone, the rest has been relocated into a PFI new-build. He then lived there because his father was the administrator for the complex. During the war the family moved out to Wembley. At which point he started riding.

I had a friend of mine who was the son of a Polish admiral. They lost all their assets and land in Poland. He took up boxing and got all the gear, and then he took up cycling, and went and got the best bike and kit. One day he bumped into Andy Burrell from the Middlesex RC who invited him round to talk bikes and see his machines. He asked me to come along. Andy lived with his mother and had this shed with his immaculate bikes – he had a Hetchins, a few other machines – and he said, 'If you're interested, I'll take you down to the clubroom in Southall.' That was the introduction.

Burrell was the club champion at 24-hours and soon involved the new recruits in his support team. 'I got up at the crack of dawn to get out to this place somewhere in Bedfordshire for the National 24 on the North Road. I handed him up a drink, and he remarked, "One of these days I will be doing this for you."' Poole rode his first 24 in 1956 at Catford, won by Burrell. It's there in the logbook, in its neatly ruled columns with a brief comment section – 'howling gale', 'hard – not fit!', 'west wind blowing'. He managed 456 miles. I look intently at the results, but the book is redundant: he remembers everything anyway.

In 1959 I did 458 miles. I asked Andy for help. He was bril-liant. I gave him a feeding and riding schedule, and he was completely reliable. It was one of those things: we'd only see each other once a year, and it was the National 24. There used to be four 24-hour events: the Catford, North Road, Mersey and the Wessex; the National event would rotate around. One by one they dropped out because of various problems, most of it the courses and traffic, and now the Mersey is the only one left.

One of the important figures for Dick Poole at this time was Arch Harding. He was a legendary figure among the 'stayers', his competition record at 100 miles a high-water mark: he man-aged 4 hours and 17 minutes in 1947. Harding helped lead the club towards the long-distance stuff. A typical weekend involved a 90-mile ride, a 50- or 100-mile time trial, followed by the ride home, clocking up 250 to 300 miles of a weekend.

Nobody had cars; we'd stop in digs the night before then ride home after. Arch was phenomenal. He liked a beer and a self-rolled cigarette. He'd keep a couple of fags in the bar-ends, put the plug in. He'd light up, mid-race. I was influenced by him a lot, but he was a very self-centred guy, as most top riders are. He used to moan. We'd ride down to the New Forest, 90 miles from Southall, without lights. This meant we had to get home quickly, chasing the onset of the dark, and he'd moan like a drain because he liked to take his time. He had a group of disciples. I used to avoid it because he went his way, and anybody else had to follow.

It could be quite difficult getting the team organised to support the long-distance races, with three or more riders competing. 'In one race all three of us turned up simultaneously and nothing was ready. There was a tin of peaches and I just took handfuls out of the tin and then carried on with peach syrup everywhere.' Burrell remained the fulcrum, and at one point suggested Poole try for the End to End, but the organising put him off. Burrell moved on and the End to End became something discussed and discarded.

The idea resurfaced courtesy of 'snapper' Bernard Thompson, who was also a member of the Middlesex. Throughout his life Thompson was committed to the pursuit of cycling. He is *the* documentary photographer of the sport, a niche incarnation of Humphrey Jennings, a poet of mass observation with a painter's eye. His images span four decades and speak of a sport that is both ageless and of its time. Thompson, or 'Bern' as he was known by the club, shared a fascination with the End to End with Burrell. He'd been snapping for Jock Wadley at *Coureur* since 1960 and working for *Cycling* magazine – known as the Comic – defining the visual language of domestic cycling at the time. 'Bern asked about the End to End. He said, "I'll take care of it." That was that. He went to the guy who organised Reg Randall's attempt, who gave us the list of all the people to get in touch with, the schedules, all of that stuff. It turned out he was using the same schedule as Dave Keeler, and Sid Ferris. We adapted those schedules.'

Thompson joined the dots and harnessed the resources needed for the attempt. He contacted Ethel Crowther at Mercian in Derby – 'he was very thick with them'. A few weeks later, Dick Poole rode up to Derby for a fitting – 140 miles out on the Saturday, back on the Sunday. He stayed over with Ethel, who was running the business after her marriage to Tom had foundered. 'They were very helpful. Ethel just sorted it.' Poole came away with a beautiful King of Mercia frame and high-end components including a new double chainset and cotterless crankset, both new developments. Time and technology had moved on.

We talk about previous attempts. I mention George Pilkington Mills and the *whoomph* from a bag of cocaine. He laughs, a real scurrilous laugh, and we chuckle at memories of Dave Keeler's strange gear system.

Amid the talk about equipment, newness and technology, Poole mentions that he went along with Ian To* on his attempt in 2018, as an RRA observer. 'They asked how I found my way. I told them I had a list of towns to go through. They were in absolute awe. They had all these technical things – GPS on the bike pointing up the road, digital mapping. They just couldn't grasp that there was no technology at all; the bike was a standard machine, no carbon fibre.'

Planning continued apace. Poole and his team had to work within the rules of the RRA, an organisation glacially slow to

---

* Ian To attempted the End to End twice in 2018, reaching Carlisle and Preston respectively before climbing off.

change. This included the insistence on secrecy before the event and the 'following cars' rule – only one 'overtake' every 50 miles. 'It made things quite challenging and we had to plan it carefully – you could only pass every two and a half hours. You had the following car and another car behind, so when you set off the car behind went ahead, dropping people off every 15 miles or so, three or four people; they'd hand up the drink, then they'd climb back in the car behind, and then as soon as they'd done the 50 miles they'd switch and repeat the manoeuvre.' It led to an elaborate game of leapfrog all the way up and along the A38.

Poole and his wife Carol lived in Essex at this time. He used the commute to central London to train, a 60-mile round trip each day along an arterial road – it gave him the distance but also the speed. He wasn't doing huge miles, 'around two thousand for the year', but in the six weeks prior to the attempt he increased that to 600 a week, through three rides to work and back, training and racing. On 23 May 1965 he went for a regional place-to-place record. 'I could tell there was a north-easterly wind, so I thought, King's Lynn, that'll be about right. I went to King's Lynn, round the roundabout, and came back again. I was on a 72-inch fixed gear. On the way back I remembered I had a racing gear on the other side of the hub. I changed the wheel round and rattled back on an 84-inch with the wind behind me.' He took thirty-eight minutes off the record, completing the 194-mile round trip in 9 hours and 11 minutes, at an average speed of 21mph.

The End to End was pencilled in for 14 June. The typed schedule was for two days exactly, two hours ahead of Reg Randall's time. In the absence of precise forecasting and given the pressures of work among the support team they 'picked a day, took time off work and went there'. Waiting was out of the question: people had taken time off work and couldn't afford to hang about. Poole is clear about this: 'unless it was absolutely awful, I was going to go. As it happened, I woke up and you could hear the foghorn going off.' Cycling journalist Mal Rees described the initial setting: 'after six months of conspiratorial secrecy, scheming and planning, Bernard Thompson assembled his team. The Met Office gave the venture the prayed-for rubber stamp. Postponement inadvisable, the oracle had spoken. Cornwall to Caithness, the stayer's ultimate in ambition. Good riding will not be enough, good luck will be required in sizeable quantities.'*

The RRA notified their phalanx of observers, and word got out to supporters in hushed whispers and late-night phone calls. Reg Randall marshalled the troops in Bristol – a role he relished, the opportunity to support fellow lunatics on the greatest challenge in endurance cycling.

Things started well, the wind picking up through Cornwall and Devon. However, Poole took a fall at Exeter. 'There were roadworks and they'd cut away the surface. Like a twit I tried to jump it, failed miserably and came off.' He laughs, thinking back to his poor technique. In photos he is hurting, a face of sharp pain, even if he downplays it now: 'It didn't seem too bad – I cut my fingers, scraped my leg.'

It chipped away at the time, and on reaching Bristol he was twenty-three minutes down on schedule. The route rolled through the heart of the city: the A38 to West Street, then East Street, past the huge tobacco factories of south Bristol, then St Mary Redcliffe Church, Union Street, up Stokes Croft, before finally heading past Bristol Aerospace at Filton and along the Gloucester Road. The support team followed diligently behind, with Bill Betton, then proprietor of Mercian, driving the works van. Like Marguerite Wilson, he hadn't passed his test and had L plates.

---

* *International Cycle Sport*, July 1965, p.27.

Bernard Thompson

After the crash at Exeter

All the while, the rain came down. It sprayed the road and rider and brought with it the cold – a pairing of elemental nastiness. By Whitchurch, at 300 miles, it was 'throwing it down'. The passing minutes mingled with the raindrops and coursed away into the gutter. He was forty minutes behind Reg Randall's time at Wigan, then got lost in the back streets of Lancaster. However, the schedule worked in Poole's favour:

> I was still up *on the record* by seventy minutes, and psychologically this was an important buffer. It was dark though, and heavy going. You couldn't see much more with a bulb than without. The following cars were also adhering to the distance and were a long way back. It was dark, wet and cold, but I don't think it ever entered my head to pack. I had to get on with it. It's very difficult if you try and don't make it. That's a hard place to be.

Shap Fell loomed ahead in the fog and mist of the early morning, a sulking, whispering menace of a climb. Huge lorries struggled against the incline, lumbering up in an unending corridor of slowness. They formed a stuttering convoy in the rain and mist, a dark woollen thread woven through and then above the road in a clumsy layman's stitch, stop-start, frayed at the edges, a triumph of force over grace. In among the ranks of Leyland Super Comets, that crawling constellation of slowness, cowered the tiny Mercian van, two bikes on the roof, then a Ford Anglia with a bike lying prone on top, and Dick Poole, 50 metres further up the road, a blurred outline of grey against grey, overtaking the convoy at 11mph. Once over the Shap, it was the long stretch across and through the Devil's Beeftub, then Moffat, towards the Forth of Firth.

Poole went through 454 miles in twenty-four hours, 4 miles down on Reg's record. 'It was slower than Reg, but you have to ride

Bernard Thompson

Shap Fell

within yourself, taking into consideration the conditions and the final outcome. It sounds simple, but that's the key to it, that self-discipline.' He began to pick up pace from that point on. He was forty-five minutes up at Dalwhinnie, tearing through the miles, feeling strong and confident, but also bemused by the strangeness of night in the depths of nowhere. 'I was struck by the wildlife. There were hundreds of rabbits hopping about in the road, things that I didn't normally see. The other thing that struck me was the people. You don't know them from Adam and never will but they come out at all hours of day and night to marshal you through a particular point, cheer you on and become involved. It's an odd experience moving onwards all the time but seeing each person.'

He continued his remorseless progress towards the east coast, Helmsdale and Berriedale. 'I rode them all where previous riders had walked. It is a tough section.' The average speed for the last 70 miles was nearly 17mph. This factored in one longer stop which panicked the helpers.

It was nearly twenty minutes. They thought I would never get going again, but it seemed to do the trick, I felt good. I didn't feel I was going to go under two days, I wasn't chasing it, I was riding to schedule. The main issue was a struggle with a bar of Kendal mint cake. I remembered it was in my pocket, but I was so tired that I could hardly reach back and get it. It took ages; I was wrestling with the pockets trying to find it. It's strange the things you recall. I had planned to eat all sorts of stuff but in the end I couldn't really take anything except Complan. I had twenty or more bottles of the stuff.

In addition to several sit-down feeds, Poole ate a 2lb fruitcake, eleven malt loaves, cream cheese, egg and tomato sandwiches, four blocks of mint cake, a gallon of rice and fruit salad, six 'rice and raisin' feeds, twelve oranges and lots of fresh and canned fruit.

After fighting with the weather, falling off his bike and arguing with the Kendal mint cake, Dick Poole made it to John o'Groats in less than two days, the first rider to accomplish this feat, stopping the watch at 47 hours, 46 minutes and 35 seconds.

It was a terrific feeling, but I was in the state you'd expect after 871 miles in two days. Straight away I said, 'Right that's it, I'm not doing the thousand.' However, Mal Rees chimed up, 'The sun's shining, you should have a go.' I hadn't slept at all, but I reluctantly had a complete change of gear and rolled out again. They said I could do it at barely club run pace. I was averaging a lot quicker than I needed to. Towards the end, they'd time every mile. You were expected to do an extra ten to take into account any discrepancies. I went down the road with the wind behind, pretty sure I was going to finish on this bit of road. At the end of this road they turned me up a hill which I wasn't expecting. I got to the top, turned right

again and was suddenly heading into the wind, and that just
did it. I struggled along for a bit, in a low gear. I was in the
early stages of hypothermia; I was absolutely smashed. My
hands were so cold I couldn't pull the brakes on.

They thought I'd done 1007 miles so got me off the bike
and into the car. I had a hot bath at John o'Groats and
went to bed.

The next morning, I went down to breakfast and the proprietor poked her head through the hatch and reeled off the
various menu choices – bacon, egg, porridge, tomatoes, you
know. I waited for her to finish, then said, 'Yes please.'

And so began the wait for ratification. Distances and routes
were checked, observation reports and forms scrutinised. The
press celebrated Poole's ride as a superlative achievement. Jock
Wadley marked the ride with the headline 'Inside Two Days':
'Poole beat the End to End record in memorable style, then

Bernard Thompson

'Yes please'

went on to take the "1000" . . .' But the last thing to be assessed was the mileage for the 1000. Word started to creep out that somehow Poole's effort wasn't the full 1000 miles.

> We couldn't understand it. They measured it again and the motoring organisations joined in and still it came out short. And it was getting to be quite a story in the papers. It took a lot of puzzling to work out what had happened. We had based our attempt on Reg Randall's schedule. The route was clear except in Scotland, where there was a choice between going straight over a mountain, which was the shorter route, or round it, which was longer, but he could ride faster. We assumed he'd gone the shorter way, and that's the way I went, when actually he went the longer way. As a result, we were 10 miles out. The RRA bent over backwards to try and make it 1000, took all sorts of measurements, but they couldn't get close enough. Two nice things happened. Reg Randall, who held the 1000, took his plaque off the wall and put it in the cupboard, saying, 'I don't merit putting that on the wall.' Apparently the RRA also inscribed on the back a footnote that I'd done 999.7 miles. It makes an interesting anecdote, it's a sad thing. But it wasn't the objective, it was an obligation – you may as well do another 130 miles in seven hours! It's one of those things.

Poole rode 24-hour races for another fifteen years. He then moved into coaching, taking his exams at Lilleshall, determined to put something back into the sport. Before long he was training others to coach, working for both the RTTC (Road Time Trials Council) and BCF (British Cycling Federation), then merging both organisations, bringing the grotty cyclo-crossers in on the act in an unusual display of collegiate approaches to cycling. Eventually, the BCF went out on their own.

I'd started the programme, taught physiology, but they told me to go on a course showing people how to go around corners. The people adjudicating were people that I'd taught, which was crazy, so I stayed with the RTTC. From there I got involved in triathlons. It was awful: all these good athletes, mostly, absolutely scared stiff of cycling, bikes in a mess, most of them on the wrong gears, position all over the place. I suggested a course for these guys, they were missing basic knowledge. We then founded the Triathlon Association and the European Triathlon Union. All of this stemmed from the End to End when people helped, watched, responded and supported me.

We look back over the photos – beautiful monochromatic images from Bernard Thompson, and pictures of Ethel, the two who met on Poole's End to End and later married. We look over the letters, the characters, the people to whom it meant so much. I feel warmth in sharing these memories with Dick Poole, at writing them down and passing them on to others, but regret for the past, the misty-eyed regret I get from looking through old images. I wonder about time and how modish our photos seem now, when everything's Instagrammed, but how anachronism will come to everything and everyone. We are already postmarked and digitally fading, pre-aged through pseudo-artistic filters.

At eighty-eight, Dick Poole still gets out on the Reading track twice a week, then comes home to Carol. Things are different now, club life and cycling culture have changed. 'There isn't the same camaraderie. When it came to club dinners people used to equivocate, but I'd say bugger that, it's the club dinner, you go. The same doesn't apply now. People are ambivalent, they don't have the same loyalties or sense of community. They are "clubs" in name only, they're not a community. That's why the End to

End is such an important part of our club cycling traditions – of family and tradition.'

I wonder if he has been back to some of the locations on the route, taken the chance to revisit the highest point of his success. He answers with laconic wit, a dryness that hovers above the truth: 'I've never been back or visited either place. I never went to Scotland before and haven't been back since. I wouldn't say I had no desire to go back, I just prefer warmth. When you think about it, it wasn't a bad ride when you compare it with the ones that followed, over shorter distances, with all the technology.'

10

Janet Tebbutt is a wonderful stayer

Sunday, 18 July 1976

Mid-July 2018. I drag the wife and kids out to a layby on the A38 to watch Jasmijn Muller attempt to break the End to End record and shout encouragement. We find a suitable spot in long, scratchy grass filled with fast food rubbish. The kids find an iPhone. Experience now tells me there are worse things to find by the side of the road. Also parked up is a yellowy-beige camper van. Next to it, holding a clipboard, is a small elderly lady.

It's not until a year later that I realise the lady was Janet Tebbutt, and she stands right there for every attempt, making sure the riders take the correct turning. As they hurtle past they nod appreciatively at this random lady. Perhaps some of them recognise that Janet isn't just a random lady with a clipboard but a previous holder of both the End to End and the 1000-mile records, but probably not.

Janet Tebbutt lives near me, in Portishead. It's just on the edge of Bristol, nestled against the Severn with views across to Wales.

She has a lovely lilting north Somerset accent. We know the same people and clubs from within the local cycling diaspora. I feel my vowels lengthen as I talk to her; my voice relaxes, gets more West Country. I can't think of anyone less likely to have ridden from Land's End to John o'Groats at record speed than this convivial eighty-three-year-old lady who makes me tea and feeds me biscuits.

Like Alf Engers, and Vic Clark, and Eileen Sheridan, her formative years were defined by the war. It was a different time; inconceivably so. She was born in 1936 in Nailsea, a couple of miles down the road. She has moved to Clevedon and to Portishead, staying within a tight Severn triangle, Kenn Moor on one side, the M5 on the other.

> The war was such a big influence on our lives. Our father was away for six years. It was so disruptive, to be away that long. On his return he had a job waiting at the shipping office, but they were short of teachers, so he did a training course in Bristol. He got a job at a new school at Backwell but the leaving age had been put up to sixteen. The pupils weren't interested in the extra year and it got under his skin, so he got a job at a junior school in Clevedon until he retired. Anywhere my sister and I wanted to go from Nailsea it was easiest by bike. I was nine when the war ended, so from about five I was the youngest trying to keep up; that may have influenced me!

Bristol has changed. The docks have drifted out to Avonmouth, brick warehouses for bonded goods replaced by mega-hangars and endless tarmac for thousands of brand-new cars. There is less industry now, the city centre full of shiny sculptural fountains that don't work and street food and shouty stags and hens from Wales and people down from London dragging sacks of equity behind them and praying that they have sourdough toast in the regions.

People moved out during the war to work in factories and industry; shipping offices were relocated. Once the war finished, the social boundaries of the countryside and city were in a state of flux. People wanted to get out and ride, to escape from work, fuelling the post-war bike boom. The Clevedon Section of the Cyclists' Touring Club was one of the first to emerge, before becoming the District Road Club because of a growing interest in racing. A surprising number of racing cyclists start out in the CTC, retaining the DNA of cyclo-tourism.

Janet Tebbutt started out on a hand-me-down BSA step-through; 'it was semi-sports, so it suited me down to the ground, but it wasn't quite as good as I thought it was'. I think of my first racing bike, how it was made of mystical materials. 'It's Carbolite 103,' I would brag to friends. It was pig-iron and putlocks. Tebbutt moved on to a lighter, shinier Claud Butler. In the back room of her house there is an Argos, one of the few remaining Bristol frame-builders. For Janet, it was the Claud Butler that opened up a world of longer-distance touring.

I'm a touring cyclist really. I would go hostelling with a Carradice – off Saturday, back Sunday. The very first was St Briavels [she says 'Brevvels' in pure Somerset tones], and we went over on the Aust ferry. We went to Minehead, Ashton Keynes, Marlborough – most of the hostels are gone. People worked on a Saturday morning, so you had to go after lunch. We'd ride down to Dorset, 90 miles or so, stay over, ride back. I used to ride into Bristol to work which saved the bus fare for the hostel weekend, half a crown each time on the bus, so I had an extra five shillings to spend.

She laughs, beautifully, at the memory of accumulating pounds and pence to pay for the freedom of the weekend, the thrift of it.

When I finished school I wanted to do accounts, but mainly I loved cycling. It wasn't good for my prospects because all I wanted was to get a job so I could cycle more! I was trained to do the accounts; they had an adding machine, but you did everything by hand. If it goes wrong you can find it, unlike now, with the buttons. After four years I got a job in Clevedon which was handy – I'd have more time to ride. Cycling was the thing; it ruled my life.

I'm lost in a reverie of the analogue world; of obsolete trades, dextrous activity, bikes, local networks, the overlapping world of work and leisure, and the centrality of cycling to a community. Janet met Alan Tebbutt through the Clevedon. His brother Michael was one of the fastest 'testers' (time triallists) in the area, regularly going under two hours for 50 miles. We talk about people in our community, such as Bridget and Ian Boon, observers and timekeepers for End to End attempts. Ian's grandfather owned a famous cycle shop on the Gloucester Road. There were more Bristol clubs back then, more cycle shops. Bridget has legendary status among time triallists after she won the North Road 24-hour, beating all the men with 457 miles. I used to organise races with Bridget and Ian as timekeepers. The racers wouldn't know what to make of this no-nonsense lady who turned up on a fixed-wheel bicycle with a tattered Carradice saddlebag, carrying her clipboard, or that she and Ian once rode 463 miles in twenty-four hours on their tandem. We talk about longstanding cycling families in the city, the names and faces, the chap who organises the marshals for every End to End attempt, making sure Bristol passes by without a hitch and silently contributing to every record. It is a vital social heritage woven through work and leisure, shared memories and experiences, and the fellowship of the road. Things have changed, the roads have changed; there is less space for races, less time for leisure. Cycling is an encumbrance, a fetish, not something to be warmly celebrated. The networks have been eroded. People live to work; people drive to work; cyclists are a nuisance.

Author photo

EVENT & DATE.		COURSE	TIME	WINNERS NAME & TIME.	
CLUB 25	3 - 6 - 56	U21	1 . 17 . 21.	M. TURNER .	1 . 15 . 0 .
W. W.R.L. 25.	1 - 7 -56	U21	1. 17. 17.	V. GARRETT.	1. 6. 30.
BRISTOL SOUTH 25.	15 - 7 -56	U21	1. 15. 33	V. GARRETT.	1. 5. 26
AUTUMN 25.	30 - 9 -56	U21	1 .17. 31.	A. MASON.	1. 15. 0 .
W. W. R. L. 10	14 - 4 -57	U1	30. 20	M. HILL & M. ROGERS.	
W.W.R.L. 15	12 - 5 -57	WINTERBOURNE	47. 10	M ROGERS .	42. 48
EVENING 10	22 - 5 -57		29. 24	M. TURNER .	27. 57
CLUB 50'	2 - 6 - 57 (First Hand 6m)	U22	2 - 33 - 8	D. BRYANT	2. 28. 28.
EVENING 15	11 - 6 - 57		43. 23	M. TURNER	43. 8
W. W R. L. 25	30. 8 - 57	U21	1 - 13 - 52	W. FRYER	1. 5. 39
EVENING 10	3 - 7 - 57		28 - 43	M. TURNER	28 - 4
PLYMOUTH CORINTHIAN.	7 - 7 - 57	S1	1 - 15 -38	M. PEARCE	1. 4. 29
EVENING 15	7 - 8 . 57		45. 3	M . TURNER	41 - 16
W. W. R. L 50.	11 - 8 - 57	U22	2 - 34. 19	B. JACKSON	2. 22. 0
EVENING 10	14 - 8 - 57		31 . 52	M . TURNER	29 . 30
ST. BUDEAUX 15	17 - 8 - 57 (2nd Hand 8 m)	S1	45. 9	B . JACKSON .	40. 10
AUTUMN 25	25 - 8 - 57	U21	1 . 23. 41	M. TURNER	1 - 19. 32
CHAMPIONSHIP 10.	1 - 9 - 57	U21	30. 59	M TURNER.	28. 30
WESTERN R.C 25	18 - 5 - 58	U21	1. 17. 30.	M. PARAMORE .	1. 6. 56.
PRIVATE TRIAL 25	15 - 6 - 58	U21	1. 17. 9	-	-
W. W. R. L. 25.	29 - 6 - 58	U21	1 - 16 - 1.	S. BALL.	1. 4. 24.

Janet Tebbutt's logbook

We look through photos taken along the A38 – the main road for all End to End attempts and the artery of the district's races. Every distance from 10 to 100 started at Patchway at the Lone Tree – no other course description was needed. Now it's buried beneath acres of tarmac and Cribbs' Causeway Mega-Mall. 'You rode 5 miles, turned in the road by Alveston church. The 25 went as far as Stone. That was it. You couldn't race in men's events; Bristol South had a women's 25. There were events up at Reading, Bournemouth or Exeter and that started the big mileages. I would get the train on a Saturday afternoon, then ride home after the event. Beryl Burton and June Pitchford came down to the A38 because it was a "fast" course.'

Janet lists more legendary women riders, many of them lost in the mists of memory: Ann Horswell, Joan Kershaw, Barbara Body, Anne Illingworth. They were incredibly fast. In many ways their stories have been subsumed beneath layers of writing about men, Beryl Burton the only one to gain wider recognition. Janet is honest about how quick they were in comparison with her. 'There was this terrific difference. June did a 1.04, I did a 1.12. That was a ladies' event at Greenford.' Janet Tebbutt was not a super-fast rider. She didn't trouble the timekeepers at a local level, let alone national. I'm beginning to understand one of the adages of the End to End: it's not whether you can ride fast enough, it's whether you can ride *slowly* enough.

Her lack of short-distance pace eventually led her to a 12-hour at Sutton Benger, a strange village near Cirencester. 'I thought it would suit me, the longer it was the better. It wasn't too bad, and I did a few more, at which point someone told me to have a go at the Western Counties Road Records, which I'd never heard of. I knew of the RRA, just not the regions. I wasn't fast enough to have people falling over themselves to organise, so it was always left to Alan and me.'

It is interesting to think of this hidden sub-level of road

records. Almost all regions had their full set of place-to-place standards – Bristol to Weston and back, and so on. These continued until recently, when most of the regional associations gradually crumbled into yellowed parchment, were digitised, and then disbanded and forgotten for ever. The RRA now has a canteen of silverware handed in to the high vizier once the regions folded, through lack of interest, essentially. Janet was drawn to one name in the record books, Edith Atkins, and her amateur status became important.

> Edith held twelve women's RRA records and the times weren't that different from Eileen [Sheridan]. She was completely amateur like I was. It was such a difference. I couldn't have ridden under the pressure Eileen rode under. She coped with the pressure of being professional and there is something extraordinary about her. She had a beautiful enjoyment in the experience. Similarly, I can't really compare myself with Edith because I couldn't have done the national place-to-place records she did, but in another way, she was a true cyclist like me, and this is the difference between cycling being your life, not just something you're doing to achieve things in races.

I wonder about the amateur spirit, what it means; the constant pressure of the day job, squeezed training and financial limitations. Does the achievement sit higher as a result? I am drawn to Janet's story because it defines the honesty and joy of an unpaid calling, a true labour of love, and it demonstrates the capacity of all of us to do something extraordinary if we set our minds to it.

Janet started with half a dozen of the regional place-to-place records. It was a mammoth task in logistical terms. The rules are strict, a car helps. 'We didn't have a car! I did everything.

I did all the schedules, typed. It's sheets of it! That's typing it on a typewriter! Again and again! No copy and paste! For every attempt!' We laugh at the madness of it, the hours spent tapping away on an Olivetti. It became a breathless series of long-distance marathons: 162 miles to Exeter and back, another to Bournemouth, or Swindon, or Dorchester, linking the West Country together. She then made an attempt on the amateur national 1000-mile record, held by Wynne Wrightson. The motivation was simple. 'I got this handbook from the WRRA and it was the only record that I thought I could get, because all the rest were short and too fast. Reg Randall came to live out at Bradford-on-Avon; he had done a 1000-mile record radiating out on lanes near here, which was useful. People thought Alan pushed me into it, but it wasn't that way at all. I had these bright ideas and he would back me up if I thought I could do it.'

She prepared in earnest, her first 24-hour in 1974. She was thirty-eight years young and 'the lone lass to attempt the distance'. 'I was the champion, I guess, except they didn't have such a thing.' She was aware of the recovery needed for the 1000-mile attempt in a month's time, taking an hour's break in the middle of the event.

It is a strange record, featuring 1000 miles of riding around Somerset, Gloucestershire and Wiltshire. I can't think of anything worse: out and back, round the roundabout, up the road, turn, back again, for *1000 miles*. She wasn't even going anywhere.

It was dry for the first five hours. Then a petulant weather front slouched in off the Atlantic and hung around from Thursday until Saturday, like a bored teenager outside a Happy Shopper. She went past her home a few times, stopping briefly but not sleeping. Friends opened their doors throughout the ride – a house in Bristol, one in Somerset – as she pedalled through villages and towns and around the edges of the city.

Janet Tebbutt

Janet and Reg Randall during the 1000

Long descents turned into climbs in the teeth of the wind. Further and onwards, to Gloucester, Tewkesbury, and back, around Oldbury, criss-crossing the towns on the saturated Severn flood plain. 'I remember someone shouting "Mind the floods", but I couldn't care less. I gave up trying to have dry clothes.' The world carried on working, sleeping and eating while Janet carried on riding, day and night. 'I don't know whether it's being mental *or* mental strength, but it is just keeping going, and that is how I ride. I just want to keep riding. Towards the end I didn't sleep because I knew it was the last day. I completed the 1000 miles in 3 days, 9 hours and 29 minutes.'

It is beyond my imaginative capacity. I think of my 200-mile jaunt to Bristol, then carrying on and doing it another four times without stopping. I'd be a seeping mess. She finished on the Sunday, then went back to work on the Monday. 'I didn't feel too bad after,' she says.

The End to End seemed to be the logical next step. It's shorter, but any hopes of an easier ride were soon dispelled by

Randall. 'I've done both, and it is a very different thing,' he said. 'The 1000 hasn't got the hills, the long climbs, Devon and Cornwall.' It was advice, rather than a warning, and in 1975 Janet set off to tackle Edith Atkins' amateur record. In contrast to the year before, it was a 'real heatwave', and the temperatures held up in the mid-twenties overnight. By the time she reached Lancaster, heat exhaustion had killed the attempt. It was a disappointment, but she knew she wasn't the first to be halted by the conditions.

She regrouped and planned for a further attempt the following year. Waiting for the right weather proved a logistical headache which was not helped by her abandonment the previous year, or the remorseless heatwave throughout June and early July. People began to doubt her ability; this is where the divide between amateur and professional becomes an issue. 'After I'd packed on the first attempt people didn't think I was going to do it. All that was left were my friends and the hardy few that went along the year before.' She was determined; Alan and the tightly knit group believed in her. When the day came, the conditions weren't right, it wasn't worth it. They waited twenty-four hours, but that threw out the helpers: they had to take another day of leave. It added stress to the occasion.

Things were hard from the start. Janet struggled with stomach problems, but overcame them through willpower. 'I just thought, I'm not having this. It wasn't something I normally suffered with.' She saw the Boons waving her on through Bristol, but the time slipped out and she was a long way adrift by Kidderminster. 'I knew I wasn't going very well. I wasn't confident, but I didn't mind being down. Going into Scotland I had a flash of clarity: I thought of all the people who didn't believe in me, and I knew I was going to do it. Shap was fine, then Devil's Beeftub, about 7 miles where I felt all right going up, but your legs can get into a set groove going for that long so when I went to go down the other side I didn't go any faster. I did away with the long breaks.'

The ride changes for everyone through the first night and into the second day. It is uncharted territory, a journey into darkness and the unknown. It is also quiet, beyond quiet – no traffic, no people. If there's a tailwind you can't hear the bike. It is a kind of dark we don't experience within our cities of endless amber light – a tar black sky and unfolding pleat of darkness.

It was open country. There was a white barn owl on a post. I looked across and the owl looked back. Towards the early morning I could hear a sound to my left in the long moorland grass, a swishing noise, like breathing. Suddenly a huge herd of deer came rushing up and across the road right in front of me, proper big red deer. It went from this rushing noise on the moorland to the noise of hundreds of hooves clattering on the road, then back to the swish of grass and a muffled thunder, all in a moment.

It is a dreamlike place where nature runs free in the darkness and only those out at peculiar times in peculiar places get to participate. It is a dream of waves of sound and nature, of isolation and the beauty of that time between night and day.

'But crikey, it rained ... and was so very cold. Your body can't withstand it. On the End to End it gets to you. These are conditions you wouldn't ride in, but here you are, in the middle of nowhere, riding in it like a madwoman. We got to Helmsdale and the road disappeared it was so steep, but the water was running down in a torrent. I was terrified, I couldn't stop, I had to go with it. It's harder on the way down.'

And all the while the lack of sleep is overwhelming and physically alienating. It is harder for women: they have to ride for longer, take on more food, need more sleep, everything. By

Janet Tebbutt

Janet in the End to End

the time Janet reached Dunbeath, the lack of sleep had begun to unpick the careful cross-stitch she'd embroidered across the rolling hills. There were 37 miles left. It doesn't seem far, compared to the 820 already completed, but it is well over two hours' riding. The proximity got to her. 'When I got to Wick I thought it was just around the corner, but I'd forgotten it was another hour. There is nothing on that road. On the hillside I saw a cottage I thought I'd seen before, like I was going round in circles. I kept stopping.' She pauses to reflect. 'It was a tough hour,' she tells me, with understatement. 'It's coping with everything on top of everything you've already coped with.'

She eventually completed the last 14 miles and finished in 2 days, 15 hours and 25 minutes, beating Edith Atkins' amateur record by nearly three hours. As many others have found, the experience of finishing was more relief than a celebration. 'I just felt, oh well, I'm here. I didn't flop down or anything. It shows I hadn't put enough in, I guess. I'm not good at putting a lot into it, this is my trouble. I had to stand and smile for a photo, but I hadn't spoken to anybody much because when I stopped it was "What do you want?" My face was set and I tried to smile and I couldn't, it was stuck in a grimace.'

It got a write-up in the Comic and wider recognition. It was and is an impressive ride, a new amateur record, and second only to Eileen Sheridan's mark at the time.

Getting home was arduous. The car broke down at Moffat and they had to break the journey a few times to sleep, once in a village hall near Kidderminster. Eventually they crept back into Nailsea, having taken longer to get home from John o'Groats than it took to ride there in the first place.

Four years later, in 1980, the RRA merged the men's and women's associations and the amateur and professional records. In 1985 and 1986 Janet attempted to beat Eileen's longstanding record, but without success. 'We made it to Scotland but it was done. We went on to the end, just to see John o'Groats again. I would have been fifty at that point. Maybe it wasn't a good idea, but it irritated me: they said it'll always stand as the amateur record, but I felt there was such a difference between amateur and professional in those days. I had nothing; the lines were so clear then. It was everything.'

She carried on riding, right through her fifties, sixties and beyond, chalking up landmarks along the way, including a veterans record for the 24-hour at the age of seventy. She always helps out at the Mersey Roads 24, the last remaining day-night event on the calendar. Her love of cycling is as strong as ever, out at the weekend to watch a time trial on the same stretch of road she rode through on the End to End, and back and forth during the 1000. Familiar places where time moves on but the ghosts of the past linger. Janet still rides along the same roads, but it's harder to get going now. 'I'm not good at making myself go out. Once I'm out I love it. I go hostelling a couple of times a year. I'm going to go back to St Briavels in April. I can vaguely remember the hostel, but nothing to do with what we did. It was a long time ago.'

St Briavels is one of the more spectacular youth hostels and probably the only one with neo-Gothic crenellations. I think back to the very different journey taken by Janet Tebbutt in 1955, on quiet rural roads alongside the river, the shipping freight heading up the Avon to the centre of the city. I compare it to now, the hack through Avonmouth and the new port, the chemical works, and the enormous lorries attending two mono-lithic Amazon warehouses. The ferry slipway is visible just below the 1960s bridge, which in turn has been superseded by another bigger, faster bridge.

'I never did tell people what I did because, to be quite honest, people don't know what a mile is; they don't know distance. There's no point me saying, "Oh, I did a thousand miles in three days", or "I did the End to End". They're baffled. If someone asks me why I did it, I think, well, it just seemed a good idea at the time.'

Janet Tebbutt

11

Paul, Mick and John pass the record between them

Wednesday, 11 July 1979

I am meeting people living lives in quiet anonymity, retired, relaxing. And then we talk about these incredible things they did forty years ago, or fifty years ago, or more, and the past springs to life in the room and the journey resurfaces in the imagination and I am awestruck. I forget about writing and become lost in waves of anecdotes. Some people exist in words, their time long before my time – Petronella, Frank Southall, Lilian Dredge – and I am philosophical. I read what others wrote about them. I am OK with that. However, I'm sad that I can't meet Paul Carbutt. He died of motor neurone disease in 2004 at the age of fifty-three, and like Marguerite Wilson, it is a hard loss to take. I hear people talking about him; his class, his friendship, his integrity, and his preternatural talent for riding bikes. He was a clay artist by profession, designing cars. I had no idea this was a profession, or that it still exists. People sculpt new cars out of clay; then they turn them into real cars. Cars made of clay – the past and the future in one. I am fifteen years too late.

It's easy to say that someone isn't like anyone else. However, in bike racing terms, Paul Carbutt wasn't like anyone else. He excelled at *everything*. For instance, he came second in the National Hill Climb on a four-minute climb of anger and pain – the Nick o' Pendle. Hill climbs are beyond niche, beyond specialist, and the sensation of taking part can best be compared to the moment Joe Pesci put someone's head in a vice in *Casino*: eventually your eye pops out and something inside you breaks and goo comes out of places it shouldn't come out of. Carbutt was at home on the violent four-minute special as well as the two-day elongated trial of torture that is the End to End. These are just the extremes; there is a full spectrum of stuff through the middle – road racing, time trialling at all distances, ripping it up in and around Crystal Palace in 1978 with Sean Kelly, Paul Sherwen and Dutch world champion Gerrie Knetemann trying to hold the wheel. Carbutt was national road race champion, rode professionally for Viking, won national time trial titles at 100 and 50 miles and came 6th at the Olympics in Montreal. He came 3rd in the Milk Race in 1976 as an amateur. He knew how to ride a bike.

I find his voice in faded copies of *Cycling*. Carbutt was drawn to the thrill of riding and went to the World Championship in Venezuela in 1977, getting a ribbing from Sherwen for his eclectic approach, but sticking to his guns: 'I was called a thick tester* ... but my answer is to get out and do it and prove a point. It's a good lesson for the younger lads to see that you can

---

* 'Tester' is slang for time triallist, someone who favours the race against the clock over the massed start. It can be pejorative when used by roadmen, e.g. 'that thick tester got on the front and it was an armchair ride'.

do anything.' The reporter got it: 'Paul Carbutt loves riding a bike just for the fun of it.' It was very hot and humid, and 'within 5 miles I couldn't breathe. The race was a nightmare. I try not to think about it. I thought Dudley Hayton was going to die. He looked like a skeleton.' Carbutt seemed unaffected. 'Strangely I felt all right. I have a skin disorder and hardly sweat. I can ride 100 miles in blazing sun and my vest will be bone dry. Others will be soaking wet.'

Carbutt set out to 'prove a point' by planning an attempt on Dick Poole's record. It had been sat on the shelf for fourteen years and required a daunting 18mph average. This is the trajectory of the End to End, it would seem: flurries of activity, a big and scary successful record, then silence. One thing worked in Carbutt's favour: the distance had been shortened by 12 miles by bridges and bypasses – potentially a forty-five-minute saving.

Carbutt rolled out in July 1979, a high-summer attempt, testing his ability to ride 'in blazing sun'. It is just one more element to add to the list of attempt-killers: too much heat. He coped well over the first twenty-four hours, despite a minor drama in Bodmin – reported to the police by an annoyed motorist for a perceived traffic violation. Cue a slow-motion chase through the back streets, a trip to the plod shop and a quick explanation, before being sent on their way again.

The night brought clear and cooler air as he rolled 'through darkened villages where shadowy figures loomed up out of the dark to give encouragement'.* Carbutt subsisted on milk by the pint, tinned rice and bacon sandwiches.

Heading up through Kendal, the first glimmers of the morning appeared with a thickening tailwind pushing across from the Irish Sea. The sun rose on a benign Shap Fell and the heat

---

* *Cycling*, 21 July 1979.

began to build through the morning, coming up off the tarmac, a slow incineration of bike and rider. On the run to Edinburgh, at 540 miles, Carbutt began to slow, head like a balloon on a stick, before collapsing. Helpers carried him from the bike, leaving him on the grass verge like a corpse. Another demonstration of the inherent dangers in long-distance record attempts. When Glenn Longland attempted the tandem record with Dom Irvine in 2014, he too collapsed. 'I could hear what was going on, they kept shouting at me, and then I'd stop and just look at them. I just couldn't move. I've never, ever, in all my years of racing, had it where I couldn't feel my legs like that.'* The End to End tests the body and mind in ways people cannot anticipate.

Carbutt lay under a blanket with ice on his neck. He had never ridden for longer than twelve hours and yet there were a further eighteen hours to go. Somehow, after ten minutes Carbutt's pulse returned to normal and they let him sleep for twenty minutes before giving him a bit of an orange and sending him onward. He staggered away, awkward limbs, slowly finding a rhythm. After the event Carbutt described it as 'like waking after a nightmare, but it wasn't a dream'.

He struggled again on Drumochter, fighting with the bike on the endless climb. Navigation became a problem through Inverness, and the last stretch was marred by an insistent headwind. Nevertheless, the last 17 miles to a 'disappointing huddle of buildings' took just an hour. He refused the 1000 immediately. Carbutt had beaten Dick Poole's time by twenty-three minutes, lowering the record to 47 hours, 23 minutes and 1 second. However, with 12 miles less distance, his average speed was lower than Poole's.

---

* www.cyclingweekly.com/news/latest-news/
end-end-tandem-record-attempt-125393#umeLcMfQwbkjGJ7u.99

The following year he went back to smashing it all over the place, chasing Robert Millar and Paul Sherwen in the National Road Race Championship and carrying on racing at every level. He was a member of Solihull CC, along with Tommy Godwin, who won a bronze medal at the 1948 Olympics at Herne Hill. Following Carbutt's death in 2004, Godwin summed up Carbutt's contribution to the sport and the fellowship of cycling: 'he always had time to chat, passing on advice and encouragement to riders of every ability – making everyone that met him feel that little bit special themselves'.

Carbutt's success reinvigorated the record, and within a year John Woodburn gave notice of his attempt. Woodburn is a cult hero in post-war British cycling who seems to crop up all the time. There is scope for a 'six degrees of separation from John Woodburn' Google exercise for all living British cyclists, maybe an app that tells you your Woodburn number. He raced from 1955, while on National Service, until 2014. During this time he won national championships, rode with Alf Engers, and turned professional in the early 1960s. He rode the Peace Race, coming 14th, and then carried on as a pro. He returned to the amateur ranks and became synonymous with the term 'supervet' in the late 1970s, effectively redefining any notions of what the over-forties can do by winning more national championships outright.

I used to see him racing in the West Country; he lived in Bradford-on-Avon. There was always a frisson of excitement when I saw his name on the start sheet: he was a bona fide legend, still turning out very quick times in his late seventies. His expression seemed permanently unreadable, straight and dour; it was hard to tell if he was smiling or angry. I later discovered when talking to Alf, or anyone who knew him, that you'd know if he was genuinely irritated. Taciturn, dry as dust, but warm, kind-hearted, generous with his time and ridiculously fast. I recall a hilly event in 2013; for some bizarre reason I'd been listed as 'scratch', i.e. the fastest rider on paper, and was off ahead of him. John rolled up, looked at my number and said, 'So you're the fast guy are you?' I looked down at my shoes in embarrassment. Later that season he gave me my prize for first senior in the series and it remains a joyous memory. He seemed pleased, but it was hard to tell.

Back in 1979, Woodburn was aware of the significance of the End to End, telling *Cycling*, 'it has a romanticism all of its own, it's the one ride that everybody remembers'. He also had pedigree, having targeted the 24-hour and completed several place-to-place records over the years. As far back as 1962 he took on the Cardiff–London record. He was sponsored by Alex Moulton, designer of a new ultra-compact frame with 16-inch wheels and sprung suspension. It wasn't regarded as a 'racing bike', more a novelty, so Moulton sought to give it some kudos by enlisting Woodburn. It required an enormous chainring on the front in order to make it possible to pedal fast enough. The smaller the wheels on a bike, the bigger the chainring needs to be. Once a chainring acquires enough teeth, typically above fifty-four, it acquires the mythical status of a 'dinner plate' – as in 'Wiggins had a dinner plate on there for the world record'. Woodburn completed the distance in 6 hours and 43 minutes. That's 162 miles at 24mph on a sort of proto-Brompton. In the late seventies Woodburn turned up with another elite time triallist, John Patston, to take on several tandem records. Both were suspended from other racing for vague crimes and misdemeanours too arcane and tedious to write about here, so had opted to chase the RRA standards.

He had a supportive employer, in this case the Post Office, where he was a telecom engineer. After an initial struggle and being turned down by Raleigh, he gained sponsorship from Jack

Fletcher, a steel magnate in the north-east who loved cycling and who bankrolled the Manchester Wheelers. There weren't many riders during the 1980s who didn't benefit from Fletcher's largesse. Jack and his wife Nora became known as true friends of cycling, much like Bernard and Ethel Thompson, a couple for whom the sport became all-encompassing, all of them driven by a consuming commitment to help people race. Stan Pike, of Crewkerne, made the machine – a local connection like Alex Moulton before him.

Woodburn had perfect conditions in July 1981, but poor health. His recovery from illness was in the balance but he started anyway. He lost time all the way against Carbutt. It was a demoralising experience and he stopped at Preston, only to be convinced to carry on by his helpers. At Perth he was visibly exhausted. He looked ill, but perhaps mindful of the phrase 'Any fool can get to Perth' he carried on, only to climb off at Blair Atholl, crestfallen because of 'all the people I have disappointed, all those who turned out to encourage me'. The sense of wanting to repay the faith shown by these supporters is compelling, the individual at the centre of a complex network. 'I was so unwell that I was letting the wind blow me along some of the time.' Woodburn resolved to go again in 1982, but at forty-four many thought time was running out for him. And waiting in the wings was Mick Coupe.

Mick Coupe and his brother Roger come as a double act. They talk in the same way they raced: one measured, thoughtful, metronomic, the other chivvying, hurrying up, making arrangements. An indistinct noise of family comes from the kitchen; something busy is happening. I'm crouched with my computer and audio recorder, using their pink velvety pouffe as an impromptu desk. Mick has a serious accent. Often I have no idea what he is saying. I listen back to the transcript over and over. The accent is tricky; 'any road' becomes *enrud*. But the dialect is something else. At one point he says 'I was fetchin' the fanwheel'. I have no idea what it means. It's a phrase that seems forged in the post-industrial past of the area, a leftover piece of linguistic memory and regional attributes.

Mick Coupe and John Woodburn were rivals in the National 24-hour Championship. Mick knew that he might not be a fast starter, but he finished strongly, and he saw Woodburn's failure as an opportunity. However, Mick's journey to the pinnacle of endurance cycling is a convoluted series of bifurcations.

He was born in 1935, his childhood blighted by rheumatic fever. 'At six years old I spent six months in bed. By the time I was allowed up I couldn't stand or walk. Your joints go solid, you can't move.' He made a recovery, but missed a lot of school. Not that it mattered. Everyone in the family was a plumber, including Dad. He wanted to be a joiner instead, right up until he was instructed to make a staircase at an interview: 'it frightened me to death – I wasn't very clever'. So he became a plumber.

'Get forward, Mick,' says Roger, 'you're waffling'.

Roger thinks I'm here for the bike racing. I'm here for the stories.

Mick carries on talking, just as he carried on riding. He would work with his dad on council houses, doing the plumbing. One weekend they were working in Kettering. Mick took his Velocette, a crazy bike-moto hybrid thing, so he could ride across to Skegness afterwards to see his sister, then back to Daventry.

It rained solidly. When I got back I couldn't put me feet down and the motorbike fell on me. I ended up in Northampton General and they found out I'd got rheumatic fever again. I had a linked heart problem; two valves weren't opening and closing properly. I was instructed to do some 'serious exercise'. Dad was a reasonable racing cyclist before the war, so he bought us a bike. I didn't want to ride, I wanted to play golf – I wanted to be a golf apprentice. Dad wasn't having it, he said there was no money in it.

The brothers started riding and racing. They rode the Luton Arrow 100-mile time trial in 1953 on a fixed wheel. 'It was Dad's idea of a baptism of fire,' Roger tells me. 'We suffered. We'd go out and he'd be on a derailleur, pushing 117 inches, we'd be on a 69-inch or so, trying to hang on his back wheel. He never dropped us but he made us move very quickly. I was never fond of it. He didn't take prisoners.' The brothers have a tendency to refer to each other as 'Brother Roger' and 'Brother Mick', or to the absent 'Brother Bill'. Brother Mick corroborates Brother Roger's story:

When I was at college they wouldn't give me a certificate for welding because I was too young. Dad was a dispatch rider in the war. 'Get on the back,' he says. We did 90mph down the main road. We get to the welding school, security bloke comes out, Dad wants to get in. He says, 'You can open the gate, or I can climb over, take the keys and open it.' He opened it. The certificate appeared in the post by Wednesday. Dad was a paratrooper, hard as cast-iron. He didn't take prisoners.

Mick used to ride the track at Bootle – now disappeared – with a long, shallow banking. They headed to Onchan Head in the Isle of Man, rode time trials, and his dad bought him a shiny all-chrome Hill Special. Mick then headed to Fallowfield at the invitation of legendary sprint champion Reg Harris. He was riding in the South Lancashire Road Club, doing 25s and 50s – 'anything else was crackers'. But time was tight and life encroached. 'I was fetchin' the fanwheel. I ended up riding 20 miles to work and 20 back, did eight hours' welding. There was no way, five and a half days, 200 miles, I could do it. I just stopped. I built myself a house instead.'

He was working at the huge Heinz factory in Wigan where they churn out a billion cans of beans a year (fact). Life was set and bikes were out – no touring, no commuting, no leisure rides and no racing. After ten years of bike-less routine, his marriage ended and he was tempted back into the saddle by his cousin, Johnny Carr.

He had an idea of winning the National 24-hour Championship. I told him he was bloody crazy. They were looking for a third man. I wasn't interested in the distance. I was at a loose end in 1976. I started to ride at the weekends, from here to the other side of the Potteries where he lived, just to get back on the bike: 60 miles there and then back the day after. I'd stay over, do his wallpapering. He had a plan to go down to Cornwall on holiday, then ride from Newquay to Bodmin every day, and then train on the beach. His idea was to be able to run as well as ride a bike. He was absolutely crazy. He hammered the daylights out of me. Seven days, 100 hilly miles every day. I thought, right, you bugger, I'll show you whether I can ride or not.

It seems like a bizarre boot camp of a holiday. I pause to listen, and also to ward off the dogs, which want to smell and lick me, the interloper in the busy Coupe household.

They got back and immediately started on a diet of long-distance racing, regularly doing a 100 or a 12-hour. After ten years off the bike Mick managed 250 miles or more, against winning distances of around 265 miles. His late blooming began to cause a stir among the promoting clubs. Emboldened, he moved up to the 24. Stronger legs and better equipment saw a significant 445 miles ticked off, enough for him to think about winning the event in 1979. Nim Carline, famed rhubarb farmer, friend of Beryl Burton and monstrous time trial rider, was the favourite for many. He started ten minutes behind and caught Mick early on, but it didn't last. 'Nim had a dinner plate on there. I reeled him back in overnight, saw him in front, and he was struggling. I caught him coming up out of Lincoln. I never saw him again, he packed. That's the only time he ever packed apart from the End to End.* I was over the moon. It was a good ride; I won the title with 492 miles and beat cousin Johnny. Uncle Jim didn't speak to me for six months.'

1982 saw John Woodburn fully fit. Woodburn was metronomic, for the most part, whereas Mick finished fast and fresh. Both seemed ideal candidates for an End to End attempt, and both made plans to ride in the summer. Derek Partington, owner of Coupe's local bike shop, sponsored Mick's attempt, with Brother Roger doing the organising. Both felt that Mick's tendency to finish fresh at the end of a 24 was a good omen. Partington also recognised that Mick had 'something different', and that it crucially wasn't about speed, but pace. At forty-six, Mick saw it as his swansong. He had made up for lost time and then some. However, there was one other important motivation. Mick's wife, Brenda, was a charge nurse at a unit for young people with muscular dystrophy in Preston. They were struggling for funds. 'It was young kids without long to live, with all sorts of challenges. They needed an ambulance with a tailgate for the kids. That's what I did it for.'

---

* 'Nim abandoned at Carlisle,' said Mick later. 'His helpers never forgave him. I never got it out of him. He got in his wife's car and went home.' Nim's unscientific approach to racing, 'hammer it right from the start', might not have helped.

Heinz got behind the effort. Mick pulls out a letter from the company, offering support for the attempt, both in terms of time and supplies; 'the Soup Group would seek a Heinz identification on the soup containers you carry, or perhaps your racing jersey'. They offered sponsorship of £1 per mile, and the workforce, 2500 strong, put £1 in each. They even bent the rules in the canteen, allowing Mick to feed up every evening before his long training rides home.

Mick/Roger Coupe

H. J. HEINZ COMPANY LIMITED

YOUR REFERENCE..

OUR REFERENCE.......jna/jlw.........................

BRANCH OR DEPT. Public Relations

DATE...... 11 March 1982

Mr M Coupe

cc Mr K Evans
   Mr C A Chamberlain

Dear Mr Coupe

Following our discussion on Tuesday, I thought it would be helpful to confirm the type of support the company would be able to offer should you go ahead with your attempt on the Land's End - John O'Groats cycling record.

Although, as Mr Evans and I explained, we are unable to contribute to the cost of staging the record attempt, our soup group would be pleased to make a donation to the charity of your choice, the Central Lancashire Authority for the Disabled. This support would take the form of £1 for each mile you cover. We also confirm our willingness to supply Heinz varieties to be used by your support team during the two-day ride.

In return, the soup group would seek a Heinz identification on the soup containers you carry, or perhaps on your racing jersey. We would be pleased to bear the cost of preparing these identifiers.

Naturally, your agent will wish to discuss this proposal with the sponsors of your racing cycles. As agreed, you will let Mr Evans know if you would like to discuss the matter further.

Best wishes for a successful result in June

Yours sincerely

John N Aspery

John N Aspery

Preparation involved 70 miles a day from December to June, Bolton to Wigan, then to Southport, through Preston, to Blackburn, over Winter Hill, then home, five days a week, with racing at the weekend. At the same time Brother Roger tackled the administrative legwork, mapping the road surfaces, the terrain, the climbs, everything. He calculated the pacing profile, rising and falling towards the end.

Come July, and fourteen people in five cars with two bikes travelled to Land's End. Derek Partington could only afford digs for a few days so a long wait was out of the question. 'Monday was bloody horrible, rain. Tuesday I had to go, as simple as that. Derek was holding me at the start and I could feel him shaking – it had cost him a lot of money. I said to him, "I would not put you through all this if I wasn't going to do it." It wasn't perfect, we had a crosswind most of the time. But the sun came out – it was great.'

No one was quite prepared for Mick's initial burst of speed: he covered the first 100 miles at 26mph. Roger was yelling at

Mick/Roger Coupe

him to slow down, but Mick was confident. 'If it had been a 100-mile time trial God knows what I would have done! I paid for it at Bristol though.' He had cramp at Bridgwater but 'spun through it', ticking off 261 miles in twelve hours, then stopped for pancakes at Knutsford. It was the brothers' home roads: club folk turned out to cheer him on, traffic lights were 'bin-bagged' to get a clear run. He went past the door of the Disabled Unit and Brenda was the night sister: 'We got them all out, early in the morning. It was lovely when he came past – they cheered, and we cheered. It's sad looking back. They were boys, they had a wonderful time up until about eighteen, nineteen, twenty. That's Duchenne's MD.* They're all dead now. You don't live beyond your early twenties.'

Coupe made it to Scotland inside twenty-four hours, the first rider to do so, en route to a new 'straight out' 24-hour record of 482 miles. 'I felt great and sat down at the side of the road for two minutes. We'd had a meeting beforehand at Derek's house. Someone said, what would you like at twenty-four hours? I said, strawberries and cream. We hit a massive rainstorm, sat in a layby, then it stopped and there was a rainbow. There was no strawberries and cream.'

Into Scotland and the wind shifted round. 'There was a bloke on the other side of the DC freewheeling at 40mph. I was riding into a gale from Penicuik and then up to the Forth Bridge. There are no buildings, an open bypass, a long drag, on and on, barely 10mph. I took such a pasting up there. There, and the Forth Bridge ... uuuuhhh.' He sighs, an elongated, dense sigh that started in 1982, dropped away again for thirty-eight years, only

---

* A severe type of muscular dystrophy. Muscle weakness begins around the age of four in boys and worsens quickly. Most are unable to walk by the age of twelve. Average life expectancy is twenty-six.

to reappear with those words 'Forth Bridge'. Coupe had ridden the carriageway two weeks before with no problems.

Suddenly word reached the convoy that he wouldn't be able to use the main road because of traffic density. Both brothers point the finger at the RRA official, Ed Zoller, who was waiting near the start of the bridge in his role as an official observer. Previous efforts had used the road. Brother Roger tenses, visibly. I can sense the anger in the room. He is still very cross. Words are not minced.

Mr Ed Zoller had his nose put out of joint because he had expected Michael to pack by then. He'd been pontificating by the side of the road where my brother just happened to be at that time, in one of the following vehicles, how he wasn't going to get to Perth – *which any fool can do*. I said I didn't care; I'm telling Mick to ride over the bridge and keep your observations to yourself. His claim to fame was that he'd ridden round France in a barrow boy's bike.

Mick agrees with him, but there was one other important factor:

I'm not good with heights. There was a bloke welding in a handrail halfway across – it was hanging out, sparks flying. It was a suspended footpath under the carriageway. I said I wasn't going; I sat down. Then it was decided that they would allow Brian Edwards to ride a bike 20 yards behind; he could ride behind over the bridge so he could assist if I got into trouble. It became a disqualification issue with Mr Zoller! It was so hard.

Stress levels were high, a combination of vertigo, conflict with Zoller and the record being in the balance. However, at Perth the wind dropped suddenly. Coupe admits this was the decisive factor. 'If the wind had carried on, I wouldn't have made it.'

17 Caroline Terrace,
EDINBURGH. EH12 8QY.
15th. October 1982.

Dear Mick,

I am very pleased to see in Cycling that your
End to End claim has been passed and offer you my hearty
congratulations.

I would like to say that I was most unhappy at
having to report what took place at the Forth Bridge after
my having twice expressed the opinion to your helpers that
having a rider accompany you would be a breach of rule 36.
My regret afterwards was that I did not suggest that a
helper or helpers could have jogged alongside you, or walked
with you, if you yourself had decided to walk all or part of
the way, so long as rule 37 was observed.

You were quoted in Cycling as saying that you
thought that the side track was a pedestrian walkway and not
for cyclists, but my letter of 23rd. April to your brother
made it quite clear that the ped/cycle track was fenced off
from the motor traffic.
                                        helped
         Local clubmen who/to marshall your ride in this area
add their congratulations.

                    Yours sincerely,

                    Edward W Zoller

Another bridge threatened, this time a brand-new one at
Kessock. So new, in fact, it hadn't been finished, and there were
'bike-sized gaps straight down into the water. The local cycling
club put lights on it and kids stood where the holes were to make
sure I didn't fall through. Dear God.'

Coupe struggled to eat throughout the last twelve hours
owing to a loss of appetite, resorting to tins and tins of Heinz
soup. Time and emotional energy had been lost and he fought
to get back on track. He no longer stopped to urinate, simply
going on the bike – one of the more glamorous aspects of long-
distance records. Think of it another way: each stop is at least a
few minutes, over two days ...

I was angry and so determined. My lights failed and I rode the last couple of hours without them. At 25 miles to go I just *went*. The only thing in my mind was to get the record from Paul Carbutt. Paul was twenty-seven, I was forty-six. It was my last ride, I knew that. It didn't matter if someone took it twenty-four hours later. I finished very fast, I was doing 25mph. How the hell I didn't run into the wall I'll never know. They got a bagpiper out. I like a glass of malt, but this guy was *drowned* in whisky. I went and had a bath. We never considered the 1000. I gave an interview, made sure I had bubbles in the right places.

They headed back later, and crept into Bolton at noon the next day. Almost immediately the phone rang.

I was dead tired, unsurprisingly. It was the manager at Heinz, said I needed to come to a reception at 3 p.m. I said to Brenda, 'Oh God, we have to go in.' We felt obligated, I guess, people had helped. I don't think we even got changed. I got to the gates and Sir Bill Beaumont* was stood there with the factory engineer; it turned out Beaumont was also involved with the CLAD charity. We went down into the canteen – it's a huge space, holds the whole workforce of 2500. I couldn't believe it: *everybody* was in there. The entire factory had stopped work at 3 p.m. for fifteen minutes, all production, the lot. They'd never done that before.

There was an 8ft board up in the canteen with a map of the ride with a light every 50 miles; they lit them when I got to a marker, for two days. Every time they went for anything to eat they saw where I was. I was tired and emotional; it was unreal, stood there with Bill Beaumont, the workforce and

* Sir Bill Beaumont, England rugby union legend.

then me and Brenda. But that wasn't all of it. They had the lads from the Disabled Unit. *That* got me.

One of the lads was severely disabled. I'd walked down in front of him and thought someone would help him, but he wouldn't let anybody handle his wheelchair down the steps into the canteen. He was one of the reasons for Brenda and me doing it, to get the tailgate. He didn't have long to live, but he wouldn't let anybody take him down those steps. He went down on two wheels, a step at a time, thirty steps from top to bottom. I shed a tear. The applause that he got was just as much as I got.

The lads were the catalyst; I couldn't fail; I would be letting down 2500 people at Heinz, Derek Partington, the lads, Brenda, everyone. There was no way.

He lowered the record to 1 day, 22 hours, 39 minutes and 49 seconds. It turned out to be Mick's last ride of note and he admits he lost his competitive edge afterwards. 'It was the culmination of everything I'd ever done in cycling. I don't know whether it took a lot out of me or what, but I didn't ride so well after that.'

Roger carries on raging against the RRA, at both their adherence to specific rules and their absence of pragmatism. 'They said he couldn't have done it, he didn't have the skills or the pedigree. It was like his first 12-hour all over again.'

Suddenly we get invaded – children, grandchildren, great-grandchildren, dogs, a family gathering. I'm up to my eyes in amazing photos. The grandchildren want to be interviewed, they are pressing buttons and asking things. Mick looks across at Roger, then at me, and the enormity of the achievement for these brothers, one of whom had rheumatic fever and wanted to be a golfer, hits home again. 'We were walking on clouds for years afterwards.'

Mick/Roger Coupe

Mick Coupe afterwards

After Coupe set the new record it became a busy fortnight for the
End to End. A week later, Eric Tremaine broke the tricycle record.
Another week passed and John Woodburn got out for his second
attempt. That morning Brother Roger looked out the window
and could see a straight southerly rippling through the trees. 'I
thought, Mick, you've had it.' Woodburn was fit and healthy; he
had been waiting for five weeks for the right conditions and had
been training through the winter in readiness. 'I've never been
a great believer in training in January, but with the End to End
you've got no choice. I'd do 30 to 40 miles a day, 50 miles on
Saturday, 80 on Sunday. At the end of June I stopped racing, and
then trained until the end of July.'

   It is one of the few attempts to have been filmed and is worth
seeking out.* The footage is lovely, the soundtrack a little bit

---

* Ray Pascoe and Peter Dansie, *2 Days and 2 Nights – Land's End to John
O'Groats* (London: Cycling History, 2003).

Mick/Roger Coupe

Woodburn and Coupe

strange. The group gather around a giant Volvo estate; flags point the way through the car park and past an ice cream van. Wife Ann rushes in to zip up his jersey, then he heads off on his beautiful Stan Pike machine, no helmet, Benotto tape, his hair neatly parted by the air flow. Everything is an early eighties brown – a brown Renault 17 wallowing across the moors, a Mini with bikes on the roof.

The hot summer air shimmers over the surface of the road. Robert Garbutt, the editor of *Cycling*, gets in at Bristol to cover the attempt in print. The ride is straightforward, just a few traffic issues through Cornwall leaving Woodburn hungry and a bit cross. 'How cross is he?' wonders Ann. Not that cross – it's hard to tell. Maybe he's smiling. 'I want some biscuits,' he says. He crams his pockets full, then carries on.

He sent his helpers off to get a fish supper from Stafford. The fish and chips boosted morale, as he admitted later: 'It was one of those dark hours. I wasn't feeling all that good, it was cold, and Shap was coming up.' His feeding was traditional, like supper at your gran's house: mince and veg, cold custard, cherries or melon, ice cream and fried fish.

He tore down from the Shap at 55mph and broke Coupe's 24-hour record by 12 miles, carrying straight on. By Perth the gap was ninety minutes, and it held steadily from then on. Woodburn beat Coupe's record by an hour and thirty-four minutes. Like Coupe, he was interested only in a soak in the bath, not the 1000. He seemed pleased when he gave an interview twelve days later, although it's hard to tell. 'I feel quite well. We had a party last night to simulate how I felt about twelve days ago.'

After a flurry of activity, the record had been put back in the box marked 'daunting'. For Woodburn, ever circumspect, it was a simple thing. 'It's mind over matter. I don't care who you are, if you're riding that kind of distance, you're going to be very tired and you've just got to live with it.'

12

Chased by an idiot from Bradford to Kendal

Sunday, 30 June 2019

I have learned a valuable lesson about the End to End. Huge, long days in the saddle are very hard work. I am going to tour the last 500 miles; I am going to enjoy the experience. Riding it the hard way is only for the hard riders, not for dilettantes and bookish, mentally fragile English teachers. I have also learned that the middle of England is a grim corridor of uncertainty. I have to postpone the next stage after getting ill. My body reacts to the long ride in February by dissolving into a mess of mucus and a hacking, vagabond's cough. I wait even longer than I'd planned. I go home, do interviews, travel to Preston to meet Gethin Butler. I worry about how to fit everything in. I apply for more jobs and don't get them. I do more crying in interviews. I am open to the elements; emotional truths threaten to explode from any combination of words or images. I seem moments away at any given moment from a wobbly lip and an impassioned *défaillance*.

I head back to Bradford at the end of June to pick up the threads and ride some more. I like Bradford. I like it because it is an angry, disenfranchised place. I like the contradictions and tensions of the city, its fractured polyglot identity. It's not Leeds, or York, it is Bradford. Or as Mum's partner Ian calls it, *Bratfut*. I'm not there long enough today, no time to go to the Kash. In twenty years of visits it has stayed the same and still feeds four people three courses each for a grand total of £30. Ian has been eating the meat and mushroom bhuna since the 1970s. It is just 'meat'; no other clarification seems necessary.

After two monumental stages I feel like I have achieved something, even if it is not fully clear what that is. The plan now is to head north-west out of Bradford and rejoin the route at Kendal. I choose to go straight through the Forest of Bowland because I've wanted to go there for years, since meeting people for the hill climb book and hearing tales of tours and rides through and over the Trough. I like the language of the northern landscape – the Nick, the Trough, Mam Tor; it is a realm of semantic honesty, where place and name are synonymous. I follow a mapped breadcrumb trail on my Garmin and I feel smug. I have big days lined up, 100-milers. It doesn't make me an ultra-nutter but it does make me hardy, brave. I'll be in Scotland tomorrow.

I choose a route I know and love, out via Haworth and Scar Top, via Wycoller. In all my memories it is empty of cars and people; houses are spartan punctuation marks in an epic landscape poem. It is joy, unconfined. The road is hard, the surface heavy. This is the vernacular – a heavy road, a grippy surface. The road takes the energy, absorbs the bike, limits progress; it is unresponsive, uncooperative. That is made up for by the stark beauty of the landscape. Ian is always a bit cagey about the road because it leads to Lancashire, and Lancashire is a dark and miserable place. Lower Laithe and Ponden reservoirs hold back the water which supplies Keighley, man-made reservoirs in the uplands, villages drowned beneath, feeding the mills. The road is a sinuous ribbon, grey against the brown upland heather, and it climbs up and up. It is a beautiful journey.

The wind gets up, or maybe the wind was always there, but it makes itself felt the further I go. It is the first time I have had to deal with a hostile wind direction and I realise that touring with a headwind for an entire day is a rotten proposition. It sucks the life out of the experience, generating anger and frustration. I am reduced to railing at the angry cycling gods. I regret doing it. I regret the ride, the planned sectors for the next five days. I know the wind is set on the forecast and I feel stupid. I am provoked into questioning the pointless narcissism of it all. At one point, somewhere near Colne, I take a turn on to a road that is a ford which becomes a river and I slide off the bike and my Carradice disappears into an eddying pool of water, and a local tells me of the delivery drivers who end up driving along it because they were told to by the voice on the dashboard. I feel a sense of hubris.

The Forest of Bowland is beautiful. I ride through it and it opens up on every side. It is waiting to be written, but I have no writerly intention to capture the beauty of the landscape, because it seems forced. I remember a talk I went to when someone said 'I am attuned with nature when riding because I am a creative' and I experienced a visceral loathing at the idea and the functional shift of a noun. I don't want to observe it with a writer's pretentious eye, I just want to observe it and leave it there. I don't want to look in order to compare, to force metaphors and bend the landscape to fit the sentence and end up with personified flowers dancing in the breeze, menacing clouds, air being vital, all those words. It is here, and it is there. A crow struts nearby, mocking my thoughts, giving me material to write about, cawing and swaggering; just out of the nightclub, like a nineteen-year-old full of piss and vinegar – pay day, ready to do something. He mocks my writing and riding, tells me I'll never see the hen harriers I'm thinking of and that I'll never capture anything and that the wind will get me.

Wycoller brings with it happy memories of beautiful Yorkshire rides, getting away from things and finding answers out of nothingness. I feel positive, that this ride will help reshape the world I've left behind. In the same breath I realise this will not happen, because I am carrying the demons with me. I am chained to an idiot, taking him for a special End to End jaunt. I realise that over the past twelve months, poor mental health has become my normal frame of reference – anxiety and mistrust and regret and anger. Surely everyone has a head full of crippling white noise and voices, short emotive impulses and a quivering sense of fear and regret? Surely everyone struggles with the accretion of everything they've ever thought? I left the security of my job for an abyss. I hope, stupidly, that the ride will create meaning and structure, and I will be hit by a flash of glorious clarity. But there is no light here.

The headwind is pushing me backwards; it hates me. It is unreasonably hilly. The Forest of Bowland is beautiful but brutal, full of steep climbs and narrow tributaries in tarmac rolling down off the moorland, the current flowing downhill, impeding progress. The road climbs up and up and up, it narrows further, the surface degrades, grit becomes pebbles, pebbles become rocks. I go past places written in the language of medieval England – Slaidburn and Gisburn. If I had the energy I'd start thinking about people and places, names and change, landscape and meaning, but the wind rises again in spiteful fury. Instead of philosophical reflection, language and people, I have painful clarity: I realise that wind destroys the End to End. It needs two days of clemency and obedience; it needs subtle changes in direction at the right time. I get none of this. The wind consumes my energy, reduces the descents to a dispiriting pedal, glues the freewheel together. I go uphill like an insect on a wall. Arrival times drift out on the ebb tide of slowness. The climb of Bowland Knotts is long and steep. It is 9 miles from Bolton-in-Bowland – medievally hyphenated – to the gap in the rock outcrops, reaching 1600 feet upwards into layers of clouds upon clouds. I should have checked this beforehand. I have a Carradice with stuff in it and my bike has the wrong gears, making it much harder than it should be. A schoolboy error.

I emerge out of the forest, blinking and broken, with a couple of miles yet to climb. The notch is visible, foreshortened cruelly, as the plateau tilts upwards towards the Knotts, a granite outcrop among the moorland. The treeless heath is the colour of builders' tea, a livery russet. A hen harrier arrives, to spite the crow, and I try to think of similes to describe its wondrous shape, to capture the moment and then write it later, but I am too in awe of the movement and beauty, and too tired to compare it to anything. It just *is*, and it hangs in the breeze, tilting this way and that, a ruffle of feathers and colour and texture, a lightning strike of white against grey and brown.

I have 30 miles left to ride and I am cooked. I am in deep trouble. I can do today but I worry about tomorrow. The wind will not change and it will be horrid. Is this at all how the aspirants feel? Wrecked and depressed? I pause at the top to sit still and gain respite from the wind, and I allow the emptiness of the landscape to claim my thoughts, repackage them, and nullify the negativity. It is downhill to Kendal and I push the pedals, trying to make up lost time, but time is lost, it cannot be reclaimed. It flees, irreparably.

I sleep in Kendal at my uncle's house. He is an evangelical post-modern Christian.* I marvel at this disjunction and at

---

* I check this later just in case I'm doing him a disservice: 'I prefer the term hyper-modernity and probably more post-evangelical. There is a new deconstructed Christian narrative called the emerging church.' If Derrida did God it might sound like this.

his fervour and commitment to the light. I am in need of the spiritual right now. I fall asleep quickly but wake just as quickly in the throes of a night terror. I know why I have night terrors: when I was nineteen years old someone broke into my student house and attacked me with a knife at two in the morning and it lasted for four hours and they made me walk to the cashpoint and I thought I was going to die. I had a catastrophic nervous breakdown about six months later. I'm still having night terrors twenty years later. The sleep clinic at Southmead called it 'a dialled-on case of adult parasomnia' – 'unresolved PTSD' they say, helpfully. They don't even bother to invite me for a wired-sleep, it's so clear. I am an exemplary page in a psychiatry textbook. I don't know anyone else who has these terrors, so either I'm special or weird. They interrupt almost every night, just before the REM phase. Something triggers something and a nightmare begins and it creeps into my waking mind and I'm caught between sleep and waking, my heart racing. I sometimes wake up shouting in terror. There is no other word: it is a primeval terror, some inexpressible fear lodged deep in my subconscious. I wonder if it drives me when I'm awake in ways I'm not aware of. I suspect the answer is yes. For this particular dream/nightmare the ceiling is open; I can see through to outdoors and it is dark and heavy and the sky begins to flood through the gap like oil. A dark roof truss is leaning down, moving, dropping in chopped movements, and it is going to fall. I can sense the trajectory, and the arc is helpfully described in the air of my dream and I can see it is going to hit me in the face and I am going to die. This is the point at which I awake, or at which awakeness begins to take over from sleep, and I sense that I might not die, but it takes a further five minutes to bring my heart rate back under control, through deep breaths. The terrifying fear in my stomach takes longer to dissipate.

This is the pattern. I sleep then wake in abject fear, petrified.

When I don't get night terrors I get demented dreams filtered through a haze of paroxetine (designed to halt the night terrors), recurring motifs. I get normal dreams as well. The night before I dreamt about Alf Engers at a dinner table. He was asking questions, putting the world to rights, castigating. Lots of cycling writers were there. One of them said he liked the cover but hadn't read the book. Everyone said I was being too domestic, not continental enough, too niche, because I didn't write stories people wanted to read, big biographies which say nothing about anything but sell by the shitload. I woke up, sweating.

13

Pauline Strong mixes it up with an acid house convoy (but sadly not on the A303)

Saturday, 28 July 1990

There is a hill climber called Andy Feather and there is an endurance cyclist called Pauline Strong. I like it when the name matches the endeavour. I try to think of a funny joke but can't make it work. Maybe if Michael Broadwith had an extra 'd' in his name and worked in internet support. I think about place names and realise it is the same for people: we used to do the work our surname told us to do. Some of us still do.

Pauline Strong lives near Doncaster and drives the biggest lorry allowed on the road, a 44-ton Class 1 Royal Mail articulated truck. She looks nothing like the stereotypical image of the sedentary lorry driver. I wonder how she ended up behind the wheel.

I had a lot of big life changes – marriage, work and so on. I wanted to work but not in an office, so I got a Class 2 licence and started driving for Royal Mail. These articulated Class 1s would come in and I'd think, Oh my God, how do you drive *them*? As soon as I see people doing an impossible thing I go and find out if I can do it. I was one of 259 applicants for five Class 1 jobs and I got it. That's a midlife crisis, isn't it?

I drive to Avonmouth to take the Yorkshire mail to Bristol to be moved on. Sometimes it's Wembley or a Scottish run. I start in the afternoon, down and back in the night. The 'trampers', the continental drivers, it's tough – they sleep in a random layby, doors open to stop people nicking stuff. A friend was doing animal waste and he had pallets and carcasses *crawling*, and he got up the next morning and they'd gone. Probably in the burgers by now. Just last week I went to Carlisle with a full trailer of Scottish mail; he brings one down, you just swap over. It was gorgeous, up over the A66 in this weather, the light breaking, birdsong.

I am fascinated. She is an Auden poem, the night mail crossing the border – Pauline who drives the biggest truck on the road, through the night, in a vague echo of her previous life: 'heading up Beattock, a steady climb, the gradient's against her but she's on time . . .' I can sense the divide between the person then and the person now – when isn't there such a separation? But like the other people I meet, it is psychological as much as physical. 'To be honest I'm one of those people now, it's odd. I'm thinking, how did you do *that*? I'll go out now, ride me bike a little bit, and I'll think, I did the *whole* End to End faster than this! And I'm *buggered*.'

Pauline Strong makes me laugh. It is the combination of crystalline honesty and caustic wit, all delivered in a sonorous Scouse accent, full of elision and tonal shifts. Pauline has moved around a lot. It isn't one house by the Thames, a calm, linear life with time flowing past in spiralling currents. It is episodic, tangential even. I'm grateful she lives 'near' not 'in' Doncaster. I last went there thirty years ago with my mum to visit a terrifying uncle who shouted at me for pulling wheelies on his son's BMX. We went shopping and followed a blood trail until it took us to a shoe shop and I came out with some shiny Adidas with lovely arch support. Doncaster to me means blood and trainers. The scary uncle is still there and now shouts at his siblings via WhatsApp.

Pauline lives away from the blood trail, to the north of the town. Her house is dotted with bike trinkets. I am comforted. The framed pictures are all bikes, bottles of wine have bikes on them, coffee cups say things about bikes. This is a bike house. She looks young and is another advert for the long-term health benefits of ridiculous bike riding, even if she says otherwise. I'm not the first person to have beaten a path to her door.

Somebody was writing a book on cycling – sixties, seventies, eighties – so he asked me as the obligatory woman. But he said he couldn't make a chapter on it. When I did the End to End I got a tiny piece cos the Tour was on. There are great people like Joan Kershaw, and I doubt if you could find anything written about Joan, yet she was amazing. I had a go at the editor of *Cycling* because there was never anything about women's cycling, and he said, 'Women aren't interested in cycling, people aren't interested in women cyclists, women don't buy *Cycling*.' That was his argument.

I'm fed up with his argument, which lingers, just as I get fed up with the arguments against equal pay, or equal prize money, rigidly numeric arguments. I'm confused by people not finding the stories. They are all there, they just aren't in the foreground, and they need to be foregrounded, which is why Isabel Best and

Emily Chappell and others write such important books. I make a note to write about Joan Kershaw, and Christine Roberts, and Bridget Boon – all of them. In fact, I make a note to nudge someone else to write about at least some of them, because I don't think it's my place to do it. Surely these stories are at least better off being told by a woman, instead of me mansplaining the fuck out of it. Maybe I'm old-fashioned in a new-fashioned way, I have no idea. I just know opportunity is limited and I don't want to take it from someone else.

Pauline's husband, Chris, is out today on a very long audax.

250K at Newark. I think it cost him a fiver. We still tour and get out from time to time. Three years ago we took a hire car to Biarritz, left it there and rode back. We did 100 miles a day, Chris carried all my stuff in his panniers. I was allowed one luxury item, so I took hair straighteners. But I was so knackered I couldn't even lift me arms up so they stayed in the bottom of his pannier. Every day he'd say, 'Are you going to use these? I've carried these all through bloody France.' Prior to that I'd done about 800 miles in the year, and suddenly had to do 600 in a week. I used to think saddles were comfy. But now I think they're bloody instruments of torture. I started riding when I was eleven, but now I'm on the other side of the fence, absolutely, and I still can't get me head round that I can't do stuff. We're all getting old, aren't we?

We talk about Eileen Sheridan. There are numerous parallels between the two, not least that they were both pioneering professionals, Eileen for Hercules, Pauline for Raleigh. I find it bizarre that more than three decades after Eileen, Pauline was the only full-time female professional cyclist in the UK.

We discuss Mick Coupe and John Williams, another amazing Merseysider. In my last book, on Alf Engers' advice, I captioned an image 'Noreen Burnham'. However, it wasn't Auntie Noreen, as John informed me politely at Champions' Night, stating that Auntie Noreen's side of the family had a contract out on me for the error should I ever show my face in the Greater Liverpool area. Pauline brings this up – 'I thought I'd known her all me life!' – and I want to hide away. That's writing. I love the moment the book is out but then live in a state of paralysed anxiety, a dread fear about the proof, the mistakes that might have slipped through when trying to write about other people's lives, followed by people telling me about them. Inaccuracies of memory, a mistaken course code, a typo, anything. It's as though the biggest Easter egg of all is showing people that you make mistakes. One chap writes to me with every grammatical disagreement and potential issue he has spotted. I am always *thrilled* to receive his communications. Nothing like a detailed list of everything you did wrong to make you feel glad you wrote the thing in the first place.

But it's Eileen we're talking about, who is ninety-six years old. 'It happens to all of us. I remember an elderly aunt asking me to thread a needle for her, and I remember thinking, Why can't you thread a needle? Now, I'm one of those. I catch meself in the mirror and realise, but otherwise I don't think it.'

Pauline's parents weren't cyclists, beyond utility – 'they rode bikes, but only cos that's how people got around in them days' – but the surrounding area was full of roadmen and women, churning out of a lock-up garage on to the streets of Kirkby, Bootle and the Wirral (not that the Wirral has streets, but it has churned out Steve Cummings, Chris Boardman, Jim Henderson and Andy Wilkinson, so something is in the water). The clubs still roll along: the Mercury, Anfield, Mersey Roads, Kirkby, Merseyside Wheelers, the names tripping off the tongue and into the archive of UK bike racing, full of domestic heroes, many of whom became a part of the institution of British cycling in later years.

We lived for a short while in Kirkdale, at the bottom of Everton valley, right by Harry Quinn's bike shop. On the way to Gran's house, me brother and dad would stop and look in the window. Maybe that planted a seed. My older brother had a Carlton and joined Bootle St Christopher's, briefly. I used to pinch it but got in trouble for putting the derailleur through the back wheel. When I was eleven Dad bought me a Hercules Harlequin, three-speed, step-through. You needed to be bloody Hercules to ride it, it weighed a ton.

It wasn't long before Dad found a Reg Harris frame amid the roadkill, rubbish and discarded clothing of a layby. Pauline joined the local club – but 'probably shouldn't have . . . I was so slow, I must have been a right pain in the arse to take round' – and began etching formative memories: night rides, tours, hanging out at the Two Mills café. 'I loved riding. It was me, I did this, no one told me to. I lived in a council house. We weren't posh with money but if I wanted to play tennis, they got me a bat with Green Shield stamps. They never said, "Girls don't ride bikes."'

At twelve she started racing; moving through the circles of riders in the area, getting advice and support. The list of clubs provided a wealth of experience – Joan Kershaw and others, bringing Pauline into the Prescot Eagle Cycling Club. Joan was the big hitter among them. She took Pauline under her wing, by this time on her new Harry Quinn. 'We'd train in the evenings. I was still at school, I could ride with her, no problem, keep up, then come the weekend she'd put two minutes into me. Eventually I beat her. She says, "I've been waiting for this day for years! You finally got your head round it!" I had it there all along but couldn't hurt meself. Later I got the hang of it: up to 25 miles and it's shit or bust, go out as fast as you can and try and hang on.'

It's something I remember former British champion Darryl Webster saying about hill climbs. Certain kinds of races are just shit or bust. It is a primitive phrase for a primitive effort. Sometimes things really don't need to be that complicated. I remember doing a hilly time trial once with a timed hill climb at the start. I went up it at hill climb pace then stayed like it for the rest of the race. I think I did shit myself a bit and something was bust.

After leaving school at fifteen, Pauline began working at John Moores Catalogue in Crosby, riding out each day from the city centre 'in jeans and that, 10 miles each way, because I didn't like to be seen in what wasn't Lycra then'. A steady improvement in pace saw the wins starting to roll in, with 1975 the turning point. After a string of strong early-season rides she was selected to ride for the national team in Montreal and at a stage race in France. 'I wasn't fit at all. I was already hitting the clubs and not doing a lot. It was around July, on what I'd been doing in April. They must have thought, Oooh she's doing well. I panicked. John Moores had a collection and I got some decent wheels, and then the company sort of recognised the international thing; they would give me time off, paid up to four weeks' international leave. It was hot, hilly, and I got dropped.'

She continued to ride and race against the strongest women of the day, soon to be world champion Mandy Jones, Denise Burton and others, in both massed-start and time trials, but with some track success, such as her 2nd in the National Championship at Leicester. In 1980 she gained selection for the World Championship, and again in 1981 and 1982, finishing in the bunch at Goodwood when Mandy Jones' startling win took the headlines. I find it amazing, to be talking to a bona fide world-class cyclist. The reality lacked glamour: 'we weren't given women's clothing, had to wear the men's outfits, at that late stage. It was all around a full-time job.' The prize list at the

1972 National Championship in Yeovil hints at the disparity: for the ladies, linen tea cloths, work baskets, head scarves and table mats.

Gendered prizes aside, women's cycling seemed to be on the up. Tour organiser Félix Lévitan decided to hold a Tour de France Féminin in a move not universally welcomed. Laurent Fignon summed up the prevailing mood among their male counterparts: 'I like women, but I prefer to see them doing something else.' Pauline was selected to ride in 1984, 1985 and 1987.

It's a three-week race. You start off eyeing each other up, but as the race goes on you become mates and share cars, help each other to finish. I knew I wasn't going to win it. It was a fabulous experience but now I think, Why didn't I take more notice of what was happening? It's just what your life was like and what you did. There certainly wasn't the razzmatazz that there is now. We stayed with families, there were no team cars. Somebody would lend you a car or pick up a van from somewhere. We'd finish on the mountain then wait for the men and they'd try to get us all down at the same time. I remember Jeannie Longo being aloof; I wasn't up there so she had no interest in me. She used to live in Grenoble. She would ride up the Alps and her husband would pick her up and she'd come home. That was her training. Longo was quite forthright.* The best day I had was in the mountains. I was 23rd, out of about a hundred or so, and finishing midway, bit above. I'm not really a climber. All the climbers would go and

---

* The French racing cyclist Jeannie Longo went on to ride for many years, before her career ended under a cloud of suspicion at the age of forty-six owing to suspected doping violations.

people would be hanging on; I'd go at my pace, and I'd catch people who would be dying. That was the way I climbed.

It's gone backwards since then in many ways. The women are highly professional now, but don't have the same opportunities, no Tour. The gap between the women and the men has closed; it used to be about ten minutes, taking Beryl out of the equation. What more is there to say about her? I thought her book was a bit like paint drying. *I did this and she did that and I won this* and so on. And I found Laura Trott and Jason Kenny's book a struggle as well. She lost me when she said she couldn't boil an egg. And she was twenty-odd. *Couldn't boil an egg!*

On her return the new manager at the BCF implied she should step aside for younger riders. She bridles, even now. 'I

Phil O'Connor

Pauline Strong in the Tour de Fem, 1987

thought she should tell the youngsters there's an old one over there, if you want a place, then go and beat her. But I was bashing me head against a brick wall, so I began looking for something else. When I was young I couldn't imagine why you *wouldn't* race for ever, like Ethel Brambleby going on for ever, or Beryl, dying on the bike. But now I knew absolutely that I didn't want to race for ever. However, my legs were full of miles on the back of the Tour and I had no races!'

She met with Eileen Sheridan and was baffled but excited by her achievements. 'I always think, Flippin' 'eck, how do you actually do that? I'd go away and find out. I'm not one to get to eighty-odd and wonder if I was good at something. I tried kickboxing, and I'm rubbish at it. And now I know.' And so the idea about the End to End percolated, grew, gnawed at her. Alan, her husband, was a driving force behind this new phase. Eileen sent a detailed three-page handwritten letter offering key advice. 'I thought it was a gettable record, it was thirty-six years old. I knew it was going to be hard. I had the strength and the miles, although in hindsight my strength was more mental than physical. I had the ability, if not the talent; Alan had the ideas and connections through working with Ron Kitching.* So, we put out a schedule for 1990. Sponsorship was hard to find, so I asked family friends, 'Would you sponsor me a tank of petrol?''

She was given some shorts and track mitts, but the bike was her own – a Specialized Allez Epic without tribars. It's a lugged carbon thing. Not many of them have survived due to corrosion and the lugs separating; they don't make good barn finds. They even approached local IT company Mitel because it was 'a big place on the roundabout at Caldicott'. They refused politely.

_____

* Kitching was a key figure in the post-war bike trade, an importer of everything and producer of the glossy trade bible *Everything Cycling*.

strength and ~~~~~~~

We had a caravan to sleep but it was ridiculous stuck on top of an articulated lorry with high steps to climb up. I only wanted a van or large car to stagger in to get warm and flop out.

Perhaps they don't stop now but if they dont, I don't know how they keep awake

Please don't think I am putting you off – you must be prepared it is not a 24 hour it is a long way.

I saw you on your bike and I believe you have the power to do this ride Who ever does this ride will have bad patches – no one could ride this distance without a bad patch.

Eileen's advice to Pauline

The build-up continued: 241 miles in twelve hours, 239 miles in Bournemouth; a few shorter-distance time trials; then a 30-mile test at Colchester. 'I went up the slip road and a car tried to overtake, before realising there was no room.' The outcome was a broken collarbone and extensive road rash. With impeccable timing, Mitel got back in touch two days later. They had changed their minds. 'It was six weeks to go before an enormous, really hard ride which I was asking them to support financially. My arm was in a sling and I looked like I'd been through the war – there was no skin left on half of it. I hid it, carefully.' Miraculously, they didn't notice and agreed to contribute. However, the collarbone remained a concern. 'They did a cold laser thing at the hospital. Oh God, it was agony. I did long sessions on the turbo. I had the base and it was only six weeks out – I didn't need "top-end".'

John Woodburn continued where Eileen left off by offering

his advice. 'I rang to ask if he could spare five minutes, because he could be a bit brusque, you know; he didn't smile a lot so it was hard to tell. Two and a half hours later and we were still chatting. He was so helpful. A few years later we had dogs, called Rominger, Pantani, Indurain, Kelly and Merckx. Then we took in this rescue dog called Woody and we kept his name. John thought we were taking the piss.'

They headed down and waited a day for the weather. The local press had come out and there was a minor frisson of excitement, dispelled slightly by a very low-key departure. 'I just rolled out to ride for two days.'

Cornwall was a static line of holiday traffic in and out of the county. Support cars were stuck in unending queues. It left Pauline riding up the outside of a 13-mile line of cars, fearful of car doors, and having to deal with what seems like the customary End to End snarl-up between Bridgwater and Bristol. Marshals at Bristol included at one set of lights 'a feller in top hat and tails. I thought, Bloody hell, he looks a bit posh! It was his daughter's wedding and he'd just nipped out! I also saw my bank manager cheering; he had given us £20 so I think he must have wanted to see what I was doing with it.' She also saw local legend Gerry McGarr out with a bugle. 'He had signs up, a big bell, and was stood on the island with his little kids making a right old rumpus – they're now thirty!' Gerry was there again in 2018, without the thirty-year-old kids but with his bugle, watching Michael Broadwith roll past.

Throughout the first night spectators appeared at the side of the road. 'There was this great big sheet across a gate, GO PAULINE GO!, in the middle of nowhere. The chap had been waiting but he had to go to work. His wife was really cross about it. "He didn't pick an old one! He spray-painted one of me best bloody sheets!"' She was humbled by the experience of all these passionate people following the record in person.

'The strangest things linger in your memory; like how at eight o'clock on a Saturday night, you've been riding for twelve hours, you're sweaty, horrible, and all around you people are going out in the evening, immaculate, dressed up, and you get this lovely waft of perfume, and it stuck in my mind: everyone is dressed up and lovely and clean and you're not. A bizarre collision of two worlds.'

After a straightforward first twelve hours, things began to drift away on a haze of English folk madness. A stop for directions led to an attempted bike theft; then came a breathless chase by wild farm dogs near Knutsford. Finally, they ended up in the middle of an acid house convoy searching for a free party. It's part performance art, part *Wicker Man*, maybe an excerpt from a Jeremy Deller film: two different folk traditions somehow inserted into each other's social history, stories to be told and handed down. I wonder where those young people are now, or if they'll read this book and recall the memories – headed to Shelley's Laserdome in Stoke for a counter-culture all-nighter, pre-Criminal Justice Act, driving round in circles for hours. Two competing quest narratives, both escapist.

Amid the surrealism, there were genuine concerns about swollen knees and a steady loss of time. 'I was losing it rapidly and thinking about climbing off, absolutely. It was a matter of timing and finding the right place. The further you go the harder it is.' Helen Edwards, close friend and teammate from the Tour, was there and gave Pauline some encouragement, tapped into her depths of determination and fear of failure. Her knees were creaking, the bandages soggy and dragging down in the rain. Her back began to subside, a lean that still affects her today. Worse still, she was suffering from an open saddle sore from the chamois seam – 'it was a weeping wound, sticking and pulling the skin off'. Before long she started seeing things – a row of people at Lancaster, except they were petrol pumps. She became obsessed with her dogs back home, that they were being neglected, and she berated the team. 'I just tore into them. "You're all sat round here and not one of you has fed the dogs!" One of the support team told me she'd fed them. "Bloomin' 'eck, cheers, Sheila!" I said. I was happy then. I cared about that, but not some of the other things.' Where previously she'd been forthright, careful about where and how she changed, she minded less and less as the ride wore on. 'I tell you what, if Prince Charles had appeared, I couldn't have cared. I'd have stripped off.'

I have accumulated such stories over time, and the scale of the undertaking has become clear, the mental strength needed for it. There are multiple further attempts scheduled; people call it the 'Broadwith effect'. Good, strong riders think they can do it and that their rigorous planning will ensure success. There is an elaborate build-up, often a social media operation that constructs a narrative of forthcoming heroism, harvesting thousands of 'likes'. There is a project, a logo, a blog, a list of sponsors. Yet it comes to nothing, and the failure is amplified because of the scale and public nature of the ambition. It is explained away – a lack of a tailwind, injuries, poor nutrition, but never 'I wasn't quick enough'. Pauline Strong bent the task to her will. 'The mental side took over. It became tattooed on my brain that I had to finish. Now, common sense says I was injured; I had lost toenails, my knees were shot. So many people think they can do it. People can ride a turbo for however long, but it's not that easy, it's not about the bike. It's so hard.'

Pauline used the A74, then an arterial trunk road with heavy traffic, now a motorway. It was cold and wet and her body temperature had dropped. After the A9 the effects of sleep deprivation were amplified through the second night on the road. She dropped down towards Inverness and began to encounter 'people in suits off to work'. Stuttered conversations drifted across from the roadside, one chap in a suit, waiting and watching, saying 'This is boring' as she rode past. 'I was all pale with 700 miles in me legs and having a really bad time. I don't know what he was expecting.'

Your mind can't cope with the fatigue. I struggled with the cold, I was shaking, I couldn't swallow, my throat closed up, my body was shutting down. It's a real eye-opener for who you are. You just can't know what's going to happen. At one point I stopped. There was a gate with a dead rabbit and I was convinced I'd passed this dead rabbit before. I accused Alan of sending me round in circles, endless times past the dead rabbit. I went off course a few times, three or so miles. At one point I followed the wrong lights, rode in the gutter, had no idea where I was or what I was doing. One of the helpers got out to run alongside because I was *creeping* up the last few climbs, Helmsdale and Berriedale. A spectator thought it was him, running for the record. He got a big cheer. I was nearly knocked off the bike. They are hard climbs.

I think of Janet Tebbutt passing the same cottage over and over and the mental degradation seems visceral. I agree that the climbs are hard and mention how I'm going to tackle them shortly, having already done some really long rides. 'Do you fancy a go at it?' she says, sweetly. Pauline Strong is amazing. She thinks I might be thinking about the record and is willing to accept that if I say I can do it then I might be able to do it. Me, the slowest dilettante in the world who struggled with a headwind for a brief ride over Bowland Knotts at an average speed of 11mph. 'Oh God no, it'd take me years, I'd die,' I say. We both laugh.

Once over the last rolling climbs, around the postwoman,

past the dead rabbit and the disappointed suits of Inverness, there was a clear sense that the record was on. She completed the last 20 miles in an hour, the weather helpful at the last, stopping the clock after 2 days, 6 hours, 49 minutes and 45 seconds.

All your aches and pains disappear when you know it's there. I needed help to get off the bike at the end though, it just hits you. My face ballooned, my eyes were like little slits, and it felt really tight. I couldn't get any of me shoes on so had to borrow some bloke's flip-flops. I didn't lose any weight either – what a bugger.

We were stood there, with the champagne, the pictures and all that, and this van comes around the corner supporting this chap in a wheelchair doing *5000 miles* round the coast of Britain, and I thought, He's in a *wheelchair* there. Took the shine off a bit! The telegram from Eileen was something though.

Pauline Wallis

After the record, the deluge. Cards, flowers, letters from across the country; family, friends, clubmates, people who knew her as a child; then club dinners, prizes, awards, veterans' lunches. 'I think I did forty-six dinners in the one winter. It was hard in one way. Sunday you'd want to ride but you'd been out at a club dinner and then perhaps a lunch on the Sunday. It got very busy.' She attended the Pedal Club at Drury Lane, a longstanding lunch club for riders and industry people. Also there was Yvonne Ricks, marketing manager at Raleigh. She warmed to Pauline, her demeanour and openness. She explored the possibility of sponsorship, then realised with a jolt that there were no women professionals in the UK. She made it her mission to change this.

> I'd had enough really. But when someone offers to pay you to ride a bike after all these years, you take it. Initially it was a one-year contract, and then I won the *Sunday Times* Sportswoman of the Year so Raleigh had to keep me on for another year, but my interest was waning. It was funny being a professional, perhaps it took the joy out of it a bit. Raleigh were paying me and I had to do the best I could, but the best I could do had gone.

She attempted some place-to-place records and planned another go at the End to End in 1991, feeling that a sub-two-day ride was possible. 'Given what I'd done with a broken collarbone, and with knowledge, and with better weather – although sometimes knowledge isn't the best thing, you're better off going into the unknown – I still think you can be faster than two days.' It's deceptive though: one mile an hour faster takes three hours off the total; but the cost of that increase is significant.

She opted for tribars and things looked promising, 247 miles in the first twelve hours and 430 at Carnforth, where she was four hours inside. But the wind was changing, and by Gretna it was 'blowing a hoolie – people ahead were telling me to stop'. She tried once more, in May 1992, but a crash early on caused too much damage. 'I caught the tribars and came off. The bars went into my side and I cut my head – I'd taken me crash hat off cos it was hot. I went as far as Wolverhampton, but I was struggling to breathe and in a lot of pain. I found out later I'd broken my ribs.'

Pauline attempted two more place-to-place records, but was hindered by the fickle hand of fate. A combination of illness, level crossings on a tight schedule and dense London traffic called time on these and, ultimately, an illustrious racing career. 'It dawned on me that I was a *bike rider* that raced, I wasn't a *racer* that rode a bike. I didn't want to train as hard any more and I didn't want to do slower times. So that was that. I look back and know I'll never be as fast or as fit as I was then.'

We are reminiscing over lunch in the garden. It's a hot day. The sun scorches the patio slabs and I drink hot tea and eat my crisps – noisily, as it turns out when I listen back to the recording. She asks if I am vegetarian, recalling something in the Alf Engers book which she has read (so much flattery … I'm always surprised when people have read one of my two very niche books). She recalls the 'bacon buns' incident. She is lovely company. I feel awed by things, but comfortable, disarmed. I don't mind telling her I am vegetarian. I'm not scared like I was with Alf when I thought he was going to feed me to the dogs. Pauline is open, honest, she doesn't dissemble. She doesn't tell you something for any reason other than it's a real thing to tell. I admire this.

Looking back, it's hard to imagine doing it. I ride along now and I just think, *Flippin' 'eck.* I don't believe it. Someone will say, 'Oh, so and so are doing it for charity over twelve days,' and when I say 'That's fantastic' I'm not being condescending. I might want to do the End to End before I get to eighty, see where I've been, take a while over it. I've always thought that, between us, you can idolise different riders. But you're nobody to anybody who doesn't ride a bike. And maybe it's an amateur thing, but it's my hobby, it's what I like doing. I'm not saving lives, not doing anything special, but among some cyclists it's special because they appreciate what I've done.

We went to Alpe d'Huez. We spoke to this Dutch couple who were camped next to us – we'd pass the time of day. When we went around Dutch Corner, I saw her there, trundling up, and she caught me. She said, 'Hello neighbour, where's your husband? You can ride with me, come on!' And I said, 'No I'm fine, absolutely fine.' And she said, 'I admire anybody of your age who tries to ride a bike, especially here.' And I felt like saying, 'When I was your age . . .' But it doesn't matter. So I said to Chris instead, 'We're not talking to them any more.'

She gives me an arch smile. We laugh, again. I think of the adage 'form is temporary, class is permanent', but Pauline puts it into much better words than my borrowed cliché. 'Sometimes you're out on the bike, you see an older figure, climbing, but the style – it's all in the style. You know they used to be somebody; they just look smooth, something about them on the bike. And you think, I can see you back in the day, up here in the race, turning the pedals, just like today.'

30th July 1990

Miss Pauline Strong

Heartiest congratulations on your great ride from Lands End to John O'Groats. I knew you could do it – but it's a long long way isn't it !?!

The R.R.A. must be proud to have such a fine new record on their books.

I am delighted for you.

For the last two days I have felt exhausted thinking of you plugging away!

Again Congratulations!

Love from

Eileen Sheridan.

14

Any fool can get to Perth – except me

Monday, 1 July 2019

The day clicks over on the calendar but the weather remains the same. I'm ready for the Shap, and to get to Scotland inside four days, spread across ten months. I cannot understand how anyone can ride to Scotland in twenty-four hours, and then carry on for a second day. It took me fifteen hours to get to Bristol and then I needed to lie down for a month. The scale of the human effort becomes more apparent with each leg of the journey and with each conversation.

I soft-pedal out of Kendal towards the climb and think about how to make things easier away from the bike. Everything has to mean something, but I am struggling to find the shape. The wind is in the wrong direction. It blows down the main road into Kendal because it knows I am here. I head out along the main road out of town, past the industrial estates that mark the messy and porous border between town and countryside. My

SHAP FELLS AND THE KENDAL - PENRITH ROAD   152

thoughts begin to unspool. I thought the End to End would be the answer. As yet, it isn't.

Shap Fell is first up. It starts in Kendal and climbs for 11 miles. It is a special place for the End to End, especially the layby near the summit. It doubles up as a stopping point, hand-me-up and photo opportunity. My mind contains a layered composite image of everyone who has ever ridden up the climb. Richard Thoday alongside G. P. Mills, Pauline with Lynne. I have a feeling that time is doing something strange, dropping out and back in, and again I wonder if today is going to be transcendent, as the real stuff begins. I am going to cross the border and keep going. The mountains are coming, and I know they hold meaning because people write about them all the time. Maybe they will add shape and texture to the mess of my thoughts. The answers will roll down off the hillside, up through the watershed and out of the texture of the Fell. Truth will emerge from the terrain.

My mind is full of truth already, but I'm not sure if it is helpful. I lack determination. I lack consistency. I am impulsive. I overthink, endlessly. My mind is full of noise. I feel defined by the wilful destruction of things of certainty, especially careers and relationships. One seems to follow the other; we choose things with certainty. My wife married a successful teacher, someone financially and emotionally solvent; not the uncertain person who ended up sobbing on a log at Blaise Castle because he couldn't finish his ride into work that day and couldn't go home. I took what I thought was the right decision and stopped doing that job – probably the only decision I could take – but became tangled in the outcome. Everything was affected. My emotional incontinence made home a horrible place for everyone. I was stuck. I recognise, belatedly, the catastrophic effect the stress of work had on my life at home. I am doing my heavy thinking on the bike. Right now, the journey allows a break in time. I relish the opportunity to escape from divisible time and place, to be somewhere which is nowhere. A layby on the Shap is a good place to start, a layby off a main road on a big hill.

Today I'm meeting Mum at Carnwath, deep into Scotland. She seemed keen on my plan to requisition the camper van. I'm envisaging an opportunity to strengthen our relationship, to talk about the past and to think about the future. At times I have idealised what the trip might be like: openness and conversations about life, warmth and happiness and resolution; the Nora Ephron version of mother–son relationships. I resolve to keep it simple, to be nice, to be kind, and not to argue, and if I manage this then maybe warmth and happiness and resolution might follow.

My thoughts are interrupted by a big blue warning sign: 'Altitude 1400ft. Winter conditions can be dangerous.' This makes me happy – it means it is a real climb. All the best climbs come with warning signs, snow poles at the side of the road, emergency bothies, that sort of thing.

At first it doesn't seem to be a climb, just a long false flat. But then it lifts; the tarmac is shaken out like a duvet and ruffled into shape. I know the road – I once raced up it in twenty-seven minutes. I am riding on top of this memory, along with my recollection of being in the support van for Mike Broadwith. Then, dawn was creeping in, the light changing and a thick mist pressing down like a shroud. We had plenty of time and stopped in the mythic layby, where a small crowd had gathered, at 4.43 a.m. Everyone there had a different narrative rattling around in their brain: the chap who saw Gethin Butler ride over in 2001, then had cancer and then got better and then decided to come and see Mike; Damian, who was filming it and thinking of his dad. The crew were there, and Gethin was there, seeing someone attempt to take his record away.

Today it is damp and dank. Cloud banks collapse against the hills, falling into the hidden plateau near the top, where farms and smallholdings sit isolated among the huge pylons running down the valley. Sheep are splodges of paint against the green canvas and the huge pylons look small. I look across to the fields and flood plain of the River Sprint. Horses dance in unconfined joy, light on their feet, light in their minds, and I resolve to be more like horses. I think about my grip on life, on normality. When my grip on things loosens, I wonder if it's a presentation of madness that initially takes control, and there is an awareness of the presentation as reality slips away, to be replaced by fractal thoughts. But then it becomes a real loss of control, a raw madness, and the distance between the surface and depth vanishes, everything is permeable, and thoughts bleed through in an unreconstructed mess. What I'm trying to say is, thinking you are mad means you are probably not mad. The time when you *don't* think you are mad – this is when you are mad. When colleagues and friends and family look at you anxiously and ask if you really are OK.

Prior to the motorway the Shap was the main route up and into Carlisle and Scotland, Glasgow beyond. Heavy, wallowing trucks struggled for hours, inching up, dropping down, then hitting the final bit. This is where Dick Poole resorted to overtaking the heavy-wheelers in pouring rain. I can sense the presence of all the riders, both the racers and the tourists, taking this route through the Eden district, Eileen and Reg and G. P. Mills and Pauline – the same challenge, the same place, only time between them. There is a steep bit at the end of the climb. Up until then it undulates gently. My youthful racing self is dancing on the pedals. In the present, I am an amorphous mass, wallowing up the hill, pedalling in spongy, inefficient circles. Nevertheless, I feel elated and ride up towards the layby, then stop, briefly, to catch my breath. It is empty. But things are going well: the climb is done and it is a downhill hurtle off the hillside from here.

The plumes of smoke from the quarry are the first sign of trouble ahead: the smoke moves south in jagged steps. The descent is heavy and does not reward my effort. I have to pedal to gain time and pace.

The flat from Shap to Carlisle is monotonous and unleavened. There is a megalithic site, King Arthur's Table. It looks peculiar, a henge of sorts; a misshapen field. I am fixated on the border, on crossing into Scotland and the symbolism of putting England behind me, moving up into the hills again. Penrith and Carlisle slip behind. I cannot remember visiting Penrith. I have no memory of it at all. I am sure someone else had a similar experience, maybe Gethin Butler. Maybe it doesn't really exist, apart from as a location on a map. Carlisle I can remember. It is big, and a friend went to university there and said it rained every single day.

The border beckons, and I cross at Gretna. I eat a sandwich to celebrate. I take a picture, then take it again because I forgot to do up my jersey. Scotland welcomes me with a horrible, grippy road surface, long drags and a spiteful headwind. There is no scenery. It is grim and grey and things turn to shit very quickly. It is the wind that does it, that and the residual ache from the Forest of Bowland.

I am running on empty, not just physically, but mentally. I have thought my way into a corner, where I don't know if I'm doing this the right way or the wrong way, or why I'm doing it. All I can do is think about why I am here. I begin to doubt my convictions, my strength, and my self-esteem plummets. The pitted road to Lockerbie is not the place to find meaning or answers. The minor road offers a view of the main road and the motorway. It becomes a metaphor for where I am in life, somewhere that is neither fast and efficient nor slow and beautiful. Everyone else chooses one or the other. I'm in a B road purgatory, solipsistic and angry. I am an idiot without a job, wanting to write a book and overestimating my capabilities on every front. I know I have to press on; but, equally, I am cooked.

When I planned the route it looked like the easiest day of all; long, but not hilly. Yet again my average speed has crashed to around 11mph. Even full-time ultra-nutters would baulk at such pitiful returns. At one point I am overtaken by a larger gentleman on a heavy bike who offers me his wheel. It makes me want to cry. I get off the bike and sit in a ditch, sheltering from the block headwind which has taunted me for the past 70 miles, and I decide to quit. I am done. I don't want to do this, I am not enjoying it. I convince myself that enjoyment is important and not enjoying things is reason enough not to do them. Any fool can get to Perth – except me. I call my mum, like an eleven-year-old wanting to be picked up from a friend's house because they didn't like the fish fingers.

It is the first time I've seen Mum in a little while; Bradford seems to move further away from Bristol each year. She drives out of the gloaming in her van – she is an angel. She asks if I brought the scarf with me. I left it at home. The scarf says 'Fuck it', and I take it to races and wave it at people because I think it's funny. And then I worry that maybe it's just rude. My mum isn't keen on it, and neither are the in-laws. The people who take photos at events don't like it either. In fact, I think it's just me.

We eat food in the van and I drink tea, away from the marauding wind for the first time. I can't control the wind, but it doesn't stop me from feeling that it is here on a personal mission, to undermine my efforts and my mental strength, and that people like me deserve better. When you have a headwind, all of the tailwind days are forgotten. There have only ever been headwinds, sometimes both ways. Today is one of those days.

We drive to the campsite and I forgo riding over the lumpy tarmac of the main road in favour of a seat in the van. I look out of the window and feel no regret. I recalculate, and aim to get to Invernahavon tomorrow. Scotland is a big place.

Author photo

15

Andy Wilkinson wasn't too bad at cycling

Wednesday, 26 September 1990

Andy Wilkinson is a bike rider with a full set of myths trailing in his slipstream. People say he once used gears more suited to going shopping to race against the fastest men in the land on a flat 25-mile course near Lincolnshire. A colleague told me he set a time trial competition record on a mountain bike. Some people say *he only has one bike.* There is a rumour that he never uses power or heart rate or any means of science to assess his progress; this is because his heart rate and power are measureless to man, like the caverns of Xanadu. Others say he pushes himself so hard in a bike race that he collapses in shuddering paroxysms and can't walk for hours afterwards. When the nuclear conflagration comes, or the climate apocalypse, whichever is sooner, only two organisms will remain: cockroaches and Andy Wilkinson.

Chester is a long way from Bristol. I contemplate riding, but

I now know that long rides disagree with me so I get the train instead. It's supposed to be a charming Roman town, with intact city walls. I see none of it walking from the station to a house in Hoole and back again. I walk past a shop called Hoole Foods which makes me laugh because it sounds like an affected way of saying 'whole foods'. I suspect the joke is on me. I'm here to see Andy Wilkinson, or Wilko, as he is apocryphally known.

I have met him once before. I was propped against a bar way beyond bedtime, talking to strangers in the aftermath of an event where I was invited to speak about something because I wrote a book about hills and bicycles that not many people got around to reading. I behaved well for most of it, then moved towards the kind of drunk where everything seems like a good idea. I asked Andy Wilkinson a polite question: 'So when you did that End to End in the Mike Burrows spaceship bicycle thing, is it true you pissed all the time out of the side in a sort of elaborate catheter thing up your penis and it went horribly wrong?'

He said, 'Yes, it is true.' He was unruffled.

Eventually, after he had humoured me for far too long, I sloped off to bed, in drunken awe, but with just enough sense of something to know that I wouldn't be able to make eye contact at breakfast because I would be struck down by a tremulous, brain-wobbling hangover, and the stuttered memories of asking my hero about being sprayed with piss.

That was three years ago. Now I am standing in his garden. It is overgrown; there is a rust-eaten Triumph Spitfire being consumed slowly by a rapacious buddleia; the curtains are closed. It doesn't look like the house of a superhero. A small, gentle-looking figure who looks like Andy pokes his head above the hedge from next door and says hello. I walk around and into his house, not his neighbour's.

We make small talk and drink tea from enormous mugs. They are bigger than tankards, more like buckets. I assume he has either forgotten our previous meeting or is choosing not to mention it – I don't mind either way. I start by telling him about my efforts, how I rode from Land's End to Bristol in a day. He smiles and says it's 'pretty impressive'. I consider my brevet card stamped and will tell everyone how Andy said my riding was 'pretty impressive'. I even tell him about my 11mph average speed when I went up through the Forest of Bowland. Again he says it's 'quite good'; and I think he means it. Admittedly it's not near the 22.5mph he managed when setting a record of 541 miles for the 24-hour, but that's by the by. Sometimes I stop and think about that record, riding at 22.5mph for twenty-four hours. My brain melts. This is what Andy did.

Andy knows everyone. He grew up and rode with Chris Boardman, Steve Cummings, Mark and Tony Bell. He knows Pauline Strong, Lynne Taylor (a close friend and tandem partner) and everyone else in the End to End fellowship. He has special words for Paul Carbutt, Mick Coupe and John Woodburn: 'they inspired me, Paul especially. He was a true cyclist, on his beautiful red and chrome Viking.' I try to explain what I'm writing about and why. Normally I say the same thing, that it's a book about cycling but not about cycling. People then look at me in a confused way, like, why would you write about something that isn't what it's written about? Andy doesn't. He sums it up far better than I can. 'It's about humans, to some degree, the wider sort of picture of why people do incredibly odd things.'

He was born in Liverpool but moved at the age of three when his dad took on a garden nursery on the Wirral, at Willaston. His dad wanted something of his own. The move was a shock. 'I grew up in a normal street, playing with friends. We moved to a detached house in the middle of nowhere, no neighbours, just fields. Mum lost all her friends and for me it was quite isolating.' It is a strange hinterland between Liverpool and North Wales, dominated by the Port Sunlight soap factory and model village. It speaks of the end of large-scale production in the UK, and the social fabric that disappeared along with primary industry. Port Sunlight Wheelers, Andy's club, was established in the factory. These things don't happen any more. Cycling clubs emerge from a desire to wear better kit, not to do better things by other people. Community is subsumed, we are much more rootless. I can't imagine a workplace setting up a cycle club nowadays, at least one that doesn't sell it as a glossy brochure and lifestyle accessory, maybe with free health insurance. The weekend we meet, another meeting is taking place a few miles away at Lord Leverhulme's old house, Thornton Manor, the latest venue in the hyper-real Brexit talks cycle as people try to redefine Britain's changing place in the world.

The bike became a necessity. 'I was whizzing around on the roads because friends lived a few miles away. I started cycling to school. It wasn't far, but I may as well have lived on the moon, out in the fields, somewhere they never went to. I felt different from everyone else. No one cycled.' Once again the bicycle offered the timeless qualities of escape and adventure.

VILLAGE SCHOOL, PORT SUNLIGHT.

Dont you think this a lovely view.

"The Unique Series."

At about eleven I got a Dawes Streak and started hostelling with some friends. I bolted on a rack using jubilee clips. By the age of thirteen we were going anywhere we could. We did a night ride to Lake Vyrnwy, Oswestry; the police stopped us for riding without lights and wrote to our parents. We went to Shrewsbury and back, through the night, because it was 100 miles exactly and my friend's dad told us there was an all-night transport café there. It was closed. We went to Shropshire, Dinas Mawddwy, out beyond Bala. I wasn't interested in racing, it was the adventure and the travel, the countryside. I wasn't good at anything at school, no good socially, but I realised as I did more cycling that I was better than some, which was the first time I'd ever been better than anyone at anything.

I grew up in north Devon and recognise the importance of a bike in a transport blackspot. It confers freedom, encourages wanderlust. However, I was riding the 9 miles to Bideford for a band practice in a scout hut, not 60 miles to Oswestry for the sake of it.

The Dawes was eventually superseded by a space-age aluminium Viscount with solid aluminium forks. I Google it and the first response says: 'DEATH FORK: UNDER NO CIRCUMSTANCES SHOULD A VISCOUNT BE RIDDEN WITH THE ORIGINAL CAST ALUMINIUM FORK.' The marque was bought out by Yamaha in 1978 who promptly recalled every fork ever made and replaced them. It doesn't seem to have fazed (or killed) Andy back in 1980, though 'it was weird, you could see them flex'. I wish our teenage band in north Devon had been called Death Fork.

The Viscount opened up more riding as he got older, including visits to the Eureka Café at Capenhurst – one of the few cycling cafés still in existence, at least from the first bike boom (it opened in 1929). Slowly, Wilkinson began the drift towards 'proper' cycling. His first race was a '10' at Huntington. 'I did rubbish. I was very small, very light and not powerful. I could climb, but I wasn't going to be quick at time trials. It was a lot of fun, blasting it like crazy. It didn't light a fuse, put it that way. At about sixteen I started schoolboy racing. There were a lot of good lads my age, some on the national squad. I wasn't good, I got sucked into it. The social life, going to pubs, living – that was part of it.'

He is reticent; I'm minded to say humble, but I just don't think he likes talking about it. I know what he did because I researched his results. He won the handicap races in Birkenhead Park at seventeen, and this seems to have been a catalyst, both back then for his riding and now, for our conversation. The memories begin to flow.

I was gaining strength and experience. In 1981 I rode the junior Tour of Ireland; it was a big race for the juniors. We did it again the next year as a Merseyside Divisional team but got in a lot of trouble because we trashed the room where we were staying and got thrown out. I began to realise I could ride away on my own, and if I could get away, I'd win. I was stronger, but still slight. I wasn't aggressive and didn't have big power. I'd wait for a climb, wait for the attacks, then attack over the top. It became obvious I could do this cycling thing, but the club was full of good riders.

The strongest was Mark Bell, national champion and a 'class rider'.* He was a cover star and is seen as one of the strongest

---

* Bell was amateur and professional national champion, and rode in the Los Angeles Olympics in 1984. 'I remember following Mark throughout his successful breakaway to win the national pro road race title in 1986, when he simply rode away from some of the greatest names in the sport,' said former president of British Cycling Brian Cookson. Bell died at the age of forty-nine in 2009 after a long battle with alcoholism.

roadmen the country has produced, capable of brilliance but, like Darryl Webster, perhaps mercurial and complicated. They rode and played hard is the short summary; Andy says 'doing the sort of stuff that lads that age do'.

By the mid-1980s I was winning stage races. We went as a club team to the Tour of Ulster in 1985. It was wet and freezing. There was a big dual carriageway with a long drag, and I wanted to get warm; I got on the front and went like hell to try and get some heat into my body. By the time I got to the top there were only two of us left. I won the stage and got the lead. For the first time in my life, I thought, I could win this race; up till then it was always an accident. I realised that I *really* did want to win it and I'd never had that focus before. The next day my teammates all got into breaks and pissed off up the road, and just left me, and I was like, Christ, I'm in the lead here with no one to help. I spent hours riding on the front. The Irish were nice about it but were like 'Mate, we're not helping you, we don't want you to win'. The only thing I could do was sit on the front and hold the gap, and that's what I did. Some of the Irish lads said afterwards, 'That was amazing, what you did was crazy.' I'd ride on the front, get to a climb, get dropped on the climb because I'd been on the front for so long, drag myself back to the front, ride on the front again. I deserved to win it and they did everything they could to stop me winning it.

I am not Andy Wilkinson, but I once won a stage of a race in South Wales. The jersey still hangs in my local bike shop. Andy doesn't strike me as someone who is surrounded by memorabilia, but I ask anyway:

PJ: Have you still got the jersey?

AW: Er ... I've still got the table.

PJ: The what? The table?

AW: I stood on the podium and they said, 'Well done, lad,
      here's your table.'

PJ: An actual table?

AW: Yeah. Me and the other lads had to bring it back
      on the ferry. There's us with a huge table. Someone
      somewhere will be pleased I've still got it. It was a
      wonderful thing really.

PJ: Wow.

AW: It's a beautiful thing. We didn't really win a lot of
      money but having a table was something else.

We eat sandwiches and I carry on drinking from the enormous cup of tea. I take huge gulps but the level seems to
stay the same.

Andy won stage races throughout the mid-eighties. A victory
at the Isle of Wight three-day brought him to the attention of
the national team led by Doug Dailey, a long-term supporter
and fellow Liverpudlian. He needed a team pronto for the
Milk Race after the Swiss had pulled out; he dragged people
off the street, called the team Britannia. As a reward for competing, the group were sent to the GP d'Isbergues and Circuit
des Mines – 'a jolly really'. Jolly? It was 125 miles against Sean
Kelly, Phil Anderson, Stephen Roche, Jean-Paul van Poppel
and Pascal Lance, whom the GB riders nicknamed 'rubber
legs' because he kept bouncing back. Wilkinson rode the Milk
Race a second time the following year and seemed poised for a
professional contract.

Doug Dailey said, 'If you're going to make it you got to
stop fucking about and dedicate yourself to bike racing.' I

was touring, I'd go on motorbike trips. He wanted me to knuckle down, but I couldn't see myself living that life; it wasn't glamorous, it was stifling. In the Milk Race there was a lot going on in the peloton. I didn't know what they were taking. People were stuffing suppositories up their arses with 10 miles to go. Injections were offered, people saying you'll be better, and I just didn't want that kind of shit. The talk was who'd been seen doing what. I never knew what was going on properly, I just knew that getting involved in that kind of shit wasn't for me. People were disillusioned. One thing I knew was that the life of a professional racing cyclist didn't suit me, and I had other things I wanted to do in life.

I still haven't finished my tea. The mug is enormous. It is becoming an endurance act in and of itself.

One form of cycling that is diametrically opposed to a racing lifestyle is the Rough Stuff Fellowship, a collective of cyclists who take their bikes far away from the built environment. Their exploits live on through the luminous pages of *The Rough Stuff Fellowship Archive*. Back then, the group was in thrall to Albert Winstanley, their pipe-smoking, long-sock-wearing founder. It was exactly what Wilkinson was looking for. 'I wanted cycling in its rawest form, I wanted adventure. I did a three-week holiday in the Alps on tracks that you can't do any more, the Gemmi and Theodul, over massive glaciers, all kinds of shit. That was my focus. It was amazing.'

I look up the Gemmi in my *Rough Stuff Cycling in the Alps*. I am not disappointed: 'often the path is cut out of the cliff itself, like a spiral staircase'. It is home to the Reichenbach Falls, scene of Sherlock Holmes' battle with the dastardly Moriarty. The Theodul is another enormous Swiss mountain pass, cresting out at 3295 metres, with a lot of snow. The book states that 'short crampons may be found useful'. It seems a good place to do some soul-searching, certainly better than riding from Bristol to Wolverhampton. I begin to see where I have been going wrong.

Wilkinson began thinking about drawing a line under his racing career, taking on a headline event, something to close the book. 'I never forgot the excitement of reading about the 12- and 24-hour races. It was just you, in complete control, it appealed to me. I loved road racing but my dream was always to piss off and do my own race.' He did a 12-hour and went off course, but still loved every minute. I went off course in a time trial once. I ended up in the genteel civic centre of Malmesbury on a Saturday morning; people were doing their shopping. I was in full bongo with my space helmet. I got strange looks – *er ... the carnival's next week, mate.*

By the end of 1989, Wilkinson was thinking about the End to End. He admired Paul Carbutt and liked the idea of the challenge. He went public at the end-of-season 'big piss-up', to an unexpectedly positive reaction: 'they all said, "Brilliant, you've been training for that for ten years!"' Cycling club piss-ups are dangerous affairs because skinny people who haven't drunk for six months and have ridiculous VO2 max tend to get wrecked on half a pint. Bristol South CC have an 'Ale Rave'. There is usually a club 'enforcer' leading the charge. It ends badly, with catastrophic hangovers and memory loss, people passing out in the cabinet de toilette, sometimes worse. There is one particular ale rave we struggle to talk about even now. Things happened that night in Bedminster, things you people wouldn't believe. Wilkinson and peers rode to the Burway the morning after their night before, with massive hangovers, to watch the National Hill Climb and see Chris Boardman defend his title. They caught the last bit of his ride, then raced back down to the pub at the bottom of the hill.

It was hair of the dog – *boom*, more beers – when someone spotted John Woodburn in the corner. He was a legend. I'd only ever seen pictures of him, read about him, but I knew all about him. Steve Tyler, our wit and raconteur in the Sunlight, went over, yelling, 'John . . . *John* . . . JOHN WOODBURN!' John looked up and saw these pissed-up riders in the corner. Steve says, 'John, this is Andy Wilkinson, he's going to break your End to End record.' John just looked at us all and said, 'Yeah, OK, hahaha,' sort of nodding politely. He might have been smiling, it was hard to tell. He was very dry.

Thus, forged on an Alpine pass and cemented through excessive boozing, the End to End was scheduled for June 1990. An initial training plan came from Keith Boardman, Chris's dad. The team found out Chris was heading to the Worlds with his uber-coach, a chap who later transformed everything about British cycling and sparked the gold rush: Peter Keen. They managed to squeeze in some time and testing on the jazzy new 'KingCycle'. Keen set about dismantling everything they had done so far. 'I was sceptical to begin with,' Andy tells me, 'but something clicked. He knew everything, it was a very important moment. It led to six-hour fasted rides, pulse meters, liquid feeding. He told me to start later and spend three months retraining, so I did.'

With the start date pushed back to September, it put pressure on the logistical side of things. Wilkinson was working for his dad at the nursery and was a partner in the business. There were tensions; his dad was sanguine, but not thrilled about the time being taken up by training. Mum was more supportive; she was always the one at the junior races. 'She saw it first-hand, she understood it. Dad was more circumspect and was concerned about the viability. He's always been dead proud, but cycling isn't his passion.' Most of the costs were met by largesse and goodwill. People wanted to be involved and were prepared to contribute with time and energy.

September brought the wrong weather. Several weekends were blown out by the wind and time marched on. It was already late in the year and there was increasing pressure to postpone. The lack of light and encroaching cold in the far north threatened a serious record attempt. With each postponement the team would change. 'People stopped helping; they saw it as a hopeless cause. To me it was unthinkable to call it off. We got a forecast which wasn't *as* bad and I decided to go. The schedule was to beat the record by sixteen minutes, which was small. Woodburn's attempt had great weather, support from Jack Fletcher, which made it a challenge. We had a new team who didn't have a clue what was happening and weather which wasn't as bad as it had been.'

The ride started with twenty-four hours of solid rain. The pulsemeter broke straight away. There was no headwind but no tailwind either, just a flat sky of solid rain. It was uneventful, too, although like Pauline Strong he encountered an acid house convoy at Preston being tailed by a police helicopter. The team sheltered for beans and toast under a lorry trailer at Penrith. At Kendal, the distance began to bite; he was far beyond his previous 'longest' ride of twelve hours. It started to slip away on the long climb of Moffat. The wet and cold crept in and Wilkinson lost time all the way. With twelve hours to go he had an almost inconceivable 17mph average to aim for, but he clung on. The new team were struggling with the schedule, the feeding, most things, and Wilkinson was struggling too, over Aultnamain, down to Bonar Bridge ... then 'it went to shit'.

On the A9 I was falling asleep, wobbling around the road. They gave me massive amounts of caffeine. After Drumochter I was on a roll – I was pinging, dead smooth. I remember the reverberation from the car engine like a perfect dream. Then I hit the wall, started falling asleep again. I was going down a steep hill and the road was covered in rabbits. I was flying down, barely conscious. The team were certain I was going to crash. I reached the bottom, somehow, still wobbling, falling asleep, hundreds of rabbits everywhere; they'd see the lights, get dazzled and run at every different angle. It was a weird dream; it was 'Rabbits – *uuhhuhhh?*' I didn't understand what was going on.

He admits to having barely any recollection of events, apart from the cold and 'shaking like crazy'. His mind had gone. He thought he had lost the record, and effectively he'd given up, telling his team he couldn't go on. One of his helpers played the guilt card, telling the rider, 'You don't have a choice; these people have given up their time for you.' Wilkinson carried on, but he remained convinced that the record was gone and just wanted to finish.

This is where things got grippier than on any End to End attempt, before or since. The mental and physical toll on the rider and the support crew created a deranged atmosphere, with only a vague sense that somehow he might still be able to beat the record; some vestige of hope, combined with a certainty that it was all for nothing. He had to average 20mph from Wick, to ride 16 miles in forty-nine minutes.

The record had gone, there wasn't a hope in hell of getting it. I just thought they were cheering to get me to the finish, showing willing. I did all I could do but I was confused. I got to the top of the descent into John o'Groats as it was just getting light. I could see islands beyond the coast, and I thought we'd come to the wrong place. I blasted down the descent, got to the door, but I knew I had failed and sat there empty, in every single way, mentally and physically. They were talking, shouting. There was a lot more confusion. After a while the timekeeper told me I'd beaten the record by *fifty-eight seconds*. People were elated, but it took me about half an hour to accept that I *might* have beaten the record. I was too tired and confused.

Of all the stories, this is the one I find hardest: 847 miles, and it comes down to fifty-eight seconds. I am in awe of this form of mental strength. For me, when things got a bit grippy I kept going for a bit, but then I climbed off near Lockerbie because it was a bit windy and 70 miles was enough for me. Andy Wilkinson carried on when everything was lost. It reinforces the underlying and absolute truth of the End to End record: you can be the fastest rider in the world but it is not enough. Terrible things will happen after two days spent cycling at the limits of human exertion, and it is the way in which these terrible things are handled that defines success or failure. 'The weather was totally unsuitable and only the people who were there knew what it took.'

In the days and weeks that followed it became clear that Wilkinson had failed at one key aim – drawing a line under his racing career. 'Before the End to End no one knew who I was, and I was fine with that. Suddenly there was a two-page spread in the Comic. I couldn't race for a laugh any more, people cared, I felt a responsibility to perform. It changed my mindset. It changed the way I felt about racing.'

It is a paradox: he wanted to draw a line under a successful career by doing the most difficult thing anyone could do and then move on to endless adventure, only to find himself defined by it. He started doing the really long races, 24s, which must have seemed like a bun run in comparison. Unsurprisingly, he won the first one he entered, and took home the hilarious headline 'Novice Andy Wins 24'. It started a love affair with the long-distance events and the arcane world of time trials. In hindsight it makes sense: he could do it his way, including from a technical point of view.

He ditched the road bike and spent the next few years trying to develop an all-purpose bike based on a mountain bike frame. It can take 29er wheels or a time trial bongo carbon disc. He brings it in from outside. I notice two things: it's filthy, and it is absolutely a mountain bike. He then took things a stage further, teaming up with Mike Burrows, an influential figure in modern bike design. Burrows designed Chris Boardman's Lotus 108 and the Giant TCR, a game-changing bike shape for the entire industry. Wilkinson had become obsessed with finding a better way of riding the End to End and knew Burrows could help. He wanted to beat the record using a 'human-powered vehicle' – a bicycle with a fairing. It became known as the Windcheetah, a recumbent with a tricycle chassis and a fibreglass fairing over the top. The fairing was the last bit of the puzzle; it cost over £5000 to make and took over a year to source. Wilkinson had trained on the chassis, but the fairing transformed the experience:

There was no wind or cooling. It freewheeled so much better. When you spin out at 40mph on a normal bike, you stop pedalling and slow down. On a recumbent, you spin out at 50mph, stop pedalling and it keeps going, or if it's a slight descent you go faster and faster. It's a crazy feeling. We took it to the circuit of the Isle of Man for a test run and set a new lap record. We were using drum brakes with 17-inch wheels, so they went round quite quick. I was touching 76mph and then had to brake to get around the corner at Kate's Cottage. The brakes overheated in two seconds. The cockpit was filled with acrid smoke, the smell was horrendous. The bike is not safe at that speed. It was a bit of fun in a way.

I once did 56mph while descending the Croix de Fer. I got a very slight speed wobble and pretty much shat myself. I wouldn't say it was 'fun in a way'. I do like talking about it though. Adding another 20mph on to that speed while sitting in a speedy plastic egg seems quite scary.

The team tackled the Liverpool to Edinburgh record, taking an inconceivable eighty minutes off the existing mark. 'Everyone was saying it'd work on the track but not on Moffat so I wanted to prove them wrong.' Liverpool to Edinburgh was the perfect warm-up for the End to End because it uses the same roads and is hilly. The team put in for their attempt and wanted it to be sanctioned by the RRA, using the same officials and observing their rules, but the RRA were nervous. 'They were worried about liability if they said it was safe. We were desperately disappointed. I was into the philosophy of it, the efficiency of human power. The RRA didn't see it that way.'

If the fifty-eight-second bicycle record was bonkers, Wilkinson's HPV record is bonkers for different reasons. It involved 60mph descents and leg-breaking climbs, staggering amounts of fluid and a huge output via a catheter consisting of an adapted condom and a metre-long tube. It would have been fine if it hadn't been for a surfeit of chammy cream; nothing would stick and piss went everywhere, coating the entirety of the inside of the cockpit. 'It was never a big problem, apart from for the people helping me.'

The riding position placed far less stress on the body due to the recumbent set-up but stretched the Achilles and leg muscles. It remains the Guinness World Record at 41 hours, 4 minutes and 22 seconds, some four hours quicker than his existing record and a superhuman 20mph average speed for the entire distance. It somehow joined up all the different strands of Wilkinson's obsessions. 'It was the culmination of all my dreams, it was amazing.' However, he wasn't finished: after that came a tandem attempt in 2000 with Lynne Taylor, a staggering 317 miles for the 12-hour in 2012, and 541 miles for the 24-hour in 2011. 'The 12 and 24 were the most satisfying. I was getting older and I'd become a lot more focused and analytical.'

I pause to add it all up – the decisions, the individuality, the determination, the brushes with authority. I paint him into the outsider artist box, where I put Steve Abraham. I ask him about this, whether he sees himself as a loose cannon, and I wonder where the End to End sits in all of this.

I'm just a bit of an individual, which worries some people. I'm not militant, not irresponsible; I have strong opinions but not to the detriment of others. I don't have regrets, I've enjoyed what I've done, and I've been very lucky. People have given up lots of time to help me.

I've put the End to End in a different cupboard. There's more to me now. I've kept in reasonable shape. Last year I tackled the 24 but I know I can't ride at that level any more; even if I could you've got to *really* want something. I can't imagine suffering like that. At the time it's perhaps best not to ask too many questions as to why you want something that much.

I can't see that I'll ever do anything with that level of commitment again.

16

Ralph demands to see the map

Monday, 10 August 1992

The individual on the bicycle is the face of the End to End record, but there are other forms hidden in the margins. These include the tandem, but also the tricycle and the tandem tricycle. The RRA values them equally, but there is a wider perception that trikies are a bunch of bearded anarchists existing at the outer limits of acceptability. Dave Keene was the nominated tricyclist in my club, Bristol South CC. He used to charge round corners on two wheels and unnerve the club run. It felt like someone was driving a lorry through the middle of the bunch; you would move in for a chat then suddenly remember the scything pair of back wheels. We had one tricyclist in a club of seventy members. We now have no tricyclists. It is a minority and mostly male part of the sport. Indeed there has been only one successful female End to End record on a trike, by Jane Moore in 2014.

After Michael Broadwith's ride in 2018, I wrote a syndicated news article. I did a couple of Google Fact Checks and was happy with what I'd written. The facts were secondary to the narrative anyway, or so I told myself. Maybe this is where I've been going wrong. Within a day or so of publication a message dropped in from Ralph Dadswell pointing out – politely – a couple of issues. I looked him up. He had thirty-nine RRA records, including the tricycle End to End, a record which was still in the book some twenty-six years later. I discovered he was an integral member of the committee of the RRA, along with his brother, Tim. They were in the group, the keepers of the flame. I felt a growing nervousness the deeper I descended into the RRA vortex. I hadn't even met John Taylor yet but knew he knew everything, and now here was Ralph Dadswell, with similar cognitive and encyclopaedic skills. I began to worry about the juxtaposition of statistics with colour, my desire to see the texture of the story set against the desire for chronological, cold facts, and how this might sit with those who have been involved in the End to End for longer than I have been alive.

However, one thing piqued my interest. I had heard rumours that Dadswell went to a very dark place during his End to End ride. Some people said that his experience exceeded even Andy Wilkinson's in terms of the visceral, mind-melting power of extreme tiredness. I resolved to ask him about this, but also about the wider context of the RRA and why it is important. The RRA is an invisible presence, run by amateurs in the real sense of the word, a governing body with 132 years of history which sits behind both the statistics and the mythology of the End to End. Ralph Dadswell is on the inside. I had other questions stemming from my preconceptions and ignorance. Primarily I wanted to know what happens to make someone become a tricyclist, what combination of events, gateway drugs and past trauma leads them to the point where they think, Oh, I must learn how to ride a tandem tricycle.

Dadswell is amenable, funny and honest. He breaks down my preconceptions within seconds. He tells me that the term 'trike' is OK to use, as is 'barrow' and 'long-barrow' for the big tandem trikes. I decide to start using these terms. I like the fact that an ancient burial mound has the same name as a three-wheeled bicycle. I feel slight regret that there is no evidence for a pact with a three-wheeled devil at 4 a.m. on a J course crossroads, no dark initiation rites, sacrifices.

Dadswell's descent to the dark side began with a careless gauntlet lobbed from a moving long-barrow.

I used to kick around with a tricyclist called Dave Pitt in the mid-eighties. He was strong and powerful when he could be bothered. There was a moment when he said, 'Ralph, you're just completely shit, you couldn't even ride my tricycle, let alone break any of my records.' I'd been time trialling for a while and craved variety and Dave had annoyed me, albeit in a positive way. When he threw his careless challenge out there I had little awareness of the RRA. I was motivated by the suggestion that I couldn't do something.

I remember someone once doing something similar to me in a line management meeting. They told me I was rubbish at my job and I needed to do things differently. I felt anger and hot tears. My scalp prickled with an intense and immediate resentment that it was intended to *motivate* me somehow. I didn't go away with a resolve to do things differently; I told him to go fuck himself, that it wouldn't work, and found another job. Maybe that's what he wanted, who knows. Yet more missteps in a lifetime full of them. In contrast, for Dadswell it became a catalyst. Without this acerbic aside, things would have been very different.

Dadswell worked through the record list, chipping away at Dave Pitt's place-to-place markers one by one, turning the tables on his mentor. Inevitably it led to an End to End attempt, in 1992. The first twenty-four hours were straightforward, as per the pattern. During the second day he needed a sleep here and there – 'ten minutes on a lilo at the side of the road, coffee, then off' – which held things together until the forty-five-hour mark. My theory, with some empirical evidence, is that it is harder for women and for tricyclists to do the End to End because things start to wobble around the forty-five-hour mark, a cumulative force which shakes people apart. If you can sneak in before that time – and that means only male individual record breakers – then you limit the extent of sleep deprivation by avoiding a fateful third night.

It was at Helmsdale, within sight of the finish, that Dadswell began not so much to lose the plot as refuse to believe that there ever was a plot, or that the idea of a plot as a construct was ever a thing. I ask tentatively about the myths I've heard and read about, that he no longer knew what it was he was doing and didn't know where he was. 'You are absolutely right. At one point after Helmsdale I persuaded myself that I'd already done Berriedale when I hadn't. Even when I was descending steeply and saw the escape area, the big sign, I kept challenging my helpers, asking what was going on, telling them I'd already been along this bit of the road. It carried on like that. I demanded to see the map to see what I was doing.'

Hallucinations are a thing on the End to End. The lack of sleep wreaks havoc; human forms emerge out of shadows in the night. For Dadswell, bin bags and trees took on ghostly shapes; what was there became distorted, melted into proximal things. Some people experience far more as the senses begin to fall to pieces. The helpers began to realise that conventional strategies to support the rider were useless. Just as Andy Wilkinson had lost his sense of time and self, Dadswell was in an altogether different place. They cottoned on to the idea that he needed some kind of mission or purpose, regardless of what it was. They issued a set of small instructions: 'you have to carry on on this road to this point' and 'keep going from here until you get to a hotel'. It involved finger pointing, simple sentences, imperatives. 'They didn't say "That's the finish hotel", because clearly that wasn't going to help. It didn't mean anything, and I wouldn't be able to do it. I had got to the point where I bitterly resented the helpers for making me do it and didn't have a clear idea at all of what I was supposed to be doing.'

With barely an hour of riding left and only an hour in hand on the record, the ride was in the balance. It led to feelings of intense frustration and despair among the team. They went for the nuclear option: they called his dad. It strikes me as the most bizarre conversation to have, notwithstanding the fact that they managed to get a mobile signal in the far north-east corner of Scotland in 1992. Ralph remembers the chat, but not the detail, unsurprisingly. He was not convinced it was actually his dad. 'I

John Dalton

Ralph loses the plot

told him I was going to have to stop and he did try and persuade me. It was all very mild-mannered – "come on, son, try and get to the end", that sort of thing.'

There is a series of photos taken by one of the helpers on this lonely strip of road. It reads like a Don McCullin triptych, a visible portrait of battle fatigue, extreme effort and utter emptiness; as Dadswell confirms, 'the journey from Wick was quite traumatic for the helpers. It wasn't put on; it was how it was.' In the first photo Hedley, a helper, looks at the camera with a look of wry exasperation. Martin Purser is remonstrating with Ralph, who looks unhinged. In the second, Ralph seems like he might be listening, trying to follow an instruction. By the third, it is Audrey Hughes' turn to look away as everything unravels. Four people surround the rider in support. There is one last photo, in stark monochrome. Purser is reduced to pointing out the direction Ralph has to go. Beads of rain sit on Ralph's glasses and he has no idea what he is doing.

Roger Hughes

'Ride down there until you get to a hotel'

I'm thrilled, vicariously, by how hard the End to End was for him. It is what I am looking for, in authorial terms – the mental collapse and the struggle, the depths and extremes of the undertaking. I wallow in it. He made it to the end and still holds the record – 2 days, 5 hours, 29 minutes and 35 seconds – but recognises, with disarming honesty, that 'it isn't the tightest record I've got'. He sent me a spreadsheet of all his records, the modern equivalent of Janet Tebbutt's logbook or Dick Poole's handwritten ledger. He now has forty RRA records. I suggest he is obsessive. I am correct.

I try to avoid obsessions these days because they bring too much pressure into your life, but there definitely was an obsession to carry on doing these things. Every time the year ended, I'd plan the next year, for sixteen years. A bit of OCD made me do one in the autumn because I'd sat on thirty-nine records for nine years and it isn't as elegant as forty. Back then, sequentially, it was the thing I was researching, planning, doing, immersed in all the time. It obsessed me.

And while the obsession and the physicality of the ride are one thing, there is one other aspect I want to ask Dadswell about; the significance of a small, almost invisible institution in all of this: the RRA. It has been rubber-stamping record attempts for 132 years, from F. T. Bidlake to Brian Edrupt, the current chair. The founding statement, 'to verify and certify the genuineness of claims to best performances on record by cyclists on the road', is deceptively simple, and Dadswell starts with that.

It formed as a credible body to ease out the frivolous claims some people were making. It established a proper and sound set of rules, and if the RRA said it was good, it was good. It remains a bit like that. If you ask the *Guinness Book of Records* 'What do I need?' they say a photo at the start and finish and the ride on Strava, no real questions about conduct. The RRA is stricter: we want to know a lot of way-points, have checkers on the road. The formal framework is there to make sure we are looking after the interests of the record breaker of the past, the one on the road right now and the one in the future.

The centrality of the idea, and the one that sometimes unsettles some people – i.e. those who exist in the present and might demand to reframe how they tackle this ride, *just because* – is ensuring the lineation and integrity of the ride, so that we know that G. P. Mills' or Lilian Dredge's ride is on a par with Lynne Taylor's. Without this I wouldn't be able to have these writerly flights of fancy where I depict past and present riders navigating through the same space and time.

The RRA provides the benchmark of effort and excellence. The framework is what validates the effort; it carries the cultural history of our sport, but is also keyed into the wider cultural history of the country – its physical and geographical changes, social changes, attitudes and values. It is an element of our identity as cyclists but reaches outwards to define other areas. It is a national journey that exists outside of cycling, whether that's people walking, hopping on one leg, in a wheelchair, the youngest or the oldest, or touring over three months, but it is defined to an extent by the competitive element. It adds something tangible. And yes, the history of the record over time ebbs and flows, in and out of obscurity and fashion. 'It feels to me like it's worth hanging on to that history,' Dadswell says, 'because it is credible and because it is important that it is there, recognising this context of epic activity. Look at the End to

End silver shields for men and women. There are giant names in there – Opperman, Sheridan, G. P. Mills, the biggest riders of the day, without question. It is important to safeguard that connection and significance.'

17

I find Drumochter, Mum finds the middle of Scotland

Tuesday, 2 July 2019

The Cairngorms and Ben Macdui sit directly between Perth and Inverness. There is a direct off-road route through the National Park. I was tempted for about five minutes before I realised if I couldn't manage the main road to Biggar in a bit of wind I might struggle when fording a river and would probably die in the wilderness and be eaten by eagles or polecats or both. I opt to follow the conventional route which skirts around the Cairngorms and runs next to the A9, but have to get to it first. Record attempts use the main road, which is now all but motorway, wide dual carriageway, for much of the route with lots of upgrade work happening north of Perth. It makes for a shitty first hour, running through contraflow and holding up traffic while looking for alternatives. The sun is threatening to come out and the wind seems less argumentative than it has been for the past three days. It is

THE GREAT NORTH ROAD APPROACHING THE PASS OF DRUMOCHTER.

drifting around from the east rather than straight at my face. I am grateful.

At Dunkeld I dip into the treeline and follow the path along the River Tay through leaf cover. I'm sheltered from the wind for the first time in three days and the sun drops down in varied dots, stippling the ground. It is respite, but not for long. Every so often I lurch back on to the A9, fast single carriageway or sudden stretches of two-lane death highway. I avoid it as much as possible and try to get some feeling back into my tired legs.

Pitlochry is awash with tourists in search of meaning and tartan. Our journeys are linked, I suspect; a search for authenticity, something better. The Clan Donnachaidh museum squats by the side of the road and has a very large car park. I ride towards Blair Atholl, skirting around the road where possible. Not for me the incessant slog of recent records. My road is beneath and to the side, stapled to the edge of the River Garry thundering below in postcard form. I think of G. P. Mills, of Harman and Blackwell, sitting high up on their ordinaries with the drop to the river below hinted at by noise but hidden by night. It feels like the Scotland I have been expecting – glens and heather and high hills. I am happy, despite the wind, and I am coping better as the road unrolls at the foot of Drumochter.

There are four End to End climbs which have a mythical status: the Shap, Drumochter, Helmsdale and Berriedale. There are others that come and go; the Devil's Beeftub and Aultnamain are now avoided, the climbs in Cornwall are a homogeneous mass of ups and downs, Slochd summit is bundled with Drumochter. The A9 is a mountain pass bisecting the sombre Munro summits of Geal Chàrn, Ben Alder and A' Mharconaich. There is no snow and I am disappointed. I had hoped to see a remnant of a crevasse, snow filling a spur or a steep-sided scree, but it is a bit too late in the year.

Drumochter, like the Shap, has a hearty warning sign: 'Cycle track climbs to 457m – weather conditions deteriorate without warning and can be severe even in summer – no food or shelter for 30km'. This is great news and signifies real adventure. Memories of Wolverhampton are banished for ever and the road from Gretna becomes a lacklustre footnote in a new narrative of courage. I am excited at the prospect of 30km of cycle track, the peace that comes from not sharing the road with cars. The climb uses a combination of the Wade Road and an undulating track on the edge of the A9. Record attempts stay up there, on the shiny surface of the dual carriageway, climbing gently for a very long time.

The path heads up through trees and creeps past deserted buildings, old farmsteads and the remnants of settlements. The light and shadow fluctuate on the side of the mountains, cloud shadows chased by the wind, the leading-edge racing across the valley floor, moments of extreme brightness suddenly dimmed by an invisible hand, then bursting out again in constantly changing colours. It is the cycling I thought I would be doing, calm and transcendent. I enjoy the physical process of the climb,

Author photo

The Wade Road over Drumochter

the way speed reduces and my passage through the environment becomes slower, so more things are seen. My field of vision widens and I look around and marvel at the glacial landscape.

The wind remains a chivvying, nagging presence, but it is easing, I am sure of that. My legs feel stronger with the miles behind me and the pattern of riding each day. The weight of anxiety seems to lift, or begin to lift, or, paradoxically, drop away down the mountain. It matters less up here why I did the things I did. I glide over the summit and prepare to freewheel for miles and miles, only that opportunity is denied by the still capricious wind, forcing me to pedal. A short drop down and I'm at Invernahavon.

I can see Mum's van, but there is no sign of Mum. This is to be expected. Mum likes to disappear. I once lost her in Bedminster Asda for half an hour as she sought bargains from the ends of the aisles, coming back with a bag of flaccid, sweaty asparagus at half the marked price. She goes into a fugue state when there might be bargains. She has disappeared somewhere, again, and there is no mobile signal here, by dint of which we must be in the wilderness. Suddenly she appears around the corner, to tell me she has found the middle of Scotland, and I laugh, mockingly.

We go for a walk a little later, up and around an estate track to a postcard view of a Scottish glen. A flash of red fizzes across the road and into the trees. We look again, in awe. There are red squirrels everywhere, all reddish tail and fluff. A cairn appears and pronounces with great importance 'The Middle of Scotland'. I apologise to Mum.

Mum has parked the van facing Creag Dubh, a sulking crag of a mountain named after the Macpherson battle cry. There is no one else here and we are in the Highlands, in the heart of Jacobite country, and I can breathe.

Author photo

Mum finds the middle of Scotland

18

Gethin Butler's heart beats much more slowly than mine

Thursday, 27 September 2001

I once read that five-time Tour de France winner Miguel Indurain has a resting pulse rate of 28bpm, as opposed to 72bpm for the rest of humanity. Apparently, Gethin Butler's is 30. He looks like what I imagine someone with a resting pulse rate of 30 should look like: calm, unruffled, precise, seeing the world more quickly and in a more measured way than me, my pulse beating two for every one of his. In previous interviews I'd read he was described as 'circumspect'. That's enough to make me nervous. This is amplified by his heroic status: I have been reading about his exploits for years.

I am sitting opposite him in the living room of his Victorian terraced house in Preston. Gethin Butler looks at me in between the beats as the seconds speed past but his heart rate stays put. I ask him what sort of a teacher he was, an icebreaker of sorts, but now I'm worried he just thinks I'm weird. He laughs, nervously.

I explain that I'm a teacher, and Mike Broadwith is a teacher, and I find it interesting. 'They'd probably say I'm too soft, to be honest. My daughter has just gone to college and she ran into students I've come across and they said I was funny, but I don't know if that's funny in an amusing sort of way, or just funny. I suppose I'm different to most people because I cycle to work and back every day. I'm not super strict. If you want to improve yourself you have to work.'

I wonder if they know that their teacher is one of the fastest bike riders of the past thirty years, or that he did crazy things on a bicycle. I suspect not, because he doesn't define himself by it. He could do, if he chose to. I looked at his 25-mile times. The top hundred times ever are dominated by those set since 2016, which goes to show how much the sport has changed recently, due to technology and aerodynamics. Simplifying it, there are four outlying riders from the last century still in the top hundred: Chris Boardman, Sean Yates, Stuart Dangerfield and Gethin Butler. The first two in the list wore the yellow jersey in the Tour. And Butler is one of the fastest straight-line bike riders the country has ever produced. 'It gets out, eventually. Oh, are you in the *Guinness Book of Records*, sir?'

The teaching is a funny thing. He trained in 1992 but then worked in the bike trade, for Hewitt's, a frame-builder in Preston. Twenty years later he started work in the classroom – a bit older and more able to 'put up with everything'.

Butler is part of a famous cycling family with close ties to the Norwood Paragon. He escaped to Preston to study Maths and never went back. His father, Keith, was a national road race champion who won stages of the Milk Race; he rode for Jacques Anquetil at St Raphael and for Tom Simpson at the 1965 Worlds in Spain. His grandfather, Stan Butler, competed at the Los Angeles Olympics in 1932 and rode with Frank Southall throughout that decade. Sister Allison came 2nd in the 1990

National Championship. Mum was a big racing cyclist too, winning national team titles. It is quite a pedigree.

What started me cycling was Allison going out with the family section of the CTC in Croydon. They had a dinner but Allison had chicken pox which she caught off me and I went instead, and was made to feel like I should go out with them, so I did. We'd do 30 or 40 miles, then a bit more and a bit more. I ended up with a hand-me-down touring bike. I had Nan's Allin with 26-inch wheels. I was on that for my first time trials. I was only ever small; Nan was five foot on the dot.

The Allin frame is another part of the jigsaw. Grandfather Stan worked in partnership with Charles 'Ching' Allin in his bike shop in Croydon immediately after the war. They made a Stanley Butler Special, capitalising on his Olympic selection; it was 'the last word in frame design and finish'. Later they made a Keith Special to commemorate his successes.

I knew what the family had done, but we were relatively naive. We lived in a cycling family, but you don't listen until you're interested, and even then, as teenagers, you don't necessarily listen. There was a brief moment when I was sixteen or seventeen and started to make the effort. Harry Featherston took an interest – his son was into it – so for a few years I went to events with Harry. We were the grandad and whippersnapper, we got on like a house on fire. I learned a lot of the TT stuff from Harry. I did the odd road race, won the junior divisional championships, lapped everyone bar one.

Harry Featherston was a lightning-quick pursuiter who missed selection for the 1952 Helsinki Olympics in opaque circumstances – i.e. when being fastest didn't seem enough.

He retired early from competition, only to return in 1982 with the Paragon, taking thirty-three victories in his first year back and beating nearly every age group record there was. He gave his experience and support to Gethin who by then had moved into the seniors and was winning regularly. He took the first stage on the Northern Ireland Milk Race, came 3rd on the Rás in 1993 and took part in the Star Trophy, the professional road race calendar in the UK. The big draw, however, was the season-long BBAR trophy. He wanted to win it; grandfather Stan had managed second place on two occasions, edged out by Frank Southall. After a ropey season, cast adrift by a bout of pneumonia after a snowy three-day race at Girvan, his form finally came good in August: he did 286 miles in a 12-hour 'like it was a club run', then a 28mph 100-mile time trial. 'Mum was in the car helping. She was "he's going to blow" for the whole 80 miles. I didn't have to hear it but it was driving Dad mad.' It came down to the last possible day in a ding-dong with Kevin Dawson, another heroic amateur of the time, and Butler won. The elation was tinged with disappointment that Stan was no longer around to see it, having died the year before.

Butler's early career is reminiscent of Andy Wilkinson's – a phase of road racing during which anything seemed possible. He rode the last 6 miles of the North Road Hilly on a flat tyre and still won. He rode the Milk Race for the Britannia team, beating some of the biggest names of the day – continental professionals, national champions. At the Pru Tour a few years later he raced with Bradley Wiggins, Chris Boardman, Jonathan Vaughters and Jens Voigt, all stars of the road scene. It seems predetermined; a career on the road beckoned. The reality is more complicated.

It wasn't quite like that. It's not sour grapes, because I'd done what I liked doing. There's a lot of riders my age could have done better but have a bit of a chip on their shoulder. British

Cycling put their weight behind Chris Boardman, who was a month or two older. Everything seemed to go to Chris. He got results as a youngster, he went on to the track, and in 1992 won the Olympics. There were riders who would have liked to have ridden the Peace Race, but Chris would go, do a few stages because it was good training, then pull out. It affected a lot of riders of that age. We loved riding a bike, so it doesn't matter in the end. The other side of it was, if you go to the continent there is a drugs problem. People had gone then come back after a year.

There is a tension here. Butler knows he could have achieved more, but also liked what he was doing and how he was doing it. He has an easy confidence in his ability and is able to list his achievements where he feels his potential was demonstrated. 'I know I'm good. I rode the Circuit des Mines, got across from a bunch to the break on my own. In 1992, when Boardman won Olympic gold, we rode the Circuit of Windermere time trial. It was an iconic race at the time. He was going for his hat-trick, and I beat him.' The lack of resources at British Cycling seems a bigger part of the problem; run by amateurs and committed enthusiasts on a shoestring budget, there was only ever room for one medal hope. Butler was selected for the Olympic squad for the team time trial but not for the final team. The reason given in passing was that 'we've got four low-pros and he's too small'. The pre-Sky and lottery-funded British Cycling was a very different beast; I think of Pauline Strong making do with the men's skinsuits, the struggle to get time off work, and just how many brilliant riders were sold short by a system not fit for purpose.

It's once again the competing thread, between riding your bike with no purpose except the joy of riding your bike and riding your bike to compete, to exact every possible drop of talent in order to reach the top step. With success ingrained in the family there were things left unspoken. 'Dad probably thought I wasted my talent a bit, but I've ended up doing what I liked.' Racing and competing, day in day out, can be a joyless process and the tension was always there, just as it was for Andy Wilkinson. Butler won the 100-mile championship in 1993 after touring throughout the spring months, 'up to the top of Durness and back. Earlier that year I went to Brittany. I'd wake up, do an extra 30 miles, then meet them for lunch. You'd spend Easter touring and come back flying fit, no pressure, getting the miles in and feeling better for it.'

He doesn't camp. I find that reassuring: I don't like carrying the extra stuff, or having to set up camp, or any of those things. Maybe that makes me a bit weak; but I like the benefits of a warm shower, a comfy bed. I recount the story of my Trough of Bowland jaunt – it was beautiful. I gloss over the horror of the headwind and the existential despair that built up over the next few days. It's about the spidery magic of lanes sketched across the OS map.

With each year Butler ticked off more of the milestones that mark out a rider as an End to End contender, the key qualities flat-out speed and the ability to ride super-long distances. He rode a 24 in 1997, the same year Andy Wilkinson chalked off 520 miles in a day. The key thing that stood out, apart from horrible, suppurating saddle sores which led to him standing up for the last couple of hours, was that he felt fine afterwards. He even went riding the next day and did a fast 100 a week later. With all this in mind he got hold of a schedule from Jim Turner of the Mersey 24. 'I'd always thought about the End to End. I'd look at the records. I liked the madness of it.' He went to a talk by Phil Leigh at the university, recounting his failed attempt. 'That rekindled my interest. He'd been all over the world, he was a local, and I'd ridden with him. He managed 600 miles before he packed.' Butler began to rewrite his training and riding in order to prepare fully. He would ride back to the family home in

Purley overnight, non-stop, a 250-mile slog. 'The first time I was on fixed, left at seven in the evening, rucksack on, didn't get in until two in the afternoon and then slept for twelve hours. The second time I was on gears, I left a little earlier, got to Bicester at one in the morning and came across people coming out of a club. Two or three drunk girls were chatting away to me in me Lycra. I must have stunk.'

Jim Turner sorted the officials, the route and the schedule, leaving Butler to focus on the ride. An initial plan to go in May 2001 was scuppered by the foot and mouth outbreak. August was a non-starter because of the holiday traffic, leaving September, when Lynne Taylor had also planned to go. Both were waiting for the wind to change. It took three weeks, and Butler got the better day. 'She went the day before, on the day I decided not to go. The amount of rain she had was incredible – she was waterlogged.' I read somewhere that the choice of day was in part driven by numbers, but I'm sure it must have been a joke. I ask anyway.

PJ: 27 September – is that a special number? Divisible by nine?

GB: (laughing a lot, a real giggle) Yes, sort of. I set me alarm clocks to be divisible by nine, stuff like that, yes.

PJ: Do you?

GB: Yeah. My alarm goes off at 6.30 now. When it changes to 7.30, it goes to 7.29.

PJ: 7.29 is a factor of nine, is it?

GB: Well yes, if the numbers add up to nine it's divisible by nine – or ends in nine.

PJ: Well, that's handy. That's a number strategy for your students, isn't it?

GB: Well yes, I have mentioned that to my classes, what you can do with the numbers.

PJ: What about if you have to leave the house? What time?
GB: It's not that extreme, it's just something silly, and I
   carry on doing it. Each number relates to something.

I go away and look up the number nine and rapidly disappear into a vortex of the nine times table. I discover that because 9 is 10 minus 1, nine times any number can be worked out by subtracting the number from ten times the number. For example, 9 times 8 is 80 minus 8, or 72. Or 9 times 123 is 1230 minus 123, or 1107. Similar tricks work for the 99 times table, or the 999 times table. I then understand what Butler means by 7.29. I don't understand how it adds up to 9, then I do: $7 + 2 + 9 = 18 = 1 + 8 = 9$. I am interested in it, but I also realise why I am an English teacher.

When writing books about certain things you become an expert on the topic. It isn't a deliberate thing; I didn't set out to make myself an expert on the End to End, but it happens when you collate all the material and stories and statistics. I can see that there is a pattern for the End to End. The ride to Bristol is fine – fresh legs. There will be traffic on the A38 which will cause anxiety. It will rain. If the wind turns you're in deep trouble. The last 100 miles will see terrible things happen. Most of these are applicable to Gethin Butler. He averaged 25mph to Exeter, beating the school run in the city. He is one of the only riders to have gone over the suspension bridge at Bristol, not under it, riding up a vile hill to get there. He flew through the city and onwards up the A38, along the time trial courses north of Filton, linking them together in his mind: the U7 or U4, leading into the K courses, then up to the Js – a time trial-list's equivalent of the Knowledge, carrying on at roundabouts instead of retracing. People were out in batches, the disarming combination of complete strangers cheering his name and lifelong friends the closer he got to Preston. It began to rain as he turned on to the London Road in Preston. The Shap lurked ahead. He climbed in thick mist, the onlookers in the layby of dreams translucent, spectral figures.

I met Gethin at the top of the Shap at 4 a.m. during Mike Broadwith's effort. It was the first time I'd been out in the countryside at that time since I was a misguided teenager in north Devon. He recalled watching Broadwith ascend to the brow of the hill, how there was an unspoken moment of recognition between the two as Mike realised he was being watched and supported by the record holder and Gethin recognised what he was doing and what was to come. 'You want to see him succeed, but in other ways you want to keep your record. There's nothing nicer than seeing people: it keeps you motivated if you're feeling a bit grotty. I felt a kinship because you know what they've gone through, you know what they might be thinking.'

It is a lasting image. Both in the same spot, at different times. Mike acknowledged Gethin with an awestruck look and was gone, impelled to carry on by the sight of the current record holder, down the descent to Penrith. It's a section Gethin can't remember. 'I've seen pictures, that's all I have. That's more frightening than anything else – it is a complete blank, like I wasn't actually there. After that I felt better. I like night riding; Shap in the middle of the night with the fog, it was silent. I came into Carlisle and it was Friday morning rush hour. My senses were assailed by the contrast of noise and light after hours of silence and dark.'

Riding through the night is a surreal experience; feeling dawn seep through in a swirl of blue ink. With the wind behind, the only sound would be the zip of tyres and the thrum of the following car – a hypnotic rhythm, headlights illuminating the road ahead, raindrops reflected in the halogen glare. Just onwards, flow, souplesse, then bang, into Carlisle and the world is awake and a very different mental and physical place. I think of being young and insouciant and out all night, walking home in the early hours when people are going to work, not making eye contact; or finishing the evening on the first Tube in the morning alongside people starting their day. Two ends of the spectrum, the straitjacket of routine undermined by different choices.

The 24-hour record was on; he was chasing 496 miles. 'It was something on the way. Even if you fail, you've achieved *something*. But it was just the first target ticked off, the lesser target.' It was done; things were looking good. But others had been this way. Some, like Christine Roberts and Roy Cromack, had taken the 24-hour record only to climb off. It was getting grippy. The rain came down – 'there were rivers running down the road' – and with it came the cold, and lots more stops; getting changed, drying off, warming up, getting cold again.

> You lose track of time, even though it's the most important thing. It's a mental thing. I'd done audaxes, I knew I could sit in the saddle for thirty-six hours, but with rest stops. You ride for twenty-four hours, what do you do for training for more than that? You've missed a night's sleep and you've been

riding so long your body is fed up. I had slept for ten minutes
in a bus shelter at Penicuik. I was conscious of stuff around
me but absolutely rock still, like a coma. I got up, clipped
back in, the ache had gone – I allowed the fatigue to drain.
It really helped.

Respite was temporary, and fatigue and mental exhaustion
crept back in.

It's 290 miles, on a good day it's a 12-hour race, but you've
already done a day so mentally you're knackered. You're looking for an excuse – not to stop, because you know you'd regret
it, but just to stop pedalling, to stop and chat. Then my wife
said, 'Don't think we've come all this way and given up all
this time for you to bloody get off now.' There's a third of the
distance to go, you've done a day, but it's not a third of the

Henry Iddon

time because you're going slower. You've still got the problem where you can't go faster than you can afford to go without killing yourself; you can only go that hard when you're sure you're going to get there. It's about riding slow enough.

Here, once again, is the paradox of the End to End: it's not about who can ride fast enough, it's about who can ride slow enough and still do it. It's why Pauline Strong thought the super-fast Ian Cammish wouldn't be able to do it – he wouldn't be able to ride slowly enough. When things got tough, the maths was a comfort: 'I have to do *that*, in *that* time'. Wife Gillian described it as 'six hours of touring mode', although it's far faster than any touring mode I've ever slipped into, and Gethin snapped out of it at Pitlochry – coincidentally where his dad Keith jumped ship to go to a British Cycling meeting. I wonder what it was like having Dad/the legendary Keith Butler in support. He laughs – maybe a wry laugh.

It wasn't that helpful. Too many strong characters. Some of the helpers were opinionated, and Dad was opinionated. Dad was good at making comments and thinking someone else would do it. But that's Dad, people are as they are. I never struggled with Dad's record, but Mum did say she thought he was jealous of how good I was, because he thought I'd wasted my ability. I came from a cycling family and my dad was national road race champion. You'd think he'd train you and teach you, but none of that ever happened. There are things I learned he could have told me years before, but I found it out by trial and error or by talking to others. He'd come out and feed, but he was not the sort of person you'd ask for advice. I know with my dad I moved as far away as I possibly could because I'm like me mum, I'm not argumentative, most of the time, and Dad was a strong character, opinionated, would argue that black is white, and no matter what your opinion was it was wrong. The only way for me to develop was to be a long way away. I've never regretted it.

When he was a lot older, a few years back, you could almost have a conversation. I said there weren't any debates in this house because it was your way or no way; Mum backed me up at the time. That's why we all do our own thing, but we are happy. I'm from a cycling family, but not in a hand-me-down way. I let him say what he wanted then I did my own thing. It's funny really, when you're a kid and your dad says 'check your bike the day before, make sure it's roadworthy'. All he did was take it to Ching Allin and he'd sort it. He was useless mechanically, as I found out. Even in his sixties or seventies he'd swear blind his bike was working perfectly while I'm there sorting it out.

So yeah, there were quite a few [who] wondered why he went to a meeting at Pitlochry when I was on the last bit of the End to End.

Gethin's accent betrays a lifetime spent in the north. I'm surprised he hasn't got the freedom to drive sheep through the city, sitting astride his time trial bike. He fits my southern, clichéd view of a northern attitude: take as you find, people are as they are.

The pace picked up once over Slochd, downhill to Inverness. The bridge is important. It promises so much with the first written sign to John o'Groats, but it terrifies in equal measure. 'It's 120 miles. People don't realise how far that is – a similar distance from Land's End to Exeter.' The last 80 miles were beset with thick, gelatinous fog, obscuring landmarks and any sense of place, or pace for that matter. It became hard to tell what was up and down, with the following car stopping at one point and taking off the handbrake to determine if they were up or down.

He stopped for a pee at Wick and the helpers tried to hurry him. 'I remember saying "I can't be bothered worrying about it", because I wasn't bothered.' The wind was ripping in from the North Sea and it became a slog. Lynne and Andy came out to see him emerge from the fog, wraith-like, on this primordial strip of land, dominated by absence and emptiness, ruins, depopulation and Pictish cairns. He waved, and flew on, the grey-out and limited vision providing a boost of adrenalin. He finished, 'fresh as a daisy', in 44 hours, 4 minutes and 19 seconds, then lined up to tackle his spell in purgatory: the 1000 record.

I got changed and waited until dawn. I regret waiting, I felt that good arriving. I'd have had the tailwind to Thurso. But it was pissing down with rain. I knew how slow the 1000 was so I had plenty of time. It was grim that whole day. Lynne did her 1000 a year later as quick as I did mine, because although I felt strong initially, I was fighting into a strong wind to Wick, averaging 14mph, then not making it up with the tailwind because of fatigue. It was cold and damp and the cold got to me, and I punctured. I had a ten-minute stop with 50 miles to go. They said I looked like Jack Eaden on a club run, an old chap who trots along at 12mph. I felt a lot worse on that last bit, fifty hours in.

It was late September; the nights are longer, and it was cold. It's hard to explain what John o'Groats and Thurso are like, unless you've been there. It gets very cold. On my slow jaunt in the summer of 2019 it was 27 degrees when I left Bradford. Five days later and it was 12 degrees at the top of Scotland. It is a long way north. Butler limped on into the wind and completed the 1000 miles. It is a demented achievement, one worthy of celebration, but the capacity to celebrate tends to disappear when you've been in the saddle for 55 hours and 59 minutes.

I felt finished. It was getting dark again. I fell asleep on the massage table – they left me there with me arms hanging down. I woke up, got off and walked down this corridor. I could hear them in the dining room. I found my room and collapsed on the bed until my wife came and said, 'Move.'

We drove home the next day. By the time I got back I had Nora Batty ankles, my knees were swollen. I went out for a bike ride at 1 p.m. in the pouring rain. I'd ridden every day of the year and I'd never done anything like that before. I finished the year like that. Now I take the first of January off to stop me. It was just something I wondered: could I ride every day? I could.

He had ticked off both the End to End and the 1000, reset the records to the extent that the End to End lasted for seventeen years and the 1000 still stands. However, the records weren't ratified for four years. I have a peculiar vision of an RRA official walking the route with a click wheel and a clipboard, just to be doubly sure. Every so often, sometimes within touching distance of the finish, he loses count and has to go back to the start. Maybe that's why.

It is a struggle to know what else there is to do after completing the End to End and the 1000, what new challenge there might be. Butler struggled with the adjustment, as many have done. He found it hard to set a new target and began casting around for something else, some other form of motivation. He did some more endurance riding, including Paris–Brest–Paris in 49 hours – a challenge of sorts but not one he seemed to enjoy. 'You just ride and it's flat and boring, it's not a nice route. There's a few lumps in Brittany. I was on me own, it went on for ever.' In the end, having a young child helped make the decision for him. Annwen had spent all of those forty-nine hours in the back of the car. That was enough.

We talk about touring and the joy of riding in France – how riding home from Barcelona, eleven days up the length of

France, remains a touchstone for me, an unbridled joy. Gethin thinks back to his Brittany tours. 'No pressure, just you and the bike. It's one way; you know you don't have to go across the same bloody road. Just lovely French towns, appreciative people.'

The racing ebbed away. He went back to university, this time to complete a sports science degree. He did a bit of racing, but not at the same level. He started to struggle a little bit. 'Not doing anything drives you nuts. If you're used to being active, even in a small way, if you stop you suddenly start going mad. Five miles to work barely gets you warmed up.' I imagine the demand competitive cycling placed on Gethin's time, energy and life, and the size of the gap left when it disappeared. It isn't as simple as stopping and finding something else. We define ourselves by things like bike racing, employment, hobbies, friendships. They generate the self-esteem we need to live fulfilling lives.

It never mattered to me what my job was when I was racing, because racing was what mattered. Once I stopped racing it mattered a lot more what my job was, and I didn't like that it mattered. It's probably best to never stop. I was getting headaches, so one day I went for a run to the park. My wife said, 'Yeah, come back in a better mood.' I did about two and a half miles, could feel my legs beginning to seize up, so I stopped. After that, someone got me to run a triathlon relay. I was the fourth fastest runner on the day. I thought I might as well do a bit more. I'd always wanted to do a marathon so I thought, I'll do that. A guy invited me to a coaching session at the track. Someone asked, 'What have you done?' I said, 'A bit of cycling.' A few weeks later he came back: 'A *bit* of cycling?' People always find out. I did the Blackpool marathon. I wanted to beat three hours but realised I could do 2.45 because I'd be jogging round at three-hour pace. It doesn't take long to find another obsession.

He says it in the most matter-of-fact way – 'jogging round' for a *three-hour* marathon. The race had both half- and full-marathon fields together. Butler ended up in the front group with the faster-paced half-marathon runners. He could see from the different-coloured bibs, and realised he was the only full-distance runner in the short group. He slowed up at about 6 miles, waited for the split at 11.

> I was left on my own, leading the race. I started the second big lap. All the holiday people watching were still drinking or just starting drinking at 10 a.m. and I didn't want to look like an idiot so I was hoping I could hold it together. I did two hours forty-five minutes and won the race, which was a surprise. I trained a bit harder, did a few more. I did 2.27 at Manchester, I had an official 2.28 at Berlin. It's not too bad. I just don't know when to stop, that's the problem.

I look up his results. Gethin Butler the marathon runner came 76th at London in 2.33, 10th at Edinburgh in 2.36 and 65th in Berlin. He is still doing them, including the Brighton marathon in 2019. 'It was dreadful. I knew after 10 miles that I was going to be hanging on.' I suspect his description of 'hanging on' might be different to mine. I'm imagining a long dark day of the soul on the Brighton promenade, a sickly Kolley Kibber being chased down by the bonk hammer in the form of Pinkie. This isn't what happened. He managed 2.47 and won his age category. However, he measures it against what he could have done, what he knows he is capable of, 'the feeling of performing rather than of winning'.

He has other plans. First up is the Three Peaks fell race, a horrific 24-mile cross-country race; 'they make you go down just to come back up'. I'm reminded of a luminous book about obsession and endurance, *Feet in the Clouds* by Richard Askwith.

I feel exhausted thinking about it. I sense a thread that connects people who take on the End to End record – a superior level of wilfulness. People like Gethin Butler and Edith Atkins who redefine things in the fullness of the amateur spirit, creating a demented joy for themselves and others, and above all creating a simple meaning which they can use to navigate through this endlessly complicated world. The End to End is the big one, for all of them, the journey that seems to both overshadow and illuminate everything else they have ever done.

'The End to End was the only time I've ever said "nothing else matters". If I'm brutally honest, it's the only thing I've ever targeted properly. At other times I just rode my bike and raced. It is the best thing I've done.'

Henry Iddon

19

Lynne is nails

Wednesday, 26 September 2001

I have to drive up north again, this time to see Lynne Taylor. I contemplate riding, revisiting the roads – they live on the route – but think better of it once I see the forecast. I also have grim memories of Gailey which are not in need of exhumation. There is a severe weather warning; I drive down the waterlogged motorway and think of what it is like to ride through water-logged air. The sky is cornflour-grey and thick with churning water. Cars are reflected in the glassy tarmac, a wobbling shimmer of light. The grimness of the motorway in the early morning is exhausting. I know Lynne Taylor rode for hours and hours in rain like this and it makes me shiver.

Meeting Lynne means meeting Lynne's dad, John Taylor. His contribution to the End to End is enormous; he is the historian of the effort, the archivist. He is the author of *The 'End to End' Story*, an exhaustive and detailed account of every single attempt, and most of the failed attempts, and the different ones, and the people who went along, and the people who didn't go along. My copy is thumbed to death, pages creased, Post-its sticking out like spines on an ankylosaur. He is also author of a book on the 24-hour time trial. In literal terms, it is the biggest, heaviest book I have ever seen. It reminds me of the phone book from days of yore. It contains a similar amount of information. John Wick could kill someone, somehow, with this book.

I don't know where I am because I followed the voice in the car, along main roads and ring roads near Cannock, into a car park surrounded by square buildings of blue glass, rendered opaque by the glowering sky. It is a retail park; there is an ice rink, some sort of huge electronics office and emporium. I wonder how long the buildings will last. In the middle is John Taylor's bike shop, a colossal retail space that seems to buck the trend of diminishing returns for the local shop selling actual things. It is exciting to see.

John is passionately invested in the story and reality of the End to End. I'm nervous: I don't want to tread on his toes, and I don't want to make any bad decisions. He is on the committee of the Road Records Association. He has been on a staggering number of End to End rides. He attempted the tandem record three times. I'm the layperson who has stumbled in with vague ideas of journeys and extraordinary people, and who has decided he is going to write a book. He has already written a book. I try to tease out the differences, speak in abstract terms. Mine is 'about people'. All books are about people, I realise, as soon as I say it. I can't do everyone; I want to do elements of the narrative, threads. By way of example I tell him I'm not writing about the famous tandem crew Swinden and Withers, who did startling things. I hear John breathe in, a measured pause, and I feel very nervous. He thinks carefully about what he is going to say. John would definitely write about Swinden and Withers: 'I rate them as two of the toughest riders ever. They were the bee's

knees for speed,' he says. He then moves away from the subject
deftly, ever the archivist. I end up writing a bit about them.

John has clearly defined views about the End to End, about
what makes a worthwhile aspirant and about the demands it
places on people. 'You may be brilliant at TCRs, win a 1600-
mile thing by half a day or whatever, come home out front,
but on an End to End, it counts for nothing. People are so far
beyond their comfort zone. There is a point in the second day
where everything else that went before becomes irrelevant. It is
deeply uncomfortable.' He is talking about the Transcontinental
Race and unsupported 'ultra' races. He feels that they are different beasts; one does not translate into pedigree for the other.
John would favour the 24-hour as the best indicator of potential
success in the End to End. Results for riders who have tried
both suggest he has a point, and that it works both ways – the
24-hour is not an indicator of ultra-endurance success. I worry
that John might tell me off about something.

And then Lynne walks in. I breathe a sigh of relief. Lynne,
like everyone I have met on this journey, looks preposterously
healthy. To borrow a phrase from another End to End rider,
'Lynne is nails'. She has ridden the Mersey 24-hour twenty-four
times – over 10,000 miles in these races alone. The family are
committed to the Mersey 24, returning year after year to the
network of roads around Prees Heath.

John Taylor opened the bike shop in Cannock in 1981. Lynne
would come in and clean one day a week; the rest of her time
was spent coaching swimming, trampolining and gymnastics,
but never cycling. Aunties and uncles all did vast mileages, up
and down the country. Dad was riding all the time but she
didn't start until she was twenty, when she headed out with her
brother for a 25-mile ride. 'I said I enjoyed it but hated every
single minute of it. I carried on. I was determined to race and
join the club.'

Even if Lynne struggled with her first rides, the idea of extreme distances was normalised within the family. As was standing at the side of the road in all weathers for an extraordinary amount of time at events like the Oldbury 12-hour. 'I used to help when I was about twelve, handing up bottles for Dad and collecting them in. Every September, that's all we knew, en masse, Mum, brothers.' The Oldbury CC in the 1960s and 1970s was a big club, full of fast bike riders, including the superfast June Pitchford – the closest to Beryl Burton in that era. The club is now all but lost in the mists of Midlands social history, just memories of weekends meeting to race on baked tarmac, the air heavy with heat and the roads empty of cars.

After a lifetime of riding 24s and supporting the RRA, John Taylor's chance at the End to End came via Pat Kenny in 1978 in the form of a tandem trike. Kenny was an important and supportive figure for the RRA during the seventies and eighties. The tandem trike is like an enormous lorry, and roughly the same weight. It is an extended tricycle, but it looks like some sort of demented charabanc. Jock Wadley was calling them 'obsolete contraptions' as far back as the 1950s. Kenny and Taylor took the Edinburgh–London record and family life began to orbit around the End to End, with three attempts in three months. They watched the pair come through at the mythical/rubbish Gailey roundabout. The second attempt was framed within a family holiday in Cornwall, waiting for the weather to change. The first attempt was the closest, with the record in the balance until a change in wind direction scuppered things with 80 miles to go. I wonder what effect this might have had, besides making them want to go again – if there are longstanding regrets.

It wasn't meant to be, with the weather, and we were running out of money. The second attempt it was 85 degrees, we were cooked. We got off near home. The third attempt was in July; it rained from Glasgow and we packed at 600 miles. I couldn't do it on my own, but with Pat I was something. Pat was obsessed with the End to End. The following year he broke the trike record on his own. He had to do it, otherwise it would have destroyed him; he couldn't think of anything else. I was so happy for him but it was a relief for me that I didn't have to do it.

John slipped back behind the scenes, organising, helping, brewing coffee for forty-eight hours on the road in a small car, and he began to think about the story, the narrative of success and failure, all the extraordinary people doing these absurd things, the challenge of it, and decided to write it all down. 'I wanted not to miss *anybody*, everybody who had even done a credible effort.' He even covered those who might have been able to do it but didn't – Beryl Burton, for instance.

Lynne waits, listens. We pick up the thread we left in Cornwall, watching Dad do his thing, not wanting to ride bikes. In the end, a pragmatic decision led to Lynne taking cycling more seriously: the gymnastics and trampolining was not good for her back. She spent more time working at the shop and a lot more time on the bike, building up to a first 24-hour in 1993. She reflects on the strangeness of the transition: 'I don't know how you get from thinking a 10 is impossible to thinking a 24 is possible in the space of five years.' The answer is that cycling, like most physical activity, is a gateway drug. It rewards you, makes you feel better. The more you ride, the faster you go – and the initial gains can be startling; it becomes an addiction or an obsession, depending on how you frame it. It is good for your mental health, mostly, until you end up grovelling and crying on a road north of Gretna and waiting for your mum, then it's not good.

Lynne kept on working, bringing her times down, chipping away. She took advice from the extraordinary Christine Roberts, who along with Bridget Boon was reframing expectations of what women could do in endurance events; the 24-hour record was under threat from both women. Lynne went along to the annual CTT (formerly the RTTC) gala event at the Derby Assembly Rooms – no longer the Albert Hall, but still a stellar event for domestic cycling. 'You could get a £5 ticket to watch. I'd see all the stars on the stage and wish it was me. The only way I was going to get there was sweeping the stage. Christine's husband was joking about the 24-hour event, and I promised to do one if she did!'

The following year she managed 393 miles to Christine's competition record of 461 miles. The path was set, in hindsight. Jim Turner waved forms at Lynne in the same way he'd ensnared Gethin Butler, luring them into the Mersey 24 each year; 400-mile rides became the norm, with 441 in 1995, before she won the event in 1997. It all began to point towards the End to End and Pauline Strong's record. You can't have John Taylor as your dad and not do an End to End.

The starting point was an attempt in 2000 at the mixed tandem record with Andy Wilkinson. 'He would ride down from Liverpool on his own on the tandem, we'd do an audax, then he'd ride home.' That was the extent of the training. The test attempt on Liverpool to Edinburgh was a qualified success, with Andy despondent in an interview with *Cycling*: 'Lynne was great, but if we go like we did on this one there isn't a cat in hell's chance of cracking the End to End.' Lynne was more circumspect, 'chuffed to bits' at breaking the record but annoyed with the things that were said and that she'd not been interviewed. She put the record straight a week later in the same magazine: 'I'm sure we can sort out the tandem. I really enjoyed it, it felt great. I'd never been over the Shap or the Beeftub before, I kept pointing out the marvellous views.' Lynne reiterated how they were really good friends; the mutual respect is evident: 'he sent me a letter with his aims in it. Everything he said he was going to do he did.'

They made some alterations to the tandem and prepared for the big one. There was to be no waiting, taking a leaf out of the Pauline Strong playbook – 'it was shit or bust'. Thick fog at Land's End muffled sound and thought. Within an hour the sun scorched through. Wilkinson lost his cotton cap on a descent. He didn't bother with sun cream, but it was a problem stored for later. There were conflicting targets: Wilkinson wanted the fastest 'outright' record, to go under two days; the mixed tandem record was 2 days and 8 hours, and much more 'gettable'. Wilkinson struggled with the paradox of going slowly enough; he'd ridden the End to End quickly. 'He was an hour down on the men's schedule, that was all that bothered him, not being six hours ahead of the mixed record,' says John. On Shap, 'the lights went out' and the support team rallied to get him to carry on. He was sick with sunstroke and it wrought havoc on his constitution. Wilkinson later admitted, 'I was miserable. The problem was having to spend over twenty-five hours more on the bike. I knew I had to finish or I would be in an even worse state. I used up more brain cells than anything else.' It shows Lynne's determination – riding tandem with the men's record holder and somehow encouraging him to continue. She seemed unruffled by the effort. 'I didn't really know about it. I could sense he was a little bit miserable. I tried to cheer him, point out stuff, like Auntie Donnie at the roadside – got him to wave. I was fine. We did 60mph after Drumochter. I can picture it now, at 3 a.m., going past cars, thinking, Oooh. It was very exciting. Andy had been dropping off to sleep but I still enjoyed it. I knew how good a bike handler he was.'

It's a scary business, tandems at speed; two people on a barn gate with wheels, gaining speed through momentum and mass – 70mph is common on an open, fast descent. It requires

Lynne Biddulph

After the tandem record

complete trust in the pilot. The combination of Lynne's determination and Andy's strength saw them through and they got
the record. Lynne felt good, Andy less so. 'It was perfect prep.
Andy said I could do it on my own, but I was worried about
finding my way. My sense of direction is hopeless!'

Lynne went straight back to racing. She had vague plans
to tour the route the following year but was put straight by
Wilkinson: 'if you check it out first it might put you off, you just
have to go for it'. The less you know, the better. So the following
year they scheduled September for the solo attempt on Pauline

Strong's record. Jim Turner and John Williams were again part of the process, with Williams signing it off. To confuse matters, John Williams has a nephew called Jon Williams, who now runs the Mersey 24 with his daughter and is heavily involved in End to End attempts, including the trek up country with Michael Broadwith. The entire Williams clan across four generations or more is an integral part of the endurance cycling community. They have a deep-rooted, familial and cultural connection to amateur sport.

Lynne's attempt kicked off the day before Gethin Butler's. She had all of the rain and none of the wind. At the time a 'same day' start wasn't permitted, but it has changed since, with a mandatory four-hour gap. I like the idea of riders on the same 'course' at the same time. There is no risk, as John Taylor acknowledges: 'If you get caught for four hours you might as well give up.' For Lynne, the weather was a long way from ideal. RRA wisdom and the runes suggested it was going to be a struggle, and by the time she hit the A38 it was heavy going. The laminated route card made for tricky navigation – no GPS or breadcrumb trail. It feels like a different era altogether. Time drained away in the rain.

'It rained and rained. We didn't have women-specific gear. I'd got very basic stuff; we were drying it on the heater to put on again. I just kept going. By Warrington I was five hours down; people were starting to doubt.' Shap had an added head-wind, just for fun, and it was as good as over. Only Pat Kenny remained in favour, saying it might just happen.

This is where willpower becomes the governing factor. I know that I lack the willpower to transcend my physical limitations or the extra hardships of horrid weather and the like – I have proved it. I am not like Lynne Taylor. 'I wanted to get there. I didn't think it *wouldn't* happen. They didn't tell me everything. They'd say, "You'll have a cup of tea in 50 miles," so I'd focus

Lynne Taylor and the layby of dreams

on that. They were all eating chips when I went in. Dad took me watch. He came and got me after an hour. They were still eating chips. It doesn't take an hour to eat chips. Afterwards I found out it was eight minutes.'

And suddenly the wind changed, over the border and running up towards Edinburgh. She needed a fast finish, 14.5mph up and over the Highlands. The hallucinations started; Disney characters leaping out of the edge of the road, dark shapes becoming shapes of definite things in the headlight halo and the rainbow of the rain, an amplified shimmer of sleepless visions. 'My eyes were really bloodshot, my vision painted out red. I kept thinking I was coming to traffic lights because of the blood. At one point I stopped in the middle of the road, and Dad shouted because there was nothing there, just a blood-red road, and I'd been looking at the dark wet tarmac and it all merged together.'

The support team, including legendary tricyclist John Arnold, were worried. Arnold said she looked 'ashen and ill'. After forty-five hours the rain stopped. It had been a process of physical and mental degradation; she might not have felt ill, but she looked it. But all the time she carried on riding, across the bleak and empty final zig-zag, despite being borderline hypothermic, and arrived in John o'Groats an hour up on Pauline Strong's record, in 2 days, 5 hours, 48 minutes and 21 seconds. She was 'chuffed to bits' and excited that Gethin Butler was on his way; she made plans to get up at 4 a.m. and watch him come in. But the record was tempered by an overwhelming feeling that she could have done better. 'Even then, sat at the end, wrapped in a blanket, I knew I had to do it again. I was thinking it all the way up. I had a shower and could see lots of flowers, really bright colours. I went to pick one off the wall. I asked if anyone had seen them. They hadn't because the walls were plain white.'

It is a frightening level of determination, an unfathomable strength. It doesn't resemble a hackneyed narrative of suffering. It is characterised by intense fitness and a willingness not to be bent back by the task, but to reshape it in the mind and defeat it. You would think that after two End to End records she might take a break. However, Lynne set out the following year to aim for the 1000 and *along the way* lower the End to End record. There is a sense, in the room when we talk, in the here and now, that the women's record should be under two days, and that with the right conditions it will happen.

Like Pauline Strong, I often think I'll do something for ever. I used to think I'd always be out bike racing; *not* bike racing was unimaginable. But then one day I stopped bike racing. Something makes people like Lynne carry on. It seems like an obsession, a driving force above everything else. 'I do something, and I'd want to keep doing it, and I'll carry on. It's a habit and a routine, like the 24 – a few years I've been saying I won't do it, then when it comes round, I'm riding it, I can't stop myself.'

The following year they delayed and delayed, waiting from August 2002 until almost the end of October. Finally, edging

towards winter and on the brink of postponement, they decided
to go. It seemed to follow the same pattern as the year before,
down on schedule with ankle-deep surface water on the A38.
One of Lynne's aunties had come out again to watch. She knew
the timings and was sitting in a car at the side of the road being
buffeted by wind and rain. She couldn't imagine anyone would
attempt it in those conditions so she went home. Lynne had
stomach problems – one of the enemies of the endurance rider,
in so many ways, physical and logistical. I don't want to think
about it, but I ask about the practicalities. Her response is unvar-
nished, the simple truth about this extreme event:

LT: I had a bucket; I just got on with it. You're used to it
     in 24s, sat on a bucket with a towel over you.
PJ: That's normal is it?
LT: It can be, especially if you get a chill. I remember
     some people coming out to see me, they'd come all
     the way from somewhere. And I was sat on a bucket
     and I kept saying 'I'm ever so sorry about this'. I was
     so embarrassed. But it's part and parcel of it.

For all the joyous and romanticised images of endurance
riding, there is an unremittingly grim side. You have to go to
the toilet; lots. It has to be a part of the strategy. It's easier for
men, both to stop and whip it out or to go on the move with a
clever roll of the leg, or to have a bulb or catheter fitted. It can
go wrong – hence Andy Wilkinson sitting inside a shiny egg
full of piss. The women have to stop. It's dangerous to try any
other method.

Time continued to leak away. Gethin Butler cheered her
through Preston but by the top of the Shap she was three and a
half hours adrift. Planned stops were abandoned and the distant
promise of sunshine was the only hope. Again, the team thought

it was a step too far, but Lynne saw it differently. 'I knew I could do it. I could feel the speed increase and I was angry. Two days four hours – I kept repeating it in my head. I related it to things: the last 160 miles were an audax, the last 45 a club run, the last 10 a time trial.'

She finished an hour up on her previous record. It was a historic achievement – the first person since G. P. Mills to hold three End to End records, the first to break their *own* record. This time there was another target: the 1000 miles, the graveyard of hopes and dreams, the point where time becomes a permeable barrier between reality and unreality, when glass tumblers roll down the road and the icy, grasping fingers of the cold unstitch the seams in your psyche.

It was still Eileen's record. It was the ultimate. I stopped, wolfed down some food, had a massage, a sleep, got up and wondered who was going to start the clock, but of course it was still ticking! I could see some cloud and rain, and I thought, Oh no, rain! Dad had cleaned my bike! But I rode away from it and carried on, stopping at 1016 miles. I'd broken my End to End and this was a bonus, in a way. When we got back Mum had put some banners up, posters. Welcome home, record holder!

The day after she went through Slochd summit, it was closed by snow.

The statistics for her ride are demented. The first 500 miles were covered in thirty hours and the second in thirty-four, with an hour or so of sleep at John o'Groats. It defies belief: End to End attempts taper, they diminish sharply, and the 1000 is a steadily flatlining race to the bottom. Not for Lynne. 'I've always been like that, it's just the way I ride. I give it my all, but I pace it.'

One comment keeps coming back to me: *Lynne is nails.* We

talk some more, as the rain drums on the corrugated roof of the shop, an incessant reminder of the conditions she faced. We talk about Christina Mackenzie who attempted the record in 2019, gave it everything but lost it on Helmsdale and Berriedale. Lynne lay awake at night dot-watching, reliving the experience, then burst into tears when she realised she might not make it – an empathy for the struggle and the desire to put everything into it, only to miss out after 750 miles. Like everyone else, she knows the record is there to be broken. The achievement sits lightly on her shoulders.

> I feel absolutely chuffed to bits. I'm not sure it gets the recognition it should, but I don't shout about it. It's nice when a customer comes in and asks if I ride a bike, and I say I do a bit of racing, and they can be a bit funny, then I say that I hold the record, and they change – and that's quite amusing. It's nice to say that I own that record. It's good for my confidence. We have a lot of ladies who come in and ask about the End to End and I can offer advice and experience. Somebody does it every week, it seems, and it's great. I'm going to carry on riding and racing. I was thinking about doing the 24, a quarter of a century of 24s. Ultimately, I'm not going to stop.

I mention that I am thinking of doing the 24, because I feel inspired by Lynne and everyone else. I want to know what it's like. I don't want to know about shitting in a bucket though – I think I'll find alternative means of ablution. Then I realise in terror that I have said it out loud. There is a pause in the conversation.

'So we'll see your name on the start-sheet next year then?' says Lynne.

'Yes . . . I definitely heard that as well!' says John.

I regret it immediately.

20

Days are where we live

Friday, 15 June 2018, 8 a.m.

Michael Broadwith is attempting the End to End, two months before my syncopated stutter northwards was to begin. There have been recent attempts by other men and women, mostly dissolving into puddles of sweat and angst just north of Preston. People climb off, adamant that if the wind was stronger, or the bike faster, or the other variables more controlled then it would have been different. Somehow they ignore the last, most salient fact, the hardest thing to say: 'I wasn't quick enough'. The rest is just details.

Four support vehicles play an elaborate game of leapfrog. The Arctic SRAM van is crammed with bikes, tyres, wheels, equipment, a larder of bike food and five hardened men. Pete Ruffhead is driving. He is the sponsor and Steve Nunn from Barnet his wingman. Tim Bayley sits in front of a spaghetti of wires and screens. Tim knows what it is like to ride along the precipice of oblivion. Jon Williams also knows. He is taking time out of his preparations for the Mersey 24 in order to observe for the RRA. But no one knows more about long, dark years of the soul than Steve Abraham, who finished his year with 72,000 miles on the clock – further than I've driven in ten years. Car two contains legendary stopwatch wielder John Pick. Riding shotgun is the serene Bridget Boon. She is among the strongest 24-hour riders ever. Friends, family and acquaintances round out the team. In car three sits team leader Helen Simpson, wife of Michael and mother of eight-month-old Poppy. I find it hard taking our kids to the park at the end of the road, let alone taking them to the park 840 miles away in Scotland. Ian Boon observes in the same car. Together, the Boons have got a competition record for something demented on a tandem which no one dares try to take from them. There is also a psychedelic camper van with signs that give notice that this van is doing special things. It contains Mike's uncle and aunt, a wardrobe of fancy dress costumes and an illuminated sign saying 'Mike'.

These are the people mad enough to drive to Scotland at 20mph with no sleep. This is the dream team, crossing the county lines in a slow-moving convoy of calculation and anxiety. I am on my way to meet them at Bristol and following on the WhatsApp group. Everyone is happy. Cornish towns are disappearing beneath the hum of tubulars and the swoosh of the disc wheel. Locals peer nervously at the curious iron horse hurtling through Okehampton. The brown stuff hits the whirly thing near Bridgwater. Bicycles are 20mph faster than cars when the road is a constipated mess. Mike is on his own, without food or water.

Anxiety permeates each key stroke on the WhatsApp thread. I volunteer to do a hand-up in Bristol. Then I realise my bottles are disgusting; I spot some sea monkeys circulating in the one I left on my bike. I smashed through my last three gels earlier in the week when I bonked massively on a 15-mile ride home from work. I run out the door to buy some. My bag sits against my back and I can feel the sweat congealing like mozzarella on a cold pizza. I already smell bad. I get the bus. It stops on Whiteladies Road and it is full of starry-eyed A Level students because it is university open day. And it is stuck, not going anywhere, and the bus driver won't let me get off. I have made a terrible tactical error. Eventually we inch forward a few more metres, within the parameters of health and safety, and he relents. I make it to the top of Bridge Valley Road and stand by the side of the Downs, waiting for a van full of men.

I have to run. It's like a post train in a western film – I'm the bag of letters and I need to be at the side of the road, by the zoo. I'm going to be bundled into the back of a moving van then hurled out somewhere north of the border while they stalk a

man on a bike for two days at about 20mph. Mike appears over the crest. He sees me and grabs the hand-up. He says, 'Cheers Paul.' It's Friday, 5 p.m., and I'm standing at the top of Bridge Valley Road in Bristol. I haven't screwed it up. I will be allowed in the van. It appears five minutes later, and I'm bundled in. Finally I am Jock Wadley and Bernard Thompson. Sort of.

The van is hectic. There is stuff and wires everywhere. The following cars converge. Mike is a hypotenuse heading northwards to the beat of a 220-watt drum. Steve Nunn wants a Cornish pasty, but it is 100 miles too late. Steve Abraham is traumatised from an experience with some Cornish cheese.

We pass through 259 miles in twelve hours, hurtling slowly through the heavy flood plain, the line graph of the Malvern Hills drawn with a ruler against the half-light. A policeman flashes his lights. It's OK; he's a big fan and has been

Author photo

Jon Williams observing

dot-watching in the custody suite. A clubman plays the bugle at the side of the road. A short stop is called by Helen – cold soup from the tin, and not gazpacho. Mike whispers conspiratorially to Helen, 'This event is ridiculous.' How do you reply? Rhetorical questions about what bears get up to in the woods spring to mind.

We press on towards Kidderminster where revellers look up from kebabs in alcoholic confusion at the slippery sight. The van stops at Wolverhampton. I smash through my burger. Jon Williams drops his chips on the floor and we leave them for the locals. We are living the dream. Steve Abraham eats more cheese. Steve Nunn still wants a Cornish pasty. There is the seductive promise of stronger winds, but also rain. We head out again and get as close as we can, headlights on full beam, illuminating the road. Mike is tapping it out at 21mph.

The Garmin stops working. The new one doesn't work either; it's running backwards and directing Mike to Land's End. Tim Bayley throws it in the back to me and asks me to sort it out. I panic. I turn it off and on again and reload the course and it seems to work. Suddenly I have a purpose again. The chain unships so we swap in another Garmin and the stop-start ends. We are off again, but it's less fluid and the undulations have increased.

Stafford arrives and people cheer. The rhythm returns. The roadside presence provokes goosebumps, with whole families out to support, before hurtling up the road to cheer again. People in different-coloured jerseys indicate the shift in district. Mike is stitching together the club colours in a thread of social history, a colourful line connecting us all in a common endeavour. Meanwhile, in the van we worry about the gilet: it's bunched up. Marginal gains. The overshoes are a hit though; 'they're like luminous Ugg boots' someone says. Steve Abraham reels through his almanac of cycling endurance stories, including the one about the abscess and the mess. I hope there won't be any further stories of suppurating lesions.

And onwards through the post-industrial northern corridor of Preston and Carnforth. Dawn carefully negotiates with night and the darkest indigo pulses swirl outwards in liquid fractals. A figure in a yellow Preston Wheelers jacket is cheering. It's Gethin Butler, the current record holder, here in fellowship. The wind picks up and flutters the feather flags of garages, drawing a fist-pump from Mike. A thumbs-up at the county marker for Cumbria, a smile. He is forty minutes up. The Lakeland hills loom with Shap Fell a silent shadow under a somnolent slate-grey sky. Shap is the reckoner; Jon Williams says it has done for many illustrious riders. A shake of the weather and the incline is enough to unsettle the legs and heart. We wait at the top in a layby, and while waiting I impose images I have seen before, riders in the fog, in and out of the saddle.

Mike's front light pierces through the fog of the summit. He is untroubled. Twenty seconds is enough for a layer and snack. Mike clocks Gethin. 'Thank you so much,' he says. It affects

Author photo

Michael Broadwith and the layby of dreams

him, he feels pressure. Gethin always turns out to support. He values the record and knows what it takes to do this as a solo endeavour and succeed.

The border beckons, and with it, the 24-hour record. The rain arrives in solid streams. Six miles are required in 14 minutes. A sprint prime. Coordinates are taken, a mark painted – provisionally an incredible 507.8 miles. Rivulets of rain arc up from the back wheel. The climbs loom like whales under the tarmac, floating up to the surface and raising the incline into enormous humpbacks of hardship. They roll and break and flumes of spray cascade down. The temperature refuses to improve but Mike pulses remorselessly onwards, now forty-five minutes up on schedule. We feel good but dare not voice it.

And then the cold seeps through, ameliorated briefly by a stop for hot food. The helpers are drenched and time is slipping, back to thirty minutes up at Kelty, the pernicious fingers of cold pick-pocketing seconds and minutes. Mike is struggling. His neck hurts – it could be Shermer's syndrome, where neck muscles go beyond fatigue and refuse to help. By 1.43 p.m., heat pads, paracetamol and ibuprofen are ready. The ride is in the balance. Optimism evaporates like heat shimmer over an arid lake bed of depression and fear. The stretch through to Perth is a purgatory and the sleep-addled support team struggle to keep things on track as the average speed plummets. Mike is broken. The record attempt is slipping through his fingers and we know it. It is over. Helen gets ready to pull the plug. Mike wants respite; he gets a bike change.

The people who are watching online refresh the tracker, hoping for more. How do you judge the moment? You know it is going to be dark, but just how dark it can get is impossible to process. Mike props up his head with an elbow on the armrest. Helen tells him to do it for twenty minutes. Then another twenty minutes. *He does this for 200 miles.* A flatter bit delays the decision. There surely can't be any more water left in the spiteful Scottish sky. The schedule is down, now only twelve minutes up, and time continues to haemorrhage. A message floats across the group – 'it is now only theoretically possible' – deflating any vestiges of hope.

Tim tries the hospital in desperation for a neck brace but they can't help unless he books in. Mike's neck might be collapsing in on itself but now is not the time to test hospital waiting times. We need fortitude and hope. Lynne Taylor provides it, calling in contacts and finding someone with a neck brace. The 1526 feet of Drumochter Pass go on for ever; time slips away down the mountain and spirits ebb with every lost second. We know what's coming: more horrible climbs, undulating coast roads and the effect of sleep deprivation, the struggles of Andy Wilkinson and Ralph Dadswell, the hallucinations, the confusion – all this lies ahead.

We wait for Helen to make the call. We support and help.

'He is begging me not to make him go on because he feels unsafe. I believe in him so much but he can't hold his own head.'

Over Drumochter, finally, and there are 9 miles of descent until Aviemore. It seems so close, but it's a long way to the finish 145 miles away. Mike resorts again to the 'Rodin's Thinker' position and makes it safely down. A full stop is planned at the Black Isle, a chance to regroup and assess. Helen remembers holidaying in Inverness with Mike. She has a plan. Mike loved Inverness. He knows it is riding distance to the finish. There is soup, porridge, a complete kit change. Everyone sets out to sell the deal.

The gloom lifts slightly, the van is warm, the kit is nice, the food replenishes and the stop is 'Formula 1 team but better', says Helen. But the anxiety and fear of everything that went before remains. Mike jettisons the neck brace. He can't breathe. Faced with a choice of breathing or holding his neck, he chooses the latter.

Suddenly, a minute has been clawed back. It feels significant.

Tired minds struggle to reconcile the figures, but we agree it leaves the small matter of a six-hour 100 needed for the record. We'll ignore the thirty-seven-hour 740 that went before. It might be possible. People are staying awake. The internet is going bananas. GO MIKE!

He can't look up, he is exhausted, but he thinks he can do it. Now is not the time for regrets; this is the moment on which the ride turns. Mike knows he can tap it out. He knows it is on. Somehow he ekes out time, stealing it from the monstrous hands of fatigue and pain. He gives a thumbs-up at Invergordon. No one knows how he is still going. He has Helmsdale, Berriedale and the coast road to go.

The late-night revellers of Helmsdale are intrigued. 'What, since eight a.m. on Friday? But it's Sunday. I don't get it. Forty-one hours?' They are thrilled and excited by the incomprehensible. 'GO MIKE!' they shout. He rips up the climb. He is relatively heavy and relatively fast and hits the climb of Berriedale next. His interior monologue is working, just not his neck.

And we all feel it, but we don't express it at the time or later. We are living a moment in time with perfect intensity and something special is happening and we are all a part of it. Only the coast remains. 'Climb after climb after bloody climb,' says Mike. Steve Abraham stands at the side of the road, then runs alongside: 'You can do this, Mike, you got this, Mike, you've got it, you can do it . . .'

And we realise absolutely he's going to do it. It is a feat beyond the imagination, a triumph of strength and determination, of support and fellowship. Everyone moves forward to take up position in John o'Groats. Mike rolls in as low-key fireworks explode gently. John Pick does his second job of the trip, pressing the stop button some 43 hours, 25 minutes and 13 seconds after he pressed the start button.

It's half three in the morning. People are shattered. Pete Ruffhead grins, broadly, tears never far away. Helen holds Poppy. No one knows what to do, how to move, where to stand, what to say; they share a look, an 840-mile stare. Mike is propped against the car door, eating food. Tentative plans are made for a celebration later. Mike wonders where people are going, what they are doing. No one really knows.

'Well done, Mike, get some sleep,' says Ian Boon.

'What are you doing now?' asks Mike.

'Er, I dunno,' Ian replies. 'What can you do in John o'Groats?'

21

Riding in circles at John o'Groats looking for Mum

Wednesday, 3 July 2019

There are two days to go. I ride into the fourth consecutive day of remorseless wind. It means stops and tea and patience and food. The wind is supposed to swing around tonight and promises kindness. The prevailing wind direction has abandoned any pretence of normality; from Bradford to here has been a dispiriting slog. I look online at wind rose diagrams and they lie to me. For all my disappointment, those heading the other way are doubtless cock-a-hoop, full of the feeling of unfettered strength that tailwind-riding confers on the lucky investee. They hurtle from John o'Groats to Land's End in joyous oblivion.

I slog across the Black Isle and skirt the Cromarty Firth. It bears witness to North Sea industry: huge oil rigs sit low in the water. They are mothballed, waiting for an upturn in the price of oil to be sent back out to sea. In the interim, they form a grid of giants tethered to the floor of the firth. It is a boneyard. I count six of the rusting arachnids as I struggle along the A9 past Invergordon towards Tain and lunch in the van with Mum. There is an added incentive in the shape of the Glenmorangie Distillery. We eat sandwiches, drink hot tea, and tour the museum. I am tempted to knock back the whisky in preparation for the rest of the ride but opt to keep it for later.

The landscape is changing, flattening and dropping away to the coast. It is emptier with each mile. Houses slump in ruins at the side of the road, collapsed crofting cottages, once short and squat, tucked in out of the wind, now condemned. Inverness seemed like the last gasp; from here it is isolation and quietude, with Wick the nearest 'big' place. The plan is for a shorter last day, 70 miles or so to finish, riding out from Brora tomorrow. Mum is parked in the Caravan Club site. It backs on to the golf club which forms an immaculate wall of green between the pitches and the sea. Time is on our side and finally the wind is dropping, just as they said it would. We walk down to the beach but are warned by the site manager to watch out for the Arctic terns. They are nesting in the dunes and get quite aggressive if you come near. I look up the Arctic tern later. I wish I hadn't. They are migratory. Like me, they do journeys, except they travel 330km per day on a 35,000km journey and they don't fret or write about it. In about a month's time they will head off to Antarctica for five months. When heading back again they don't follow the same route but loop up in a huge S pattern. I am chastened.

The beach is beautiful. It is a stand-in for the Caribbean, a meme: people post it and everyone says it's St Lucia, or the Seychelles, when really it's the north of Scotland. The temperature is dropping: four days ago it was 27 degrees in Bradford, now it is 16 degrees and falling. Within moments the terns start circling, screeching and dive-bombing as we walk on the beach. They hover and scream, swoop to within centimetres and roll away, before coming in for another sortie.

There are jellyfish, huge hallucinatory blobs of colour and squish; raging angry purple colours, brain shapes and alien matter. I walk around them, but poke one with my toe and it quivers, a gooey mass. I try not to see it as a metaphor for something but fail. This would be my hallucination, coming out of the trees in the depths of sleep deprivation, a seething ocean creature come to colonise my brain and scare me to death. It is my mind, squishing out in a horrible mess, beached somewhere.

Brora is a transcendent place. There is no one here, just me and Mum. We mug for the camera, laugh, take selfies. We go back to the van and drink whisky. I have nearly finished. I think I can do this.

Author photo

Mum at Brora

THE HAIRPIN BEND OF BERRIEDALE HILL, ON THE ROAD TO JOHN O'GROATS. A.4253

The next morning I dance on the pedals as I ride out of Brora. Finally, the wind has changed. Would I have swapped four days of headwind for one day of tailwind, on the last day? I am uncertain. It has been hard, but now I feel liberated by things. I am the horses in the field and the strutting crow combined into one messy, shaking, excitable person. The bike swooshes and I am flying along the road. Helmsdale barely makes a sound, a long and draggy climb through huge tweed swatches of moorland heather. The wind is with me at last. Helmsdale collapses into Berriedale, which is steeper. It has the mythic hairpin sections. Heavy machinery is doing something to the road; it is possible the hairpins may be untethered from the edge of the climb, consumed by progress, with the road placed directly across the top. There might be no more photos of people walking or riding through this particular amphitheatre. It is steep, a challenge, but I enjoy every inch of the road, knowing that there are no climbs left to do. I'm being pushed up by a heavy hand and it is a joy.

The road drops down and slides towards the end, green on either side with the grey of the North Sea sitting silently on my shoulder. The road is grippy, the tarmac uneven, and the rain begins to come down. I remember Eileen Sheridan saying how the right wind usually brings the rain, and she is right. It starts to whip across in drizzly waves as the fields slip down to the sea. I pass Latheron and then Bruan Broch, a crown-shaped turf mound, thousands of years old. The landscape is littered with cairns; it is primitive, atavistic and unnerving. The life has been sucked out of the area in a process of gradual depopulation. People no longer want to live at the edges, they move to the centre until the periphery becomes the place we go to get away from the centre. Outbuildings and granite outcrops merge beneath grey, lumbering clouds. The road falls apart as it falls towards the sea, past Pictish place names like Lybster, Occumster, Ulbster and Thrumster; they all slip beneath the tyres. Wick is a real town, full of people and chain-stores, a generic high street made of dark granite buildings and a certain civic pride. The angular streets give way again, suddenly, to greenery. There is no blurred boundary here between country and town, just a wall and a fence.

It is featureless and flat, the green of the fields divided from the sea only by a sultry, blurred line of hedgerow. The highest thing is the dry-stone wall and the gorse growing out. I feel deflated; the beauty of the landscape is behind me. The place names speak of waves of occupants: Skirza, Huna, the Vikings taking over from the Picts in the kingdom of Cait. They would recognise it today.

I sense a change in myself. For the first time I feel like I'm repairing something – confidence, capability perhaps. I am proving that I can do things. I thought the journey would be a steady process of restorative calm and ideas and phrases would leap up out of the road surface. I did not realise that I hadn't quite got to a restorative point. I realise that now. I wanted to write a book which mapped a landscape and other people and ended up instead mapping the contours of my mind. It is an

unfortunate coincidence that my life of employment and structure and regularity fell apart at the same time as I was supposed
to be articulating what things mean. I think about what I
have done, or not managed to do. I threw everything into this
adventure, the staged process of mapping the landscape and
seeing how and what other people had done. I tried to be brave,
to demonstrate that I had willpower and could ride my bike a
really long way if I wanted to, only to discover that willpower
is not enough for me. The feeling that I will be finishing soon
hits me hard. I think of Eileen, and Mike, and Lynne, and all
the others, but that isn't it. It is the thousands of other people
who have traced this line on a map and done this thing, and
lived purely and absolutely, both with joy and with staggering
misery, in that time.

I ride past a bed and breakfast offering sea views. It is called
Sea View. At last an unbroken connection between sign and sig-
nifier. One last limpid brown promontory and I can see the sea
ahead and a view of islands in the grey waters, the same islands
that confused Andy Wilkinson. The sign offers a 'welcome at the
end of the road', and the one-storey whitewashed guest house is

Author photo

The best-looking guest house in the world

the first to greet people, the last step before the road drops down to the last hotel before the ocean.

It is cold and now really wet, and John o'Groats is a terrifying place. It has all the romance of the end of the known world, amplified by a Scottish summer. The sea of the Pentland Firth is a violent, swirling cauldron, the ocean roaring through the gap between the mainland and Stroma, a once-inhabited island in the tidal stream. Orkney lies beyond. It is the grimmest place in the world. It exists in unrefined, unwelcoming beauty and I feel a profound sense of anti-climax, standing at the sign in the heaving rain and wind, taking a record of the moment the ride finished and real life began again. I think back to Land's End, to Harman and Blackwell, and their words ring true in my ears: 'the 20 miles to John O'Groats requires no description. There was nothing to be seen but bleak moor and ditch. I cannot help expressing my disappointment at the celebrated terminus, and surprise that so many tourists should ever go so far ...'

Mum is not here. I am not surprised. Mum is never where she is supposed to be. I head back to the car park and find the van. It is empty. There must be bargains somewhere. I remember our day-trip to the Whitworth. We went to Sainsbury's first thing to get a croissant. She disappeared in the aisles, returning ten minutes later with a 5kg bag of potatoes because they were 'cheaper than in Morrisons'. I struggled to carry them round for the rest of the day in my bag. No, it doesn't surprise me that she is not here. In fact, it seems entirely right and appropriate. To her credit, she had calculated that I might be a little while because I had been so painfully slow and late over the last few days.

There are two or three shops and a café. I remember the time I was six years old and got lost in Banbury's department store in Barnstaple. I ran around in circles looking for my mum. This is the grown-up version. I ride around in circles at the literal end of the road and look for my mum. Finally she emerges from the rain and mist. We hug, then try to take a photo in the rain and wind. It is not one for the family album. Some people ask if I've done the journey. I say yes, sort of. Mum chimes in, 'Yes he has, and it took him a lot of effort and I'm really proud of him.'

On the way home, Mum decides to enact her own ultra-endurance event by driving from the tip of Scotland to Bradford in one go. I realise this quite early on from the steely look in her eye. She has had enough and wants to go home. I do not argue. She has been riding her bike a lot more these days with the Queensbury Queens, a ladies' group near Bradford who do wonderful things for participation and for women who want to get out on a bike but need guidance. It emerges that she hasn't yet sought their advice on whether you wear pants with Lycra, and asks me instead. When I tell her *no*, the response is inappropriate and unprintable, so obviously I'm printing it here.

'You mean you don't put the pants on? Oh Christ, Paul, I been putting the pants on. I been putting lard and butter on. It's rubbed me raw.'

I never want to hear any of these words in this order ever again.

I look out the window at Dornoch Firth. Up ahead a cattle lorry is creeping along the road. Every time it goes uphill a river of liquid sewage pours out of the back and covers the front of the camper van. The windscreen wipers succeed only in smearing it back and forth, the screenwash diluting it into an opaque, hot-chocolatey smudge of cowshit. It is not the best end to a ride.

The journey is as exhausting as the days prior to it. We stop at Perth and eat supermarket veggie burgers. I still feel deflated. I have been looking so hard for meaning, yet even at the last no truth shattered the air. I am no closer to knowing what to do with my life, how to be a better person, how to cope with things and what to do next.

*

I get home. I have more horrible job interviews. I spend a memorably shitty day being grilled by people who have a lazy hypothesis about me. I know they are wrong and one day it will fall apart around their ears. Their certainty will collapse because it is an unmortared wall of arrogance. This doesn't help me while I sit in offices as part of an egocentric powerplay, and when I go home I feel bruised and cry about it. But something *has* changed, some small kindling spark. Maybe it was the hostile interview process, but I begin to recognise that the choices I made weren't fickle, terrible errors. They were the right decisions, for my family and for my fragile mental health. It doesn't make the fall-out from them any easier, but it helps to be able to see it from outside of myself.

I have an interview to be a writer, full-time, and I don't cry in front of the panel, and I might even have made a good account of myself in front of people who seemed genuine and thoughtful and nice and caring. I dream about writing the word 'writer' on my passport. They tell me I'm not the right fit; they say I'm a long-form person and that I have a niche and this job isn't really these things. I know they are right. I go back to my niche manuscript, secretly grateful because I hadn't told my wife how much – how *little* – the post paid.

I have another interview for a full-time job. Teaching interviews are bizarre. Everyone is herded into a room and you spend the day trying not to upset each other. I keep quiet because it seems too complicated to say 'Oh I used to do this but then I lost my mind and then I did this and I do this writing and stuff and try and make sense of myself and the world around me through long, awful bike journeys that show how wonderful other people are and how rubbish I am.' I allude to 'projects' and 'time off' so as not to unsettle the other candidates with a bizarre work history and too much emotion. Everyone is full and frank about their current experiences, unencumbered by baggage and younger – so much younger, with taut skin and a sheen of innocence. Everyone seems to have chosen Greta Thunberg for their non-fiction teaching task and I feel adrift. I like Greta Thunberg but I never would have thought to choose her. Instead I have chosen an extract from Harman and Blackwell.

Someone mentions driving home for six hours in one of the winter's named storms and I feel like I understand this; I see it in deeply figurative terms. I think of Wolverhampton, all the A roads I've ridden in the course of this book, and I start romanticising and I can't stop. I say, 'Yes, you must have really lived during that time, been alive through the storm, thinking in different ways, and living in a way that the M6 doesn't typically allow you to live.' The room goes very quiet.

I manage not to cry at the interview, but it is close. My bottom lip quivers but I bite hard and hold it in. Instead I cry down the phone when they tell me I have got the job. My wife finds me crying and doesn't know if I've got the job or haven't got the job. I am a different kind of John Woodburn and it is hard to know. I tell her, and she holds me so close, and I never want to let go of her, of this moment when things feel better and repaired and full of love. I feel a forgotten feeling of pure, untempered happiness. I wonder how the other candidates reacted. '*What?* You gave it to the silent older bloke who made the gnomic comment about driving in the rain and taught a lesson about bikes?' And I laugh at the madness of it all.

22

The Cowdenbeath Carnival

Monday, 19 August 2019, 11 a.m.

I meet up with Helen Simpson and Mike Broadwith to talk about everything. It has the trappings of a bit of family therapy, trying to process this monumental thing that happened, and what it means. We are in the churchyard of the Oxford college where Mike studied Maths. It is removed from the aimless smudge of tourists. The chimes, conversations and echoes of the city drift across in a heat haze of summer sun. I ask how things were in the aftermath, using the words 'head, limbs, undercarriage'.

> When we got back to the hotel I couldn't sleep so I sat with Poppy in the foyer trying to process the WhatsApp thread. I didn't feel too bad but I went downhill badly once we got home. I was entirely awake at 3 a.m. every night. I had all these cold sores by Wednesday. I went to the doctor, who said, 'What did you expect?' I phoned Gethin on the Friday

and he had felt the same, had gone to the doctor's and had a similar response. It was reassuring in that it was expected.

Helen and I noticed a slight difference in posture, a slant. There was other damage. 'My hand was totally numb; I had a few issues eating with a fork. One finger feels like it's made of rubber.' Or as Helen puts it, 'When he drank a cup of tea he looked like he was doing that thing where you stick your pinky out.'

I struggled on the way back from the record attempt just from being in the van. I couldn't sleep and was wide awake on a train for ten hours, my mind racing in a state of addled exhaustion. It took most of the team a full week or more to feel normal. I mention to Helen that I think it works on two levels: it's physically and mentally exhausting, but at the same time it's a very peculiar thing to do; you go to a strange place and you need some form of reintegration afterwards. What was normal before is now strange because of the extraordinary nature of the experience, the geography of it, both inwardly and outwardly. A change occurs and the nature of this transition is hard to explain to people. Mike agrees. 'Land's End was ordinary, there were normal people there having normal meals, and it's a normal holiday place. However, John o'Groats was anything but. There was no one there, it was a weird twilight, an intense location with rough seas and everyone lacking sleep. Dave [Hill, the driver of Helen's car] said he stood there looking at the sea for a long period of time, unable to process where he was or what had happened.' Or as Helen puts it simply, 'The crew had spent forty hours not doing anything without knowing what the next thing was, and suddenly there was nothing to do, and it's a long way to Inverness and you can't be bothered and you go from extreme structure to nothing whatsoever.'

We piece together how all of this came about. Mike toured from Land's End to John o'Groats when he was nineteen, taking three weeks to do it with friends Rob Pitt and Rich Taylor, who later ended up on the support team. They did crazy things – stopped to climb Ben Nevis, went clubbing. Mike resolved to come back one day and do it a bit quicker. He liked 'maps, extreme places, islands, bridges, peninsulas'. He used to race against Gethin Butler and 'always got thrashed . . . I never dreamed I would be good enough to do it, but I was interested in his story, had a bit of hero worship.'*

It changed, as it did for many, with the 24-hour. 'In my first 24 I went so much further than I'd ever dreamt of going so it opened up lots of conversations that I hadn't expected.' I think of Jim Turner, the Williams clan, John Taylor, their eyes lighting up – they see the possibilities. The paperwork appears, gentle conversations, a nudge here and there.

> We did the 24 again the next year. I had a bad time. It was my own stupid fault. I took a couple of bottles that I found in a garage that were really old, gave myself low-level food poisoning but still won it by a long way. I then started having the conversation with Helen and with work. The hardest thing is getting to the start line. There are no other competitors. If you did 44.08 no one would give a shit. You can't say 'I'm the second-best person ever'.

Helen was good to go, until she became pregnant and did what I did, resigned from her job. 'Suddenly it seemed like the worst imaginable timing – three kids, got to find a new job, tiny baby to look after. I didn't appreciate the scale of the task. It's a

---

* After I met with Gethin some months later I mentioned it to Mike. He wanted to know what Gethin felt when he came out on the Shap to see him come past. I say, 'He felt solidarity.' Mike was overwhelmed. The validation, the kinship. It's all we want. To be recognised by those we look up to.

moveable feast; you don't know when you're going and people have lives to lead. I resolved to do it properly. No dodgy bottles!'

We talk again about the picture of Dave Keeler in the fog of Aultnamain. It is the same course, the same event. They are teammates across time taking part in the most amazing thing. Helen recognises the affinity. 'It has changed, but the images are the same, the pictures of exhausted people handing up bottles, helping in the darkness, the same climbs. Eileen and Michael discussed Berriedale. It is the same timeless experience, both in 1955 and 2018.' Mike is animated by this.

> Everyone has ridden the Shap, crossed at Gretna. Those key parts of the landscape are the same. And it means something extraordinary to people. Yes, different things to different people; but intense meaning is what defines it for the individual. The burly chap with the red jacket on Shap, no one knew who he was. He wrote me this letter. He had cancer and had watched the Woodburn film when ill. There is a scene in the film of Woodburn coming up the Shap. This guy recovered and he set himself the task to ride from Land's End to John o'Groats and he said he stopped in *that layby* and cried and cried, looking out over the scene. He had got over cancer and felt this affinity with Woodburn. When he heard I was going to ride it, he knew he had to be there at that moment.

It is the layby of dreams. I have stood there, overwhelmed by emotion. Anywhere can be a place of pilgrimage, a Madonna del Ghisallo,* because it is about what a place means, not what

---

* The Madonna del Ghisallo is a small chapel at the top of a hill near Lake Como. Pope Pius XII confirmed the Madonna as the 'patroness of cyclists' at the request of local priest Father Ermelindo Vigano. It is a shrine and museum with artefacts from the sport, along with an 'eternal flame' for cyclists who have died.

it is. I felt the ghosts of every rider who had crossed the summit. A record attempt stitches a thread through the landscape, joining together all of the interested people, the club jerseys, caps and colours, their stories and feelings. These ripples of meaning move outwards from start to finish and write new stories on top of the old myths. In prosaic terms it has changed my life. I've spent three years writing about it, talking to people. I think about all the other people who give up their time to ensure the individual at the centre can achieve this dream. By give up time I mean nearly five days in total, existing on a sleepless diet of garage snacks and stress.

> People were falling over themselves to contribute. Bridget said, 'So you want Ian to come as well?' We've kept thanking people, for time and support and enthusiasm, and saying, 'What do we owe you?' And they say, 'No, thanks for letting me be a part of it!' Timekeeper John Pick said, 'It'll be the biggest honour of my timekeeping career to do this'. He must have said thank you over a million times. He was in tears in the end.

Being a timekeeper is probably one of the easier jobs, pressing the same button twice, two days apart. No printouts. Just be careful you don't accidentally switch it off or something. As well as local legends like the Boons and Pick, they also had cult hero Steve Abraham. 'He had total faith, more than anyone. Even in the lowest points, he said, "You can still do it." When I was moaning about my neck, I thought, As if Steve would give a shit if his neck gave up.' I sense these outsider figures throughout the End to End, the obsessives, artists of a sort – a single, unambiguous passion.

From the start of Broadwith's ride, currents of meaning flowed outwards in disparate ways, sparked by encounters and chance. 'At the start this guy from Penzance Wheelers came out with his two little kids. They came and spoke to me and I thought, Wow, you two little children think I'm someone worth talking to. I gave them a little maths test.' These children are part of a chain of memories which link together into something so much more coherent and bigger. Mike recalls others, some less benign, but equally a part of the narrative and the myth:

> Outside Penzance a chap in a purple Nissan Micra pulled alongside, wound down the window, said, 'I hope you fucking fail!' and then drove off. I laughed. He was stuck in traffic. When I got to Bristol there was this little old lady going 'Mike, it's this left', and I thought, Who are you old lady? Wow, brilliant, what's going on? I've entered an alternative reality. But of course it was Janet Tebbutt, *the* Janet Tebbutt.
>
> I remember these snippets of people cheering, shouting hello, a little old lady in a deckchair clapping at 1.30 a.m. I have a friend, Laura from Penrith, she made these savoury snacks. She phoned her dad who is in a nursing home to tell him I was coming and he needed to be outside to watch. I went through Penrith at 5.15 a.m. and there was this old gent outside a nursing home waving a stick – 'Go on Mike!' – and I realised suddenly who it was. 'You're Laura's dad?' I said, like he didn't know he was Laura's dad, but I wanted to make sure that he knew I knew.

But none of these can hold a candle to the Cowdenbeath Carnival. It came immediately after the darkest bit of the ride, when it was pissing down with rain with a long way to go. Mike had a bit of a wobble, took a while to get going again, but managed to keep moving. They took a right turn in Cowdenbeath, following the map, when suddenly a ROAD CLOSED sign and endless cones blocked the road. A deus ex machina in the form of a Tring expatriate living in Edinburgh hurtled round the corner on his bike and yelled, 'It's the Cowdenbeath Carnival, Mike, go for it!'

> They came out of the holding pen as I came through, and there were floats with bands, majorettes, the whole town marching, in the pouring rain, and I thought, This is the world's shittest carnival ever. People were hiding under bus shelters, these poor, tiny majorettes were soaked, hoodies stretched down to their knees by the weight of the water. There's me on a time trial bike coming through. Over there somewhere is reality and this is not it. Cowdenbeath is not the prettiest place at the best of times but this was the greyest, wettest, crappiest day. The guy from Tring followed me to make sure I didn't get lost. God knows what people thought – a guy on a high-tech road bike looking deeply confused, then another guy on a road bike chasing after him.

I imagine they thought it was part of the procession, some sort of tableau with an intense folk meaning. It is part of the ritual – Pauline Strong and the acid house convoy.

I see fit to ask Broadwith about the interior monologue. This is because when I ride, I talk to myself. Not always, but I do. It is a solitary activity and it keeps me company. I imagine everyone does this, but I am increasingly aware this might not be the case. I ask people anyway. Mike seems to know what I'm talking about.

> I decided to tell myself off if I went too hard on the climbs. I would say it out loud: 'Don't overgas . . . You're overgassing.' For my sixth formers the phrase of the day is 'Mr Broadwith, that's calm', so when I was sat on my power I was saying 'That's calm, no overgassing, that's calm', and I said it a

lot. At one point I hadn't said anything out loud for about eight hours, then I said something like 'Good', and I heard it and replied, 'Oh, hello internal voice, well done, thanks for coming back in the game, nice to have you back,' and then the internal voice would go, 'That's all right, you're welcome, cheers.'

Helen tells him he sounds like a fruit loop. Mike says you may as well talk to yourself. The experience for Helen in the car was the other extreme: a polyphonic array of voices, both real and rendered.

The support was fantastic, but became overwhelming; so many voices, at the side of the road, inside the vehicle, on WhatsApp, in the other car, Twitter, Facebook, every single direction. At points I had to block out the noise because there is only so much you can process on a massive lack of sleep and you have to choose what it is. Dave Hill was really important. He was calm, unassuming, got the event, got everything. He allowed me to manage everything else. You ask people to do stuff all the time which you don't do in normal life, and it feels bossy. The changes had to be sharp, you instruct, with no real sense of how people are responding. The decision about whether to get Mike back on his bike, I was eaten up about it, but he got what I was thinking. Your decision-making is hampered by lack of sleep, and it's your husband. Dave didn't pander to it or belittle it. He gave me a hug at one point when I needed it most.

I'm struck again by the scale of the team effort, from the Arctic team manager Pete Ruffhead – who seems to own a business selling air conditioning for the sole reason that he can fund a race team – to Tim Bayley, to the auntie and uncle in the camper van, everyone doing everything they can to make this happen and doing what Helen tells them to do.

We creep around to talking about when things started to go wrong. I've been avoiding it. I ask about it, delicately. Mike says, 'Oh, you mean when the weather began to turn and it all just slowly went to shit?' I nod. It felt like moments away from ending. Helen picks up the unspooling thread. 'It wasn't *moments*, it was a single moment away. Mike said, "My vision's bad, I don't feel safe, my neck is a mess," but there was a single point where he said, "You just don't understand, it's not safe for me to be out on the road, I need to stop. I'm really sorry, it's over."' Mike recalls it.

> In hindsight I was trying to convince Helen to let me stop. It was getting worse and worse, and I kept stopping. People were cheering me on and I thought, 'Why are you cheering? This is all over.' Then I did a really bad thing: I pitted Helen against Tim. I said to Tim, 'What would you do? Would you stop?' And Tim said, 'Of course I'd stop, this is ridiculous.' And I said to Helen, 'Tim knows,' then something bad like 'I can't see properly.' But the truth is I was just desperate to stop.

Tim and Mike go back a long way. They ride and race together. Tim is calm, mild-mannered and highly respected in all matters relating to bikes. It put Helen in a bind. 'Tim pulled me to the back of the road and said, "We shouldn't be doing this." In his mind it was over. The WhatsApp chat was full of people saying "well done", "Woodburn failed first time" and so on. I remember thinking, Oh God, *Tim* is saying it. I was frustrated, because although it was a psychological low, he was mentally very strong and the legs were strong.'

I suddenly remember it was me who said 'Woodburn failed first time'. I thought it was over. I was trying to help soften things. People felt crushed by disappointment, that this thing was falling apart.

At the centre of it, Helen made a suggestion.

Helen said, 'Can you do twenty minutes?' and from somewhere this fire of indignation came back – '*Of course* I can do twenty minutes.' She said, 'Off you go then.' I'm sure within three or four minutes I was totally back in the game. It warmed up and stopped raining, my mental state changed. Steve said, 'Get to Aviemore, it's 30 miles of descent.' I got there and it isn't anything like that, but I was laughing about it. 'Steve, you cheeky blighter, you had me!'

Inverness was a turning point on the ride for three reasons. The A9 is really shit and can be dispiriting. It is quieter after Inverness and the roads are more interesting. Mike and Helen went on holiday to the Highlands and to Inverness; it holds happy memories. And lastly, Mike really likes bridges and there are some sexy bridges on the last bit of the ride. We have some great bridge chat. 'I just really like bridges, from all points of view – aesthetically, symbolically. I am quite happy to sit on Wikipedia and read articles about bridges.' We both get quite excited about the bridge and tunnel that links Sweden to Denmark, discuss the saucy bridges in Norway. He is the opposite of Mick Coupe: no quaking, record-stopping terror at the Forth Bridge. The Kessock Bridge has come to matter more than most.

At the Kessock Bridge, people were still trying to persuade me to cheer up but I knew I was going to do it. I remember going through Helmsdale. I got to the top, it took a while, and I thought, I'm going to be all right. I rolled down to Berriedale, conscious that after the summit this was the key moment – effectively we're done, two hours to go. Helen was stood at the bottom bend and we knew it was Berriedale but I still asked her, and she said, 'Of course it's Berriedale.' It wasn't the question that was important, it was the shared recognition that we were *here*. And that's when I was suddenly conscious that I had to remember it, that everything I've ever done and thought about in getting to this point is happening right now, and the danger is I'll go through it and won't remember it afterwards.

My aunt and uncle were on the first hairpin, and then everyone was there and delighted to be there in that moment. I was climbing but with no effort and it was intense and overwhelming because everything that I wanted the ride to be was happening at that moment; and it was dark, I was within the glow of the headlights, and all the people I cared about were there but also everyone else who had ever done the ride was there: John Woodburn was there, Gethin, Eileen, Dave Keeler in the mist, and I'm on this bike, adding my name to that list, and I was overwhelmed – not by the effort, but by all of that. I just thought, This is me, living my very best life, living the moment I always wanted to live in the perfect intensity.

Tears itch in my eyes as he speaks and I do that funny breathing thing when you know you're going to cry. It is about being a part of this extraordinary thing, but there is also a realisation of what things mean, of some absolute truth, of what happens when you reach for the stars. Later on, listening back to the tape, I cry at the forcefulness of the moment, the visionary nature of it, and the fact that very few things ever have that force and power or occur in such a way. I had thought that all along the road when I was riding this would happen, and it never did. But it is happening now and I think I get it. Helmsdale and Berriedale are where it happens, because with the best will in the world, John o'Groats is not the place for damascene visions. I marvel at the silent and strong community, all of the people involved in this extraordinary thing over the years, the links between them when it comes to the record, the encouragement, but then the wider subtext of this being a journey that everyone has done and which means something to everyone.

> Huge numbers of people have done it, and for everyone it is a meaningful journey in their life. So many people have said to me 'I did it', and they start being all self-deprecating – 'Oh, it took me seven days so you won't care about me' – and every time I want to reply 'That's incredible!' Clearly for everyone that's what they've taken into work – *I did Land's End to John O'Groats*. They've enjoyed the journey, just like me, Pitto and Rich did twenty years ago. We were full of it, he still dines out on it. The time is irrelevant, the journey is the thing.

I did it. I pretty much imploded on the way. It created some breathing space of sorts, it muted everything else. The layers of meaning probably undermined me in the end; I was doing it to make sense of other people doing it, to know what people meant when they said 'Berriedale'. This in turn meant that I didn't ever really access the kind of feeling that comes from just *doing* it. I made it unnecessarily complicated with huge long stages and strange gaps. But I've come to realise, slowly, belatedly, that this book is the journey, and some other profound changes have been happening at the same time. Like the baddies in *Raiders of the Lost Ark*, I've been looking in the wrong place. This book is the End to End, not my painfully slow rides spread out across time like a stain on a tablecloth. I rode to gain experience so that I could write with clarity and truth about the journeys people take, the reasons why, the thoughts they have and the changes that happen to them.

Before all of this, in the immediate aftermath of leaving my job, I flew to Barcelona with my bike and rode home. It was an End to End through France. I did it, in the words of Janet Tebbutt, 'because it seemed like a good idea at the time'. It had meaning for me; it was joy and ambition combined. It became transcendent because I wasn't looking for transcendence and I wasn't writing about it. I thought of nothing. I rode up a huge climb and plummeted down to Perpignan, crossing the border on a gravel track, and I ate baguettes and cheese and saw huge eagles in the mountains and kingfishers in a fizzing flash of cobalt along the Canal du Midi. I tell Mike, while I try to keep my emotions in check, how these rides are important. He knows.

At heart, the reason I race is because I don't have the time to go touring and have adventures. One summer we were in Norfolk, our son Olly was with us, we just got on our bikes and rode. We had lunch and then rode back. It was the middle of the afternoon. We stopped and fell asleep in a field, woke up and rode home. That was a day when we thought about nothing, *nothing*, apart from cycling to a pub, to a field, sleeping, home. The journey became life, it became everything. One summer Rich and I toured for a whole summer in Pakistan, thinking of nothing all day – wake up, here's a map, let's go. It is those days, when everything is about the journey and everything you worry about normally – mortgage, work, that you haven't done your marking – is gone. The End to End is that journey for everyone.

Michael Broadwith and Eileen Sheridan

Bibliography

Books

Best, Isabel, *Queens of Pain: Legends and Rebels of Cycling* (London: Rapha Editions/Blue Train, 2018)

Chappell, Emily, *Where There's a Will* (London: Profile, 2019)

Cox, Peter (ed.), *Cycling Cultures* (Chester: University of Chester Press, 2015)

Green, Roy, *100 Years of Cycling Road Records* (Taunton: RRA, 1988)

Harrison, M. John, *Climbers* (London: Gollancz, 2013)

Hillaby, John, *Journey Through Britain* (London: Constable and Company, 1968)

Hudson, Mark (ed.), *The Rough Stuff Fellowship Archive* (London: Isola Press, 2019)

Ray, Alan J., *Cycling: Land's End to John o'Groats* (London: Pelham, 1971)

Sheridan, Eileen, *Wonder Wheels: The Autobiography of Eileen Sheridan* (London: Nicholas Kaye Limited, 1956)

Taylor, John, *The 24 Hour Story* (Cannock: Btown Bikes, 2005)

Taylor, John, *The 'End to End' Story* (Cannock: Btown Bikes, 2005)

Thompson, Bernard, *Alpaca to Skinsuit: 50 Years of Time Trialling* (Gearings of Ashford: 1988)

Whitfield, Peter, *12 Champions* (Charlbury: Wychwood, 2007)

Whitfield, Peter, *Time, Speed and Truth: A History of Time
    Trialling 1890 to 2010* (Charlbury: Wychwood, 2013)

Williams, Keith, *John Woodburn: Fifty Years at the Top*
    (Charlbury: Wychwood, 2006)

Wilson, William, *Marguerite Wilson: The First Star of Women's
    Cycling* (Poole: CMP, 2015)

Woodland, Les, *This Island Race* (Norwich: Mousehold
    Press, 2005)

Wright, Fred, *Rough Stuff Cycling in the Alps* (London: Isola
    Press, 2018)

Magazines

Archive issues of both *Cycling Weekly* and *Coureur* have formed a
significant part of the research and inspiration for this book, and
have been quoted from widely. Harman and Blackwell's account
of their journey appeared in *The Wheel World* in January 1882.

Films

Pascoe, Ray, *Racing the Clock: UK Time Trialling 1979–1983*
    (London: Cycling History, 2019)

Pascoe, Ray and Dansie, Peter, *2 Days and 2 Nights – Land's End
    to John O'Groats* (London: Cycling History, 2003)

Acknowledgements

I am indebted to everyone who gave freely of their time, welcomed me with tea and biscuits and spoke about their experiences. It was humbling and wonderful to be able to talk to the following: Eileen Sheridan, Dick Poole, Janet Tebbutt, Mick Coupe, Pauline Wallis (neé Strong), Andy Wilkinson, Ralph Dadswell, Lynne Biddulph (neé Taylor), John Taylor, Michael Broadwith and Helen Simpson. Mike in particular has been a mentor and guide in this fascinating journey.

I would like to thank James Spackman for believing in the idea and supporting it from start to finish, and Richard Beswick, who saw something in the proposal. Without them the book would be gathering dust in the corners of my mind. I am grateful to Daniel Balado for his attention to detail and to Nithya Rae for her help in managing the process of publication.

It has been an intense two years and yet amid the struggle, sometimes to do the most basic things, there are people who have had a profound and positive effect on me, even if perhaps they haven't realised it. It was in the decisions they took, the small acts of kindness and of faith. Thank you to Adrian Bell, Andrew Hobbs, Nick Kemp and many others.

My mum's contribution to this book is extensive. I am grateful for her support, now and at every step, and for her camper van. She is kind, thoughtful, a bit hectic, but always there.

Lastly, thank you to my wife Helen, always, for your presence at the darkest possible moments and your desire to find a way forward. Thank you for your patience and willingness to see that things will get better, for giving me the time and support to get through, and to write this book.

Index

Page numbers in *italic* refer to images.